After the Bombs
My Berlin

Heidemarie Sieg

A Memoir

ABQ Press Trade Paperback Edition
Second Edition

Some names and identifying details of some
characters in this book have been changed.

ABQPRESS.COM

ABQ Press
Albuquerque, New Mexico

ISBN 978-0-98443024-5-1

Many people have encouraged me along this journey.

I will always be grateful to my writing friends: Kitty, Lisa, Sally, Margot, Jeannie, Christine and Bill, who convinced me that I have a story to tell. I thank them for listening, questioning and helping me to be clear and historically accurate.

I thank Trent, my husband, for his patience and support. He nudged me to keep on writing and read every draft and revision.

Most of all I am thankful to my mother. She waited countless times, holding her next sentence, when I said, "Wait, I have to write this down!" Also, for reminding me often that all people are the same, "only by accident of birth are we different."

Table of Contents

Introduction

Chapter One
      Family History - The Early Years   1

Chapter Two
      World War II Years   21

Chapter Three
      After the Bombs   47

Chapter Four
      On my Own   212

Postscript
      Berlin 1989   254

Introduction

To Jason, Andrea and Derek

It never occurred to me to write a memoir. But, as I have learned over the years, everyone is raised in a different environment. Even within the same family, people's memories differ.

Recently I read an interview where a German writer was quoted: "I didn't know anything about the war. Nobody talked about it. I just learned that my father was in the SS during the war and I started to ask questions."

Well, to me it is inconceivable that people didn't talk about the war, or the years leading up to it. In my family, at birthday and holiday gatherings, the conversation always led to, and stayed with, the recollections and sharing of experiences of the past, including World War II.

In 1992, during one of my visits to Berlin, my sister relayed with great astonishment that she just learned that Uncle Helmut was wounded in Russia and still had shrapnel under his skin. Occasionally the shrapnel bits appear closer to the skin surface, requiring hospitalization to be removed. I was startled that this was news to her! Was she not listening when "war stories" were traded?

Then I remembered. When we were crowded around the holiday dinner table, sooner or later we were excused with "you can go and play now." Magic words for my sister Margot and cousin Dorit. They instantly disappeared. Cousin Ingrid and I stayed. We snuggled close to our favorite Aunt Hille, stayed very quiet, hoping nobody would notice, and listened...

Now I see how Margot could also say, "We never talked about the war." I understand why people in general have the impression that Germans didn't talk about World War II. Not true!

All of this, along with the fact that all records regarding our family were lost when the statistics office was leveled late in 1943, is my motivation to write down what I have heard and experienced. There will always be questions about my family background.

This is all I know.

My Turn

Written in 1987 as commentary for the newspaper, *The Times Argus,* Barre, Vermont.

When you listen to the Germans today, "There never were any bad Germans during Hitler's time" is one of many incredible quotes frequently heard.

Every time a case against an alleged World War II criminal unfolds, the media reviews Nazi atrocities. The Germans are the bad guys and the generic Nazi label is applied. For me, this is a time of contemplation and soul searching.

When I read these articles I think, "Will the Germans ever have a chance to change this stereotype?" It is unjustly assumed that because Nazis were in power in Germany for many years, all Germans are Nazis.

While growing up in postwar Berlin, I was deeply troubled by what happened before and during the war. It was incredible that so many innocent people were sent to their death. I must have asked myself a thousand times "How could this happen? Were my parents in on it?"

My father was born in the Ruhr Valley in 1910. As a toddler, his father shipped him off to relatives. Little children were a nuisance in his eyes and "kept the woman from doing her job." His mother died a few years later. Once old enough, he went to Berlin and built up a flourishing vegetable wholesale and retail business. By 1935 he was well established.

My mother was born at the eve of World War I in Berlin. Her father was the type of German who is always described when pre–World War II Germany is discussed. A master tailor by trade, he was a loyal Party man. He was an autocrat. His wife suffered in silence, his sons didn't like it, and Mother absolutely hated it. Her brothers joined the "Hitler Youth." There was no choice; it simply was done. Mother also had to join.

Grandfather was not a leading Party official, but he was very intent on staying in the good graces of the chairman. Mother was forbidden to date; but at Party events, of which there were many, he ordered her to go for long walks in the woods with sons of higher-ranking officials and told her to be "nice to them." That's just one small example of what went on for years. On her twenty-first birthday, her parents' consent no longer required, she left home.

Mother worked as a secretary for the Otis elevator company. When all businesses were ordered not to employ Jews, Otis had to let them go, but Otis employed them at home on the sly. Co-workers took turns delivering and picking up work, such as bookkeeping. On those trips, they also took food and, for Jews, hard-to-get items as often as possible. They kept this up until the beneficiaries asked that it be stopped. They feared for their safety and those who were lending a helping hand.

It was a fact that not only Jewish people, but many Germans also disappeared. Yes, the Germans knew that people were arrested and never seen again, but the public did not know what fate they were dealt. Of course, Hitler threatened to eliminate all non-Aryans from Germany. But nobody interpreted that as a death sentence.

"If we knew, what could we have done? People were arrested just for uttering a doubt!" Mother explained. When your life and that of your family is on the line, you have no options. Not everyone could or wanted to leave Germany. It is, after all, their homeland, and the human spirit always hopes for the next day or year to be better.

In the late 1930s, fear was well established. People didn't dare speak up in public or even show sympathy.

At the beginning of the war, my parents married and planned to raise a big family. Because Dad was in the food business, he didn't get called to active duty until 1941. Mother took over and ran the fleet of trucks with women and old men as laborers. One by one, though, the trucks had to be taken out of service because tires were confiscated by the army. Naturally, business came to a screeching halt, and so did a lot of the food supply lines.

Before the Russian's invasion of Berlin, we were evacuated to a farm in Poland. By then my parents had two daughters, and mother was expecting a third child. Their business compound, including office and living quarters, had been destroyed during an earlier air raid.

The new baby, born in April 1945, died of malnutrition within six weeks. After Germany surrendered, Mother packed our belongings into a baby carriage and started the journey back to Berlin.

She was hopeful. Although we had lost much, she was looking to the future. The war that seemed as if it would never end was finally over. Dad, she knew, would find a way for us to survive. Together they would rebuild.

In Berlin she received the news that my father had been killed during the fall of Berlin. There would be no rebuilding together.

Her brother Werner died during a military training accident before the war. Helmut, her younger brother, was a prisoner of war in Russia.

My grandfather chose to disappear in East Germany. "He would have been lynched had he shown his face around here," Mother stated.

The postwar years were tough. Food was already scarce, and then came the Blockade of Berlin. My younger sister contracted tuberculosis and spent two years at a treatment facility. Hard times did not want to end.

Looking back, I don't believe the chain of events could have been altered by the Germans. Any 20/20 hindsight can be shot full of holes, because the hypothetical scenarios I have heard wouldn't have worked in the reality of Germany in the 1920s and 30s.

I lived in several countries before coming to the United States. Many accusations have come my way directly, like, "You're not wanted here. Go back where you came from." My children, born Americans with an American father, have been called "Nazi brats."

It once was very important to me that people understand how it all happened. It doesn't seem possible. It looks as though humanity won't be ready to forgive, or understand, in my lifetime.

I cannot reverse history. Today I believe I have been given the opportunity to learn from the mistakes of my ancestors.

Chapter One – Family History
The Early Years

Edith Richter

Mutti, my mother, grew up in a castle...sort of.

Home was a castle estate in Naugard, Pommern (Pomerania), which has belonged to Poland since World War II. Pommern was known for its gentle rolling hills, dense forests, castle estates, and gentlemen farms. Being only thirty miles from the Baltic Sea, it seemed you could sometimes smell the salt air.

The castle had been converted to a county prison, where Mutti's grandfather, Herman Baumgarten, was head warden. His wife, Auguste, was in charge of the family. All of their children completed school, and each one learned to play an instrument. Some continued on to business school. Auguste was both creative and industrious. She owned the first sewing machine in the region and also taught her thirteen children—seven girls and six boys—how to master it.

Mutti's mother, Margarete, my grandmother—I called her Oma—was the youngest of the thirteen children. Oma and her sister Anna, Aunt Anni, left home to find work in Berlin in 1907 when she was eighteen. Oma started to work with a young tailor named Paul Richter. Paul, who became my Opa, moved to Berlin from the Spreewald, a lake and forest area close to Berlin, to become a tailor.

Oma and Opa lived together, had two children—a son who died at birth and a daughter, Elizabeth—before they married in May 1914. Edith, Mutti to me, was born a couple weeks after the ceremony, on May 29, in Berlin.

The heir to the throne of Austria, Archduke Franz Ferdinand, and his wife, Sophie, were assassinated on June 28 in Serbia. The event sent shockwaves through Europe. Countries began mobilizing their armies. Opa, who joined the army in 1911, was called to active duty immediately. Germany declared war on Russia on August 1st and two days later on France.

With Opa in the army, Oma was left alone in the city. Together, they decided to send the girls to live with their grandparents. Elizabeth went to Opa's parents in the Spreewald. They took Mutti to Oma's parents in Naugard. The countryside would be a better place for small children during wartime.

Most of Oma's brothers and sisters still lived at home, and Mutti's grandparents and aunts and uncles welcomed her into their large family. Her aunts Lottie and Marty were put in charge of Mutti. They remained her lifelong favorites.

Naugard's main road led into the countryside of mostly open meadows from which Castle Road branched off. From this point on, the land was government property. The poplar-lined Castle Road was straight and led directly to the castle. Outside the castle were a farm, gardens, and houses for prison staff and their families. The road went to and over the drawbridge. The actual prison was inside the castle walls. Mutti's grandparents had a house on the prison grounds, and when the children were old enough, they worked there also. The eldest son already was managing the adjacent farm.

The prison was completely self-sufficient. The inmates operated the farm, the extensive vegetable gardens, a bakery, laundry, print shop, and more. The farm outside the prison raised beef, chicken, and pigs, and produced by-products like soap and other goods. Whatever the prison population could not use was sold in the town's open market.

Mutti mostly tagged along with her aunts. It was a busy place. The bakery, kitchens, laundry, tailor, workshops, and more were located underground in what were once vast caverns. All the windows for the various spaces had been placed near the ceiling to get some daylight. On the outside, the windows were level with the ground, where water had once slowly moved around the castle's moat. From this vantage point, Mutti could spy and watch the activities going on below. She also had a regular daily routine of rounds, stopping to say hello. Everybody knew to expect her, and all had treats handy— some morsels of sweet dough, a piece of smoked bacon, inches of pretty ribbon—and all along the way, teasing her shamelessly. She loved it.

The laundry under the prison was busy every day, but at grandmother's house the laundry was done once a month. Mutti spent much of her time watching the activity of the laundry.

Imagine the loads and loads of laundry for that big family. Before dawn four inmates came to help with sorting and soaking. A fire was built under a huge tub filled with soapy water where all the whites were boiled for at least twenty minutes. After that, the water was changed and heated and the routine repeated until all the whites were clean. Then, the dark laundry went through the same steps, except for having to sit in boiling water. Next, the laundry was scrubbed on a scrubbing board and rinsed twice. Then everything, one item at a time, was pushed through a wringing machine to extract as much water as possible.

From there the laundry was hung on long clotheslines to dry. If it happened to be a rainy day, laundry day was put off. It was usually dark by the time everything was dry. The following morning, they started ironing and folding. Ironing alone took over a week.

Something was always happening to interrupt the routines of the day. A pig would escape its pen and run around the yard, a new prisoner would arrive, the mailman brought letters, and so on.

Quite often, a prisoner's escape would stir great excitement. All of the houses and apartments had alarm systems. When the alarm sounded, all but regular personnel had to stay in their quarters until the culprit was caught. Mutti and Lottie would watch from a bedroom window. While they were waiting, they would imagine what they would do should they run into an escapee on the grounds. Once a fellow was caught hiding in a bush under their window. It was the main topic of conversation for weeks. Not much happened to the inmates except to be put under stricter supervision, and that would end their escape plans.

Sundays were always leisurely. Everyone dressed up for church and remained dressy the rest of the day. In winter, there was sledding on the hills or skating on the big Naugard Lake. In the evening, the musical family held their own concerts. Mutti learned to play the piano and could join in when she was six years old. She later remembered "low lighting and warm camaraderie in the air."

During the summers, everyone changed into more comfortable clothing after church. The siblings went on long hikes through open, sunny fields leading into damp and dark woods, always singing folk songs and songs about hiking. Mutti was wishing that the hikes would never end.

Once the country fairs started, they visited all of them. Each small town had its own fair where they played games, ate lots of food, and danced to a band well into the night.

Summer also brought leisurely Sundays spent at the Baltic Sea where the family had a small cottage. Armed with loaded picnic baskets, they whiled away the time at the water's edge, with beach chairs providing shelter from the sun. Mutti watched the fishing boats go out and then return with their catch. Fresh fish was their standard dinner at the cottage. Life was good. To the end of her days, fish was Mutti's favorite special food.

The years passed, and World War I ended in 1918. Mutti's parents visited a couple of times every summer, but she stayed with her grandparents at the "castle."

Grandmother Auguste died suddenly in 1922, Mutti was eight years old and had to move back to Berlin with her parents.

She thought of those years in Pomerania as her happiest. She felt loved and wanted there. It was a carefree life. Someone was always glad to have her company.

The years ahead were going to be the most difficult ones of her youth.

Earliest photo of Mutti
in front of a basement window at 'the castle'
1917

Paul and Margarete Richter

Herman and Auguste Baumgarten
Mutti's grandparents

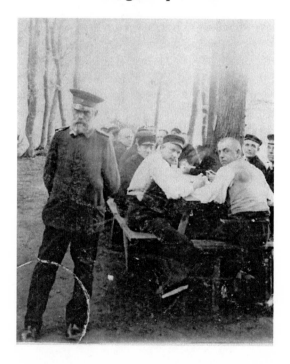

School Years in Berlin

In Berlin my grandparents, Oma and Opa, had a typical small apartment on the third floor of a large apartment building on Emdener Strasse, a working class neighborhood.

The apartment had a small, narrow kitchen and an adjacent large room that served as dining room, living room and bedroom. Although both rooms had a window, the high surrounding buildings totally obstructed the sun. The toilet was on the stairwell a half floor below.

When Mutti moved back to Berlin, the family had grown to include two boys, Werner and Helmut. Opa was a master tailor and operated his shop from the apartment.

Oma was working with him, as well as two employees. So, the small apartment was taken over by two sewing machines, a cutting table and a couple of 'fitting dummies' with suits in progress at various stages. The kitchen table served as cutting, ironing and sewing table. The living room also was a sewing area, as well as a reception and fitting room for visiting clients. The apprentice worked in the kitchen and Opa and his assistant in the living room.

Mutti started school and when she came home she did her homework in the kitchen. She spent the rest of the day there as well, having to stay "out of the way." At that time children led a very disciplined life. Playing was considered frivolous. Maybe because they were in the city, playing outside with other children was not part of a daily routine. The political climate probably also contributed to those habits. People, in general, were very formal, reserved and private.

Supper was taken in the big room and then the room was converted for sleeping. Opa and Oma had a double bed; the boys shared a sofa and Mutti slept on a settee. Bathing was done in the kitchen either under running cold water at the sink or at a ceramic bowl with some water warmed on the stove. Mutti would get up while everyone was still sleeping so that she could have the kitchen by herself. If she got up later she would have to wash with everyone coming in and out. This was especially bothersome and embarrassing for her as she turned into a young woman. There simply was no privacy.

Mutti was quite homesick for her aunts and uncles but found little understanding. "If you don't like it here, go back where you came from," or a plain "we don't want you here either," were the standard replies from her brothers and parents. "You're a girl. You get what's left over," was another comment often coming her way.

During four short weeks of school summer vacation she could visit 'her family' in Pomerania and get a reprieve.

Opa joined the Nazi Party because that is what you had to do, especially if you wanted to stay in business. He became a leader: first in the apartment complex; then his block on Emdener Strasse; and then for the whole neighborhood, covering several square blocks. His business was flourishing because he was an especially capable and talented tailor and also because of his Party leadership. His assistants worked seven days a week.

Besides attending school, Mutti's social activities were limited. She was allowed to join a gymnastics club (Hitler highly approved of exercise) and participated in all club activities, most of them on Saturdays.

On Sundays she had to go with her parents to Nazi Party activities. Her brothers were members of the *Hitler Youth*, membership was mandatory for all boys between ages 10 and 18. Mutti had to join the *Bund Deutscher Mädchen, the* Hitler Youth Organization's branch for girls 10 to 18.

Oma had an upright piano in the apartment. Mutti rarely played it because she was only allowed to play when no one was there.

As she grew older, Opa became increasingly active in the Nazi Party. Almost all his clients were Nazi officials. He was very conscious to ingratiate himself to the Party at all times.

Mutti, her mother and brothers had to do the same. Grandfather gave the orders. To object was unthinkable. In those days a youth did not dare speak until spoken to. Parental rule was supreme. It is a German law that parents are completely responsible for their children until they are twenty-one. A son or daughter cannot do anything without their parents' written consent. They could not travel, get a job, go to school, or move out of the house without specific permission.

Some parents, like Opa, carried those rules to the extreme. What little effort of objecting Oma made was squashed with violent arguments at home.

That pretty much was the way the country started to be also. After Hitler became Chancellor, objections to anything were immediately and harshly squashed. Very effective. After a few of those examples, people just went along for the sake of peace and quiet.

Mutti was under the control of her father and basically the rest of the family too. Opa didn't have any use or understanding for his daughter, except to use her when it seemed to his advantage, so why should her brothers or mother be more human. It only would bring down Opa's wrath

Mutti grew up under Opa's supervision. She was not allowed to date. When indeed she met with anyone else and Opa found out - his network of contacts was widespread - he was waiting for her return by the main house entrance, leather whip in hand. And he used it right there, no questions asked.

Opa was different, though, when on the many Party-organized outings. During spring, summer and fall it meant picnics in Berlin's forests. Opa would choose a boy and send Mutti with him for a hike in the woods without a deadline for return. Those "hikes in the woods" usually meant kissing, groping and some young man's demands for more. Mutti absolutely hated it, always shaking with disgust when she recalled those days. She was not allowed to date except handpicked party officials' sons. She started to have severe migraine headaches as soon as the weather turned warm. "The migraines made me physically ill. I threw up a lot. Sometimes it saved me from having to go on a picnic."

Mutti started working as a stenographer for Otis, an elevator manufacturer, when she turned sixteen. It was the start of some sort of freedom. She could socialize at work, made friends and also joined a hiking club.

Opa still held a tight rein and she had to account where and how she spent her time away from home and had to observe a strict curfew. Buses and trains ran with German precision – they were always "on time." It was easy for Opa to keep track of Mutti's time. If she was late coming home he would be waiting for her at the building entrance with the leather whip ready.

A few times Oma did not follow orders. It was known that when the state police came to take people out of their apartment, they would not return. A couple of times Oma was able to hide Jewish couples in the apartment at the last minute. Once, the police stormed across the interior yard and up one of the staircases. "Their footsteps were loud and echoed throughout the complex. You could count the steps and knew where they were on the staircase." Due to the square design of the apartment complex, grandmother's living room window was next to another couple's apartment. The man and the woman jumped into Oma's living room. Because of Opa's status, the police did not raid Oma's apartment in search of the missing couple. She declared innocence to Opa's questioning afterwards.

Another time the police stormed up grandmother's stairwell around three a.m. They stopped on Oma's third floor landing, broke down the neighbors' door and dragged them down the stairs. The neighbors never came back.

With Mutti's job also came vacation time and her activities were pointed towards those two weeks of the year. From her small salary she had to give most of it to her parents for living expenses, and she saved the rest. She saved more by walking to and from work, three miles each way, and skipping meals at work.

Her vacations were always with the hiking club, traveling to the Alps in Germany, Austria and Italy. Shorter trips were taken during the holidays Germany observed: May Day, Easter, Whit Sunday and Veterans Day. But even then, if she did not arrive home on time, her father would be standing by the entrance of the apartment complex with leather whip and hit her right there.

It was also around those years when Hitler was working hard at making every adjoining country an ally. All youths and young adults had to 'volunteer' their vacation and help the farmers in the fields. Mutti was sent to Alsace in France. It was a very hot summer there and the migraine headaches started as soon as she arrived by train. It was impossible for her to work in the fields. She was put to work helping in the kitchen where breakfast, the large mid-day meal and supper were prepared for the farmers, their helpers and the volunteers.

Lucky for her and for us, she thrived in the hustle and bustle of the country kitchen. It reminded her very much of her childhood at 'the castle.' She would get up before dawn, hurry to the kitchen where the women hustled to have breakfast ready by six. Work in the fields started at seven. It would be dark before the kitchen was clean again after supper. Mutti was intrigued by the different food and happily learned the steps and recipes. From then on, everything she cooked was influenced by French country cuisine. The month in France went by very quickly and then it was back to Berlin

Mutti could not wait until her twenty-first birthday when she no longer required her parents' permission for anything. She arranged to rent a room that a widow offered in the center of the city. For months before her birthday Mutti moved her belongings little by little on her way to work, careful not to get noticed.

On her birthday, May 29th, she left for work and did not go home again.

1922
Emdenerstrasse Courtyard
Far left: Brothers Werner and Helmut - Mutti far right

On Her Own

The room Mutti rented also included the use of a private bathroom. What luxury! Her routine did not change much. She walked to and from work, one hour each way, and continued to save for vacations and outings with the hiking club. She could have friends and come to her room without having to answer to anyone.

She met many very nice men who pursued this petite woman with a great sense of humor. However, she made it clear to anyone who needed to know, that she was not interested in any relationships whatsoever. After the years at home with her father and two brothers, she had a very low opinion of men and marriage, and did not want any part of it.

The social life provided by the gymnastic club and the hiking club was totally fulfilling. With like-minded friends from both clubs she went to the theater, the movies and countless cafés on Sunday afternoons for coffee and pastries. Although everyone also enjoyed wine and beer on their outings, mother learned quickly that she could not tolerate either, but she enjoyed their parties as much as anyone.

Mutti's duties at Otis now also included bookkeeping. Otis was the largest company of its kind in Germany, employing thousands of people.

We are now in the mid-1930s, when the Nazi government was in full power and people became aware of the different status of Jews. At that time Jewish citizens had to wear a yellow star on their clothing. The star was to be on the front left side on whatever they were wearing in public. Then it was announced that they could buy food and other goods only on certain days and times. A short time later all German-owned businesses were ordered not to do business with Jews. If a Jew going into a German shop would be reported by someone, both the Jew and the shopkeeper were arrested.

Then companies were encouraged not to employ them. A huge conglomerate like Otis could afford to ignore those suggestions. Mutti remembered how her Jewish colleagues could not go to the cafeteria for food. So the secretaries would get extra helpings and then shared it back in their office. The time came when the company was forced to let all Jews go.

Otis kept the Jews employed on the sly. The secretaries took turns taking bookkeeping work to their homes after dark, hoping not to get noticed. Knowing that the lunch at the office was the only meal their friends were getting, Mutti and the other secretaries always took food along with the work. Finally their former colleagues asked them not to come anymore, because they felt they were being watched. Mutti does not know what became of them.

In order to save extra money for clothes and travels she took an evening job as bookkeeper in a store. After a year there she heard of another opening. In 1938, she started to do the bookkeeping for the busy merchant August Sieg.

Although she had left home, she was always in contact with her family, being a dutiful daughter that included her father. Her actions often were not reciprocated

Rationing of food and other goods had been in place for several years. Each person had to go to social services monthly, show their identification and receive their vouchers.

Mutti's younger brother, Helmut, was in the military and was dating Else (Elschen) Freier for several years. They were married a day after his twenty-first birthday when he no longer needed his parents' permission.

Before Helmut married, Oma asked Mutti to give up her vouchers for food for the small reception after the civil ceremony. Mutti complied. She was not invited to the gathering but learned later that Elschen's brother was.

Werner joined the Hitler Youth and, at 16, the Army. He didn't like school and barely managed to graduate, but he loved the military and advanced regularly. Mutti kept up a regular correspondence with him.

Werner dated Hilde, Aunt Hille, for several years and planned to get married. He died in a military training accident in October 1939. Oma was devastated and very bitter about losing her favorite son.

August Sieg - The Early Years

My Father August, I called him Pappa, was born 1910 in Bochum, near the Ruhr River in western Germany. The Ruhr Valley was mostly known for the production of coal. Coal mines dominated the area and with it the seemingly always present black dust clouds from the mines. The tunnels stretched for miles under the towns, making many homes shift ever so often.

My Grandfather, August Sieg, had a vegetable and potato business and also a grocery store. Grandfather ran the vegetable business and Grandmother was in charge of the grocery store that was adjacent to their small apartment.

A few days after Pappa's brother Alfred was born, my grandfather told his wife, who was still in bed recovering from childbirth, "I'll be gone for a couple of days and I'm taking August with me." At that time a woman usually stayed in bed for at least two weeks after birth and then slowly returned to her daily duties.

Grandfather took Pappa by train to Treuburg, a small town in Ost Preussen, East Prussia, where grandfather's sister Anna and her family were living on a big farm. Ost Preussen was the easternmost German state bordering Russia. Pappa's father left him at the farm, he was only two years old. Grandmother only found out when Grandfather returned to Bochum without him. Little children were a nuisance in his eyes, "Keeps the woman from doing her job." She did not have any say in the matter.

Anna and Friedrich Nowotsch, Pappa's aunt and uncle, and their four children took Pappa in. Emilie, Emma, Friedrich Jr and Willie ages 17 to 8, worked on the farm and 'adopted' Pappa as their baby brother.

The farm produced vegetables and many varieties of potatoes, a staple in the German's daily diet. They bred and raised Trakhener thoroughbred horses as their specialty. Chickens, ducks, geese, rabbits, pigs and sheep also were part of the farm's menagerie.

Right from the beginning Pappa was helping with all aspects of raising crops and taking them to the market.

The responsibilities were always adjusted to his age and ability. He was learning well and living happily in the country. He grew up on the farm and also finished school there.

When Pappa was sixteen, grandfather brought him back to Bochum to attend business school. In the intervening years, Pappa's mother died in 1918, when she attempted an abortion. Grandfather remarried. When Pappa rejoined the household in 1926, the family had grown with the addition of his sister Elfriede, who was born a couple of years after he was taken to the farm. Grandfather had two additional boys and a girl with his new wife.

Looking over the family history we were always amazed at the similarities of the children from both marriages. The first boys, August and Fritz, were much alike in complexion and stature, fair-haired, a receding hairline at an early age, strong boned and good-natured. The second boys, Alfred and Erich, were dark-haired, slim and even in those days considered wheeler-dealers. Last were the girls, Elfriede and Klara, both had a twin that died at birth, had very similar facial features and complicated dispositions.

While going to business school Pappa also worked at the family business every day. Grandfather bought vegetables from farms in the surrounding countryside and brought them to his business yard in Bochum in large covered wagons. At the yard he had ten, sometimes as many as fifteen, horses to pull flatbeds. The goods were unloaded from the large wagons and distributed to the flatbeds. The men would fan out into neighborhoods to sell the fruits and vegetables. Pappa learned from grandfather the give-and-take and bartering with farmers. Then again there was bartering and give-and-take when selling from the flatbeds to customers. The goal was to sell everything and come back to the yard with an empty trailer.

Pappa excelled at business school in Bochum. Business suited him, and he graduated with honors. A while after graduation he moved to Berlin to start his own business with money he saved and also a bonus Grandfather had given him upon graduation. It was 1930, and Pappa was twenty and dreaming big.

Moving to Berlin

Pappa didn't know anyone in Berlin. He found the railroad station where the boxcars with produce to be unloaded arrived. Beusselstrasse Station was a large rail yard next to Westhafen – West Harbor, at the time the largest inland harbor in Germany. Most goods came from Bremen, by the North Sea, by way of connected waterways to Westhafen. All supplies were unloaded to boxcars and moved to the tracks at Beusselstrasse Station. Merchants came to the station from all over Berlin with their trucks and wagons to buy fruits, vegetables and potatoes.

To be located close to the station, Pappa scouted the adjoining neighborhood and rented a big yard in the back of an apartment complex. He started to operate his business – August Sieg Vegetable Merchant - with one truck, one flatbed trailer and a horse from his yard at Waldstrasse across the railway.

Everyday he drove to the station and bought produce from the boxcars. Back at the yard, one worker was waiting to help unload part of it onto the flatbed. Then, Pappa with the truck and the worker with the flatbed started scouring the neighborhoods, selling until all was gone. This routine was repeated six days a week

The yard on Waldstrasse included vast underground cellars. They would be used in the fall to store tons of potatoes for selling throughout the winter. There also was a small three-story house at the edge of the yard; garages and stalls for horses at ground level, and a two-story apartment above where Pappa lived.

By 1934, Pappa's business had grown; he really wanted a friendly face to come home to in the evenings. Elfriede, his younger sister, came to run the office and keep house for him. He now had several trucks, a fleet of horse drawn flatbeds and was the largest produce supplier in the borough.

His brother Alfred also moved to Berlin and was working with Pappa most of the time. They split duties between unloading at the train depot and supervising the regrouping at his yard.

In 1935, he bought the sales yard and the house he was living in, as well as the attached three 5-story apartment buildings. The owners, Professor and Frau Schneider, continued living rent-free in a third floor apartment in the complex.

It was Elfriede who hired Mutti in 1938, mainly as a much needed bookkeeper. Elfriede continued to run the household and some of the business logistics.

1937
Unloading potatoes at Waldstrasse Freight yard
Above: Pappa
Below: Uncle Alfred, far left, and the crew

An Eventful Date

By 1940 Mutti had been working for August and Elfriede for two years. She had noticed in the past that his birthday was totally ignored. She gave him a box of chocolates for his birthday in October. In return he asked her to go out and celebrate with him.

At that time the use of private automobiles was already restricted. So, Pappa put a couple sacks of potatoes in the trunk and bags of onions on the back seat pretending to make a delivery, in case they were stopped.

They celebrated all right. On the way home visibility was restricted due to blackout on streets. All street lights were out and headlights had to be 95% covered. Pappa went off the road and hit a lamppost. Just a fender bender for his midnight blue BMW convertible, but Mutti's head hit the windshield and Pappa had to take her to the hospital. She had a few cuts on her face and a concussion.

She was in the hospital for a week. Pappa came to visit with a bunch of flowers and a sheepish apology. He promised to take her out to dinner after she'd recovered and to bring her home safely that time.

The romance was on but they had no plans to get married.

Mutti and Pappa 1939

Chapter Two – World War II Years

1941

In March of 1941, Pappa was called to active duty in France. Pappa and Mutti decided to get married. My parents' wedding was a civil ceremony, just the two of them, on March 10, 1941, at the nearby Tiergarten District City Hall. Pappa reported for duty at the barracks the next day.

Until now Pappa had only been drafted. Because he was a food supplier, he was left in Berlin to keep the business running and the goods flowing to the neighborhood. Although supplies were getting a bit slimmer, Pappa was expert at finding new produce sources in the countryside. He often brought back more than vegetables.

Upon the announcement of their marriage, Elfriede promptly moved out and left Mutti alone to run the business. Alfred was already on active army duty.

All the men and few women working for Pappa were not fit for army duty. They were too old or too sick, but had been working for him for many years. They all knew the ropes and routines. Pappa had been a most fair employer and Mutti was reaping the benefits. All were loyal and hardworking. First of all, they wanted to keep their jobs and secondly they wanted to keep the business going for August.

They also continued the well-established "secret feeding of war prisoners." Prisoners were assigned work duty, but citizens were not allowed to make contact or feed them. A truck brought them to the rail yard and then picked up again in the evening. In between they were expected to work at anything and for anybody at the railway.

On the street corner across the street from Pappa's business was the neighborhood bar. They were a German 'Mom and Pop' tradition. Beer on tap, *Schnapps* and traditional pub style food was available almost around the clock, although those supplies also had dwindled. The neighborhood police station was in the building next to the pub.

The prisoners, first French and later Russians, "young men – almost boys," worked for several businessmen at the railroad station. For food they were only allowed water and slices of dark bread. The men already were just skin and bones. Pappa organized a secret feeding routine for the prisoners. Merchants at the station culled potatoes, vegetables or portions of whatever they were unloading that day.

Pappa took everything back to his yard and a stew was cooked in large vats in the yard. Potatoes were always boiled there for the horses, so another vat would not raise any suspicion. When the meal was ready the bins were carried to the police station across the street and then through a backdoor to the pub.

Later the prisoners would arrive in small groups at the police station and via the back door at the pub where those stews were the only solid food they got.

When supplies got really scarce, they all felt it was too dangerous for the pub, all involved and the prisoners, so they finally had to stop this practice.

Oma came every day to help in the house and Mutti supervised the men. She kept the retail yard open and people could get their rations. Booths with vegetables and potatoes were set up every day in the open-air yard.

There were not many Jews left in the city and one rarely saw a person with the telltale yellow star displayed on their coats or jackets. One of Pappas friends – Ernst, an accountant, was one of the few still around. He would come to the yard with a briefcase clasped under his arm that covered the yellow star. Ernst strolled along the booths and slid supplies in his coat pockets. Everyone looked the other way.

One time Oma happened to be at the house and noticed Ernst from the kitchen window. She became very agitated and called Mutti to the window. Mutti asked her very firmly to ignore what she was seeing, "This is August's friend, and he has been coming ever since August started the business. Don't tell anyone." Oma promised, but was really angry with Pappa. Mutti does not remember when Ernst stopped coming. She lost track and after the war nobody knew what happened to him.

Pappa's army duty was driving supply trucks for the troops on the front lines. First, he was stationed in France, then in Russia and later in Czechoslovakia.

Pappa sent letters regularly, coaching and advising her to keep her chin up. Mutti was able to save a few.

One at a time Mutti had to stop using the trucks. First there was the lack of fuel and later the army confiscated all tires. The trucks were put on blocks in the storage hangars and just the horse pulled trailers with iron–clad wooden wheels continued to make their rounds. She also had a large portable stall with potatoes set up in the yard. Pappa came home often, sometimes officially on leave, and sometimes he made a detour from his supply missions. He continued his specialty of supplying everybody. His truck turned into a wonderland of butter, eggs, bacon, and meat, all items already very scarce in Berlin. He spent a good part of home leave time 'out and about,' visiting neighbors and buddies and carrying presents of food. Mutti learned to squirrel away some butter, flour, etc. for herself, "Or August would have given away everything."

An excerpt from one of Pappa's letters:

May 6, 1941
Dear sweet wife!
 After I received advanced notice in your dear letter, the three packages arrived today. For everything my heartiest thank you and many dear kisses. I can tell everything was prepared with unbelievable care and love, especially the strawberry jam.
 Please do not be too upset with the remarks or seeming lack of interest in the business in my previous letter. In the circumstances here I experience heavy mood swings and some days are very trying.
 I'm forever indebted to you for carrying on the daily routine of the business. The experience will only strengthen our relationship and partnership for life and help us both to weather the storms that life has in store for us. When I am back from the army, life will be easier, better and more beautiful for us together.
 All work-leave has been canceled- no explanation. It would be so good if I could be home for the early potato harvest to help.
 Now to business. How is Fritz? (younger brother). Be nice to him and keep him close. As you have already learned not everything works out the way you would like.
 I hope to be home for a day visit very soon...

Letter to Mutti
May 6, 1941

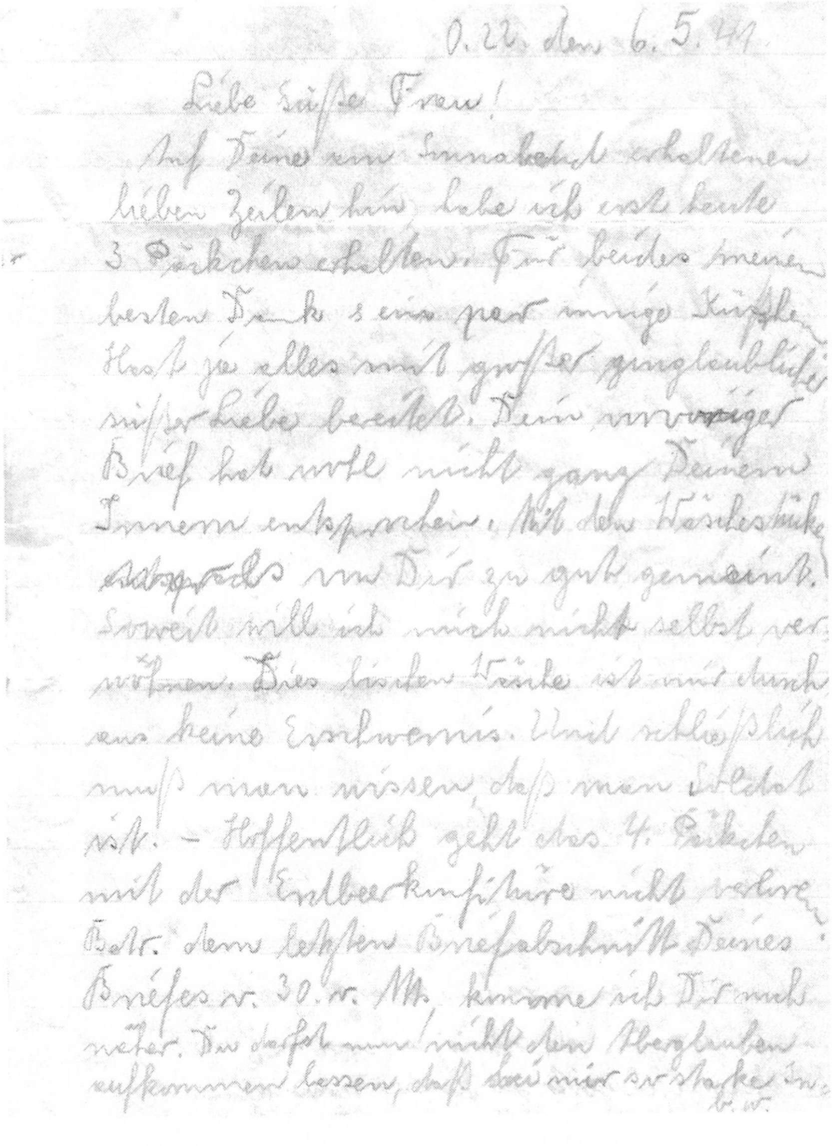
O.U., den 6.5.41

Liebe süße Frau!

Auf Deine am Sonnabend erhaltenen lieben Zeilen hin habe ich erst heute 3 Päckchen erhalten. Für beides meinen besten Dank u. ein paar innige Küßle. Hast ja alles mit großer unglaublicher süßer Liebe bereitet. Dein vorvoriger Brief hat wohl nicht ganz Deinem Innern entsprochen. Mit den Wäschestücken [illegible] von Dir zu gut gemeint. Soweit will ich mich nicht selbst verwöhnen. Dies bißchen Wäsche ist mir durchaus keine Erschwernis. Und schließlich muß man wissen, daß man Soldat ist. – Hoffentlich geht das 4. Päckchen mit der Erdbeerkonfitüre nicht verloren. Betr. dem letzten Briefabschnitt Deines Briefes v. 30. v. Mts. komme ich Dir noch näher. Du darfst nun nicht den Aberglauben aufkommen lassen, daß bei mir so starke In-

b.w.

Pappa in Uniform
1941

Pappa's activation pass March 12, 1941

1942

Berlin was under air attacks throughout the war. When the warning sirens went off, everyone was supposed to go into the cellars below all buildings. The cellars created an enormous tunnel system, a virtual 'underground city.' All were connected but could be closed off with heavy iron doors. The doors were designed to keep fires from spreading. Also, if a house should be hit and the regular stairs were blocked off, people could move to other cellars and get out. Mutti, like everyone else, went to the cellars only in the early years. Although these cellars saved many lives, as the war dragged on, many people waited out the attacks in their apartments.

The sirens would go on again once an air raid was over. People would then go out and check for damage. Mutti would first check our house, then the apartment buildings and then go to Emdener Strasse to Oma's apartment and on the way pass by Helmut and Elschen's building on Wiclefstrasse.

I was born on a cold and snowy February 9, 1942. Mutti walked five blocks to the school turned hospital (later my high school) on Turmstrasse. Women had to bring their own supplies to the maternity ward: several sets of linens, nightgowns, food (rationing gave pregnant women extra food allowances including extra malt beer – non alcoholic but considered very nourishing) and baby blankets and clothing. Carrying all that, and having contractions all along, made the five blocks a very long walk.

Pappa quickly came on baby leave and visited a few hours later. 'Heidemarie' was Pappa's choice for my name. Mutti was not in favor and the deal was made that she could name the next baby. Mutti did not want Heidemarie because it was a most popular marching song the soldiers sang all the time.

One family highlight was my christening in April. All relatives including the men who were able to get leave came. It was a big day, an excuse to make the effort to get together. Luckily some photos of that day were not lost or burned.

First outing with Heidi
1942

With Ingrid in front of Waldstrasse 32.
Note the entrance to freight yard in back.

From back to front: August Sieg Sr.,
Pappa, Herr Freier with Ingrid, Uncle Emil

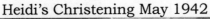

Heidi's Christening May 1942

Back: Aunt Hille, Frau Freier, Frau Bahr, Aunt Anni,
Front: Aunt Elschen, Oma, Mutti

1943

Bombing became heavier. Our street was especially hard hit because we were so close to the train depot. A big section of the building complex was destroyed from bombings and fire. The front apartment building was still standing.

Pappa came home on emergency leave. He also kept an apartment on the fourth floor of the main building that he previously rented out. It was empty now and they carried some dishes, a white iron bed frame, a landscape painting, a kitchen table and a couple of chairs upstairs.

Pappa had an option on a farm with 75 acres in Fehrbellin, about 60 miles north-west of Berlin. He made regular payments towards it throughout the war. The plan was to move the family to the country, raise crops and deliver and sell directly from his shop in Berlin. He borrowed a truck, loaded it with the larger furniture, china, linens, scrapbook, clothes and anything else that could be salvaged and drove to Fehrbellin. Everything on the truck was stored in a barn there.

Mutti was pregnant with Margot at the time and we moved in with Oma at the tiny apartment in Emdener Strasse. Berlin was bombed heavily during that summer. They did go to the cellars every time. It was during those raids that Oma's apartment complex came closest to damage.

A bomb came through the roof and stopped. Everyone covered up, held their breath and waited for the explosion. Nothing happened. After the 'all clear' they found the bomb stuck on the second floor in the staircase. The bomb squad came and defused it. Oma's entire block on Emdener Strasse was spared during the war. Yet, the next block was completely leveled on both sides of the street. And so it went throughout the city.

After Mutti moved in with Oma, she went to Waldstrasse after every raid to see if the apartment building was still there.

Margot was born on September 7, 1943. This time Mutti only had to walk one block to the same hospital and Oma helped carry the supplies. Mutti's middle name Margot was obviously chosen for this baby.

Just a few weeks after Margot's birth, Pappa came home and decided to take us to Nowotch's farm in Ostpreussen where he grew up. We went by train and it was a very long trip. It was standing room only; everyone was fleeing the city if they could. Pappa's father and sister Elfriede also moved to the farm at that time. The farm was large enough for all parties to have their own room. Mutti was very happy to leave Berlin behind, hopefully for a long time.

Ostpreussen's businesses and farms, including Nowotch's, were under strict government control. The farm kept producing vegetables, potatoes, varied livestock and the thoroughbred Trakhener horses. All crops and livestock were inventoried weekly. An official was present during slaughtering to assure that the appropriate percentage was delivered to the government.

But Pappa's cousins, I called them all just 'uncle' or 'aunt,' had built an underground slaughter facility where they also raised some animals that were not accounted for. There was always plenty of food at the farm. The Poles working on the farm went along with the deception and did not report anything to the authorities. Neighboring Poland was under German occupation and it could have been in their favor to report the cheating. But they turned the other cheek, like most people.

Food was plentiful. To Mutti's frustration, I was a very finicky eater and would not eat any chicken, eggs or cheese, all goodies that had not been available in Berlin for quite a while.

In the fall Hilda, Alfred's wife, and my three year old cousin Werner also came to stay with the Nowotch family.

Nowotch's Farm

The uncles and aunts, Willy, Friedrich, Emilie and Emma, loved having children around. None were married and had endless patience. Their parents, Pappas Aunt and Uncle, were also living on the farm. I called everyone either Aunt or Uncle whether they were relatives or not. Friedrich and Willie took over my care. They took me everywhere.

I showed a particular interest in the horses. I didn't miss a day in the barn, Uncle Willie took me along. I was there when they went out to pasture and again when they returned in the evening. I knew all 25 of them and called them by name as they galloped past us into the barn. In the spring when a new foal was born I was allowed to choose a name. He became 'Freundchen' – 'Little Friend.'

During the winter, when I was sick Uncle would bundle me up and carry me through the snowdrifts to the barn to see the horse over the protest of all women. I'm told I had both Uncles wrapped around my two-year-old little finger.

Pappa came for Christmas, as did Uncle Alfred and also their younger half brother Fritz. It was a cold and snowy Christmas. Trips into town for supplies were taken with a big sled. Everyone was dressed in many layers. Blankets and furs lined the passenger part of the sled. Several heated bricks were laid on the floor to keep people warm along with the cover of several furs. It was an adventure.

1943
At Nowotch's Farm
Back: Emilie, Mutti, Elfriede
Front: Hilde with Werner, Pappa with Heidi,
Emma with Margot

1944

Springtime was wonderful for running around. When we were not 'helping' Uncle with chores, Werner and I explored barns, wagons, and fields far and wide. We never had so much space and freedom and, along with the fun, we got into all kinds of trouble. Here are some of our adventures that were told and retold when we visited in later years.

Often we were playing behind the barn. There were open fields and a huge manure pile that had accumulated over the winter. Next to the manure pile was a pond that actually was the cesspool with runoff from the manure pile. We always chased each other and one day I fell into the pond, head first. Werner was horrified and ran for help. Everybody on the farm heard him screaming and came running. Luckily the pond was fairly shallow. Uncle Willie waded in and pulled me out.

I was hosed off outside the house, followed by several sudsy baths in a tub outside. Finally I was rinsed with vinegar which seemed to cut the last lingering smell of you-know-what.

A few weeks later we played catch-me-if-you-can around a long picnic table jumping up and down between table and bench, up and down, up and down—until I fell under the table and broke my right upper arm.

Again, Werner ran for help. Uncle took me to the doctor in town. The doctor put a heavy cast on my arm and I was told to keep the arm in a sling. The sling hung loosely around my neck the minute we got back to the farm. The cast did not slow me down at all. I was as busy as ever moving about, usually dragging my arm behind. It healed just fine.

An excerpt from one of Pappa's letters:
Brünn (Czechoslovakia), April 17, 1944

Dear sweet Edith!
Many 'thank yous' for your dear letter that arrived with the afternoon mail. I had planned to write at least once a week so that you don't worry.

Easter with you was special even if it was too brief. In my wildest imagination I could not think of anything more beautiful. In quiet places true beauty survives. Most important is that we have more waiting for us in the future. I did not even feel down on the journey back and still feel very happy.

Just to make sure that there are no misunderstandings I want to tell you now that you make me very happy and I am deeply happy with you. I am at peace knowing that you and the children are in good hands. After the war, unless fate has other plans, you will be the same breath of fresh air and healthy busy-body that I love.

Ultimately it is the inner strength of both husband and wife that will carry us through the highs and lows of life all the way into old age.

Be sure to get along with Uncle and Aunt as you have all along. Sometimes allowances need to be made for the older generation. Hilda shouldn't carry on so with Tante, over a bucket of water yet! When some days seem to be quiet and never ending try to remember the busy unhappy ones.

We arrived in Berlin at 9 a.m. with a two-hour delay. Elfriede and I took turns sleeping on my coat on the train's floor. I was running around the remainder of the day. Stopped at Mother's (Oma) briefly. She is of the strong belief that the end (of the war) is very near. You can even hear propaganda to that effect here and there. It should be settled within a few weeks.

The car, being repaired at Alkett's garage, is not ready yet.

To my unbelievable surprise I was able to have roasted kid (young goat) for dinner yesterday! The heart was especially tender. Can you imagine that!? This feast will carry me several days at least. It was a rare treat indeed.

Summer started early, it got very hot. The uncles set up an old feeding trough between house and barn. They kept it filled with water for us and we played either in it or around it all day.

It was during this time that I was chased by a gander. Maybe I splashed him with water. Nobody knows. All I remember is that I was chased around the farm. The gander, flapping his wings as he was after me, looms huge in my memory. I remember a lot of noise from the gander and me screaming. Again, Werner to the rescue, he yelled and screamed for help. Everyone looked up from their chores. Uncle and the farmhands dropped what they were doing immediately. They ran towards me and diverted the gander with food in another direction and I was sent into the house. To this day I avoid anything with wings.

Werner and Heidi

In July, the Russians were advancing and the German government evacuated all Germans from Ost Preussen to Sudetenland, which was German occupied territory at the time. Today it is part of Czechoslovakia. Mutti packed up and started the move to Sudetenland.

The Russian's move into Ost Preussen was the last straw for the Nowotches. This was the second time they had had to leave everything behind. In World War I, they lost their homestead also.

Tante and the aunts and uncles packed a wagon with their belongings and left with twenty-three horses in tow. They started on the 730 mile trek to Bochum in Germany's Ruhr Valley.

Thousands of people fleeing the advancing Russians clogged the roads. Food and water for people and fodder for animals was scarce to nonexistent. Along the way one horse after the other was slaughtered for food.

The Nowotch family made it to Bochum with twelve surviving horses. They rented an apartment in Grandfather Sieg's building. The uncles built up a transporting business, and the aunts ran the household and took care of Tante.

Sudetenland

Nobody could go outside one's area of residence without official German government issued papers, not even for shopping. ID papers had to be carried on one's person at all times to be able to pass random checks. We went to Sudetenland by train with official papers for the whole family. This time Mutti traveled with two children, our belongings stuffed into a suitcase and baby carriage, all she was allowed to carry with her.

The train stopped often, usually more people got on. It was very hot and the train was jammed with evacuees heading to Sudetenland. Then, the train stopped again and this time it did not start moving again.

There were rumors of an attempt to assassinate Hitler, the date was July 20, 1944. There had been assassination attempts before, none were successful. The train stopped for three days. People had to get off and everybody and everything was thoroughly searched. No food or water was in sight, only what people carried.

People shared what they had and always gave a little extra to Margot and myself. Mutti said, "It seemed like time stood still. Everybody was tired of moving around and so tired of war, and now we were just waiting and waiting. There was nothing we could do but wait."

Finally without any explanation the train moved again. Mutti's papers designated exactly where we were supposed to go. We were billeted to an empty farm near a railway station. At first we could use the entire house but soon more people arrived and every family had one room. We were lucky to have a room with a bed. Most people slept on straw mats, sacks that were filled with straw, a buffer between the body and the hard floor.

Toward the very end of the war in April 1945, we had to share our room with another family that was fleeing from the Russians.

Not far from 'our' farm were two big farms, Hackers' and Schwarzes', which were still active. Hackers and Schwarzes became good friends with Mutti, but separately. These two farmers had been feuding for a long time and remained enemies throughout the war. They were very generous and helped the displaced people as much as they could.

Margot and I were sick almost the whole time we were there. Scarlet fever, measles, whooping cough, all in a row. First I and then Margot, and no medication.

Some Russians were stationed in the area for work details. One Russian took care of the herd of sheep for the army, their traveling meat supply. The man was a teacher in peacetime. Mutti volunteered to do his laundry. This way she also was able to get extra food for us and it also gave some sort of protection from some of the wilder soldiers.

Looting and rapes happened. Whenever she was outside and soldiers moved through the village, Mutti put dirt in her hair and on her face and black shoe polish on her teeth to look as old as possible.

Once a big, burly Russian came into our room and locked the door behind him. He went towards Mutti, who was sitting on the bed with us. She pinched both of us really hard and we promptly screamed at a high pitch. The soldier backed up. Mutti dashed to the kitchen table, picked up a butcher knife and pointed it at the soldier. We kept on screaming. The Russian backed up, quickly unlocked the door and took off.

The shepherd soldier, our protector, reported the incident to his superior, a Russian Colonel. This kind of behavior was not tolerated in the professional Russian Army. The big, burly guy was executed in a field shortly thereafter.

Pappa was stationed in nearby Brünn and could visit often. If he could not get leave, Mutti would make the short train ride to Brünn.

In the fall Mutti realized that she was expecting another baby. With the war dragging on she was not sure she wanted to bring another child into the world. But Pappa was adamant. He wanted a big family. In one of his letters he wrote,

"The war will be over soon. All signs point to that. Then I'll be home again and we will have more than enough to raise this one and maybe more."

This was one of their few arguments. "It was a big one and Pappa won," Mutti told me.

Mutti, with us in tow, was a regular visitor at Hackers' or Schwarzes' farm. She helped where she could, often in the kitchen. Again she was able to get extra food and we could play in a more peaceful environment. The two farmer's families became good friends with Mutti. With most of their farmhands serving in the army they finally made some sort of truce and helped each other. Extra help was always needed when animals were born, planting and harvesting and storing of the crops. Hackers and Schwarzes managed to survive by pitching in on the other's farm and with the help of the evacuees in the surrounding area.

Pappa came to visit at Christmas time. I remember him playing with me in bed. He made a slide for me with his legs. He put me up on his knees and down I went, landing on his stomach, over and over and over again. That is a very vivid picture in my mind. It is the only recollection I have of Pappa.

1945

The closest village was Chiech, five miles away. Mutti and several women, fellow residents in 'our' house, went on foraging trips often.

During one of those trips they were caught by a bombing raid as they walked along the mountain road. Everyone dropped whatever they were carrying and jumped into a ditch. They lay face down and prayed for it to be over. Mutti said that was a worse memory than all the bombings in Berlin.

I remember that Mutti never liked firecrackers or fireworks when I was growing up. A car backfiring would quickly bring back that afternoon on the mountain road.

In early March 1945, the Waldstrasse complex received a direct hit. The business complex was totaled and their small apartment building partially hit; two Mercedes trucks, Pappas BMW convertible and the flat bed trailers in the hangar were burned. The neighboring building also was hit and burned to the ground. The fire spread to the lone standing apartment building and burned the roof and the 5th and 6th floors. Pappa's apartment on the fourth floor was spared. The fire stopped at the living room ceiling.

Pappa's last writing - a request for furlough:
April 2, 1945
Request for Furlough
To the Company:
I am requesting a 5 to 7-day emergency leave from the company.
Reason:
My wife and two children were evacuated to the Sudetenland. She is close to the delivery of a third child and her return to Berlin is imminent.
Our apartment at Waldstrasse 32, Berlin, was severely damaged during a bomb attack. A few days leave will enable me to prepare another apartment for her return. At the same time I could look after my business that also received severe damage and is affecting my livelihood.

My Sister Hella

On March 31, my sister Hella was born. While Mutti was in labor, Margot was laying next to her sick with whooping cough. Hella was a big baby weighing almost twelve pounds. Mutti sent a telegram to Pappa, April 6, 1945: 'Big strapping girl arrived – all well.'

But Hella was sickly. Mutti could only nurse her for a couple of weeks and then realized soon that 'something just was not right.' Hella could not tolerate cow's milk. She needed a special formula from the pharmacy. But we were Germans in German occupied Czechoslovakia; Germans were not liked. Mutti could not get a prescription for the formula. Hella literally starved and died in July.

The farmers fashioned a little white coffin and helped Mutti to bury her. I clearly remember the white coffin as it was carried out of our room on the shoulders of the men.

End of World War II

On May 8, 1945, the end of the war was official with the
unconditional surrender of Germany. It ended the most
widespread war in history, involving over 100 million
personnel. It was also the deadliest conflict in human
history, resulting in 40 million to over 70 million fatalities.
That number includes Holocaust victims.

The Russians occupied the Sudetenland now.
Everybody just wanted to go home. Farmers Hacker and
Schwarz evacuated to West Germany, leaving all they
owned behind.

Mutti didn't want to go back to Berlin with the first
big mob of people. Stories of looting on the trains got back
to her and she decided to wait until the biggest mass
movement quieted down some. We were relatively safe in
the farmhouse in the countryside. During this time she
had her hands full with Hella not doing well and the two of
us to boot.

In late July, after Hella died, Mutti applied for travel
papers and in August we started the long trek to Berlin.
She was allowed to take anything she could carry and one
suitcase. She packed the baby carriage high with sheets,
blankets, pillow, and some food and put Margot on top.
Mutti stuffed the suitcase with clothes and wore two
winter coats. What she couldn't carry she had to leave
behind.

Local people helped us to the train station. The
trains were still packed with people leaving the Russian
occupied country. It was a long trip for us. Because of
broken train tracks there were many stops. We had to get
off the train at every second stop. At the first border
check, everything in the baby carriage was confiscated by
border guards, no explanation.

The trains did not run at night and everybody had
to get off. One night was spent near Leipzig. We camped at
the railroad station. The station was full of Russians; they
were trying to get home too. The Russian soldiers helped
Mutti make a bed for Margot and me and shared their food
with us.

Back on the train in the morning. Off the train, on the train. In Karlstadt we had to change train stations. The stations were about three and a half miles apart. On the way there, the baby carriage broke. People tried to help fix it, but it was hopeless. Mutti dragged the carriage, and other people helped carry the suitcase and us.

Back on a train and onward to Berlin. At Georgenstadt, the Czech border, the suitcase and silver baby spoons and a camera, the last valuables stuffed in Mutti's coat pockets, were taken from us by border guards.

Berlin, August 24, 1945

Finally, after eleven days and nights, we arrived at Anhalter Bahnhof, one of Berlin's main train stations, on August 24th. More than half of all structures in Berlin were reduced to rubble.   70% of the population was homeless.   What was once the pride of the German railroad stations; Anhalter Bahnhof was completely flattened during the final bombings of Berlin, only the train tracks remained.

We got off the train. Mutti pulled everything together and looked around for a familiar face. Trains really were the only mass transportation left after the war and the stations were a hub for people trying to find one another.

She noticed a man who had been a truck driver for Pappa. She asked him about August Sieg. He didn't recognize Mutti and said "August Sieg is dead."

This, Mutti was not prepared for.

Pappa survived so long that she didn't believe anything would happen to him. Suddenly all life seemed to drain out of her body. She couldn't think. She started wandering around the train station aimlessly. What to do? Where to go? What's next? She could not focus. Margot and I started trailing her as we were used to doing. Round and round she walked. Someone gave us a ride to Oma's house.

There she was, back in Berlin – with nothing. All household goods and other personal items stored in a barn in Fehrbellin were lost to the Russians. Moving into our Waldstrasse apartment was not an option at this time because it was temporarily lived in by other neighbors, Herr and Frau Büll.

Their fifth floor apartment was completely burned out in March 1945, when the building next to us was totaled and our roof caught fire, burning the attic and fifth floor.

Throughout the war people moved into others' apartments as needed when they were displaced by bombings. As repairs started, people were able to sometimes get back to their own homes.

We stayed with Oma.

Berlin 1945

How Pappa Died

The German Army destroyed Stalingrad in 1943. Russia wanted revenge for that and Berlin, the capital, was the ultimate goal and prize. Russian Generals Georgy Zhukov and Ivan Konev were in charge of finally taking Berlin. The shelling of the city started April 15, 1945.

The Russians officially invaded Berlin on April 20. The tactics were simple. Artillery and phosphorus-filled rockets would knock down and burn everything that might have given shelter to enemy troops or snipers. Sometimes heavy siege guns, firing shells that weighed more than half a ton, would be used as well. A Russian reporter traveling with the troops recalled, "Our guns sometimes fired a thousand shells onto one small square, a group of houses, or even a tiny garden."

In Berlin, German women uglied themselves as rumors of Russian retribution flooded the streets. The general's first echelon troops were proud and disciplined veterans, but the second echelon, filled with replacements recently freed from prisons and concentration camps, committed heinous atrocities.

The troops looted stores and banks, shot innocent civilians, and raped countless numbers of women. Casualties were high. The Russians did not take prisoners, people were shot instead. Official conservative estimates state that 22,000 civilians and 30,000 troops perished during the Fall of Berlin.

Soldiers knew that Berliners were seeking shelter in cellars. That's where most of the rapes were initiated. Whether they were girls as young as eight or old women, the soldiers did not discriminate. They were vicious and relentless. Over 90,000 women visited doctors in Berlin as a result of rape. However, an unofficial estimate puts the numbers at several hundreds of thousands. No one knows how many simply kept silent in shame.

Berlin officially surrendered May 2, 1945. The Fall of Berlin is considered one of the bloodiest battles in history.

Pappa was in Berlin for a day in late April, just as the Russians invaded. He wanted to get to Fehrbellin (60 miles west of Berlin) and make the purchase of the farm final. Pappa went to Oma's to borrow a civilian suit. He knew that she had lots of them in a closet left over from Opa's tailoring days. He also knew that he was a dead man, should the Russians catch him in uniform. Oma refused. She was bitter about the loss of her son Werner. She wasn't going to help anyone. (Relayed to Mutti by Oma).

Pappa went to one of our damaged storage cellars to sleep, before driving to Fehrbellin in the morning. The cellars weren't used by anyone.

On May 29, Herr Ulbricht, the house janitor, followed a persistent odor and found Pappa's decomposed body.

Pappa was lying on his back in a sleeping position with one arm under his head. One bullet hole in his forehead was visible. No money or his watch was found. Apparently the Russians stumbled upon him.

News spread quickly. Herr Ulbricht alerted the men at the police station across the street. Pappa was very well known and respected by everyone, including the patrolmen. They made a coffin for him out of crates. It was a great honor. Because of shortages of everything, people were buried as they were or maybe wrapped in a blanket or paper. Pappa was buried in the neighborhood's Catholic cemetery, a small plot of land next to the red brick church.

A few years later the Catholic Church exhumed all non-Catholic bodies and transferred them to other cemeteries. Mutti was notified. We walked to the small cemetery on that day.

Standing on the street we watched the men digging in Pappa's grave. The remains were moved to Plötzensee, the main cemetery in our borough.

Mutti felt they should have left the graves undisturbed, leaving the remains where they were originally buried.

Chapter Three - After the Bombs

Emdener Strasse

Although the whole neighborhood of five square blocks received heavy bombings, Oma's block on Emdener Strasse was unscathed, rising like Mount Everest out of the rubble.

Oma's apartment was small, barely 400 square feet. It was on the third floor in back of the building where the sun never reached the windows. A heavy wooden door opened to a tiny hall with two more doors, one with two milk glass window led to the narrow kitchen and the other one opened into the large living room, doubling as a bedroom.

Sharing space was nothing new; we crunched into Oma's rooms. The kitchen was the only room with running cold water, it also was the washroom. The toilet, one john with barely enough room for your knees, was half a flight downstairs and shared by four apartments.

Mutti usually went scavenging for food alone. Margot and I stayed in the apartment alone at those times because Oma was working six days a week.

Like all Berliners, she was required to help in the cleaning up and rebuilding of the city. As part of a work crew Oma was recovering, cleaning and sorting bricks from the rubble where ever they were sent. Whole bricks were carefully stacked for reuse; broken ones were tossed on a pile. Those piles of broken bricks were trucked to the Grunewald forest where a huge hill was created, 'Monte Klamott' (Mt. Rubble) nicknamed by the citizens. Years later it turned into a winter sports center complete with downhill trails, cross-country ski tracks and a ski jumping venue.

Most of the day was spent in the living room where we played and explored the same small space over and over. We also played hide and seek endlessly. Being still very small we could hide behind the tall tile oven, in the broom closet, under the bed, behind the fluffed up cushions on the sofa, under the desk, behind the piano, and so on.

The upright piano was close to the window. We were allowed to 'play' it softly and did so often, but instead of softly, we hammered away. I can't imagine what it sounded like – nobody ever complained.

At night Oma and Mutti shared a double bed. Margot and I slept on a sofa, each having our 'own' end.

Moving In

Mutti was waiting for permission to move into our apartment at Waldstrasse. The housing department was controlling occupancy in all buildings. In the spring of 1946, an apartment at Waldstrasse became available. Bülls got permission from the authorities to move out of our apartment into the vacant one a floor below.

Mutti heard about it and hoped that she could finally move into her own apartment. She applied at the housing department at City Hall to be allowed to move back.

One day, at mid-morning, the mail-mistress dropped a letter through the mail slot in our door. We rarely got any mail and Margot rushed to bring the letter to Mutti who was making lunch in the kitchen. She opened it immediately. It was from the housing department stating that she had a place to stay and the apartment would be given to someone else.

Mutti was so upset at the injustice of not letting her move into her rooms that she stopped making lunch, yanked off her apron, told us that she would be back soon and slammed the apartment door hard as she left.

City Hall was about four blocks from Emdener Strasse. She reached the offices just before they closed for the two-hour lunch break. When it was her turn the clerk again calmly told her that she had a place to stay and they would not assign her the apartment in Waldstrasse, because it had been given to a single refugee.

At that moment she lost it. At the top of her lungs she recited all she had experienced throughout the war, stopping only after relaying learning of Pappa's death and living with her mother in the one-room apartment. "You mean after all this you will not let me move into my own apartment with my two small children?!!!!"

A long silence followed, as Mutti recalled later. All clerks, about twenty of them, in the huge square office looked up from their work and were staring at her.

"I'll be back in a moment Frau Sieg," the clerk quietly excused himself.

He returned with the supervisor, "I apologize for the mistake, Frau Sieg, we didn't realize this is your own house and your apartment," he said and stamped a moving visa allowing her access to our apartment.

Meanwhile Margot and I were hoping Mutti would be back soon to fix our lunch, as we were hungry. When we heard the key sliding into the door lock we quickly went into the small hall. Mutti was very quiet and went straight into the living room. We followed her and could barely hear when she said, "I have a big headache, and it hurts so bad I can hardly see." She went to the window and closed the drapes and then she just took off her shoes and slid under the comforter on the bed. "Oma will be home soon, just wait for her." We pulled the door shut.

Margot and I spent the afternoon in the kitchen trying to be very quiet and waited. Our stomachs were growling. We were not allowed to touch anything in the kitchen, because this was Oma's place, and so we waited and waited being very hungry. We couldn't tell time yet but knew Oma always came home toward the evening meal. Finally she arrived home.

First she went in to see Mutti. We listened at the door, but all we heard was murmuring. Then Oma went with us in the kitchen. She quickly made us a sandwich and said that we would be moving to Waldstrasse.

The following morning Mutti felt good again. She told us that going to the housing department had given her such a migraine that she felt like throwing up all afternoon and that's why she stayed in bed.

After breakfast we went to check out our future home. Bülls had already moved into their apartment. Mutti rang their doorbell to make sure all was in order before we went up. They were home, invited us in and showed Mutti how well all their furniture fitted into the rooms.

Onto the floor above and our apartment where the name plate 'Sieg' was still next to the doorbell! The apartment had a small hall, a kitchen with a window looking out the backyard, an oblong bedroom for Margot and me to share, also with a window to the back and a larger square room with two windows facing the street. This would be the living room and Mutti's bedroom as well.

It was the room with the most damage. About half of the ceiling's plaster was missing, revealing a hole close to the outside wall. The hole was about four feet in diameter, showing charred lath and nothing but darkness above. When a bomb totaled the adjacent building, the floor above and the attic burned, only the brick walls were left standing. The fire was stopped before it could consume our apartment also. The roof was patched with tarpaper.

The next day went to the apartment early. First Mutti opened all windows, "to bring in fresh air." The kitchen had a white cupboard for dishes, a white wooden table and two chairs. It also had a small tile oven for cooking and heating and a two-burner gas cook top next to it. The small sink with a single faucet was close to the kitchen door.

Next we checked a room to the right of the kitchen. Mutti told us, "This is going to be the bedroom for you to share. I'll sleep in the other room." The room had a *Kachelofen*, an upright tiled oven, for heating in the corner next to the door. At the far end was a south-facing window. Below the window the frame of a white iron bed and the metal box spring were leaning against the wall, no mattress, no sheets.

The other, larger room with its two street-fronting windows would be the living room and also Mutti's bedroom. It was empty except for a big landscape painting on one wall and a *Kachelofen* in a corner by the door.

Mutti let out a deep sigh, "I don't know where I'm going to find enough for us to sleep on!"

Mutti took us along when she went to call on each tenant to say 'Hello, we are back.' Of course, everyone had lived in the building for a long time and knew Mutti. During the conversation the emptiness of the apartment always came up. In the process, almost all neighbors volunteered something they didn't use or need.

Bülls had extra sheets and could also give us three towels and washcloths, "They are a little worn but we saved them anyway."

Aunt Schneider, in the apartment below, had a small sofa in her living room that she really didn't need, "I have two and just kept it because I didn't know what to do with it." Her adult children, Lutz and Susie, would bring it upstairs when they returned from the schools where they were teachers. She also had extra dishes and a couple of pillows and blankets.

Mrs. Schenck, in the store on the ground floor, would send her husband up with several pots, a teakettle and a frying pan. She also had curtains for us, stored in the attic in the building next door that miraculously escaped all bombings, "I've had them forever and bought new ones just before the war started. I'd be very pleased if you could use them. Oh, and we also have a mattress in the attic that we don't need."

Mrs. Fülster, on the second floor, said "We have an extra table at our summer cottage. We will bring it back and you can have it for the living room."

Mrs. Broczinzki, living with her mother and sister in the apartment next to us had a *Schrank*, an armoire, which she would like Mutti to have, "When I moved in with Mother, I brought it with me. We now have three of them in our small living room and it is really too much."

Slowly our little apartment had all the necessities and Mutti got busy setting up the bed for us. When Mr. Schenck brought the mattress, the bed was ready. He came back one more time with the curtains that his wife had offered.

By now it was about one in the afternoon – time for lunch. Mutti bought a quarter of a loaf of dark rye bread and cup of milk at the grocery store across the street. We huddled around at the kitchen table and dunked bread slices in a bowl with the milk for a yummy meal.

After lunch Lutz and Susie brought up the sofa for the living room; it became Mutti's bed.

Later in the afternoon we walked the few blocks back to Oma's apartment. She was home already and had bags packed with our things waiting for us. A neighbor loaned us a small flat cart with a long string for a handle to help with moving. We watched Oma and Mutti carry the stuffed bags down and load them onto the cart.

Oma pulled the cart along the street avoiding the up and downs of the sidewalks. Mutti walked along one side and Margot and I on the other, making sure none of the bags fell over. We didn't look up until we maneuvered the four blocks to our house.

Now everything was carried upstairs. Mr. Schenck who was still at the store came out to help and made one trip upstairs with two bags. Oma and Mutti managed the others.

Oma helped unpack and looked around the rooms. She was surprised, "Where did you get the sofa and the *Schrank*?" Mutti went on to relay the events of the day as they unpacked. It did not take long. Oma had packed some basics for us: flour, a few eggs, a dollop of butter, a bit of salt, some cooking spoons, a small piece of soap, etc. Last out of the bag were a couple of small candles. Candles were a necessary staple. Electricity was severely restricted; at first we only had power for two hours in the morning and from 6 to 8 in the evening.

Finally Oma said her good-byes. Mutti opened the living room window and we leaned out and waved to Oma as she walked home, stopping now and then to turn and wave back. At the last corner she turned and waved one more time.

It was getting dark and we had to get ready for bed. We washed our hands and face at the kitchen sink under the cold running water. Mutti lit a candle and led us to our room. We crawled into our new bed and Mutti kissed us *"Gute Nacht"* - good-night. She left the room with the candle and closed the door.

It was dark now and silent in the room. It felt strange. We had never been in a room alone at night. As far as we could remember there always had been at least one other person around. We were both lying there wide-awake. Time went by.

"Are you asleep?" I asked. "No", said Margot. "Do you think we can sleep with Mutti?" We got out of bed and carefully made our way to the door in the dark. We went across the hall, found the living room door handle and opened it. In the dim candlelight we saw Mutti settled in on the sofa. She was propped up by a couple of pillows reading a book. We rushed over and crawled in next to her.

"What is all this?" she asked us smiling. "We can't sleep!" I said. "Well, all right, you can stay here for a minute, but then you have to go to your bed. This sofa really isn't big enough for all of us."

She added, "You'll get used to your room and you can keep each other company."

Just when it began to feel warm and cozy next to Mutti she said, "Now it's time for you to go to sleep." She led us back to our bed in the dark, tucked us in and gently closed the door. We fell asleep quickly then.

The next morning Mutti called us to get up and we started what became our usual routine.

The toilet room, just a toilet – no sink, was off the stairwell half a flight down and shared by four apartments. It was our last stop before going to bed, hoping we did not have to go in the middle of the night. In the morning it was our first action. We grabbed the key and made a dash downstairs, hoping that it was not taken already.

As usual we went together. Going downstairs to the john, often in a dimly lit staircase, felt creepy. Margot and I never went alone, giving advance notice, "Hey, I have to go to the john soon." In the mornings we didn't have to give notice.

There was no light or heat in our stairwell 'outhouse.' When it was dark we lit a candle and carried it, hoping it wouldn't blow out from the draft on the stairs. The lights in the staircase were on a timer and always out when we were ready to go back to the apartment. The flickering candle made weird shadows on the wall as we hurried upstairs.

Meanwhile Mutti heated water in the kettle for our morning sponge bath in the kitchen. In a big bowl she mixed hot and just enough cold water to comfy temperature. After I was done scrubbing myself from top to bottom, Mutti emptied the bowl in the sink and made fresh water for Margot. I proceeded to brush my teeth at the kitchen sink. We did not have many clothes, just one outfit for weekdays and one for Sundays. It did not take long for us to get dressed.

Then it was time for breakfast. In those days it would be a slice of bread with a little butter scratched across the surface.

Mutti went out to see what she could get for food. We usually stayed home. Everything was still rationed. The only food always available was bread. Other than that

Mutti often came home with very little in her bag. Our standard lunchtime meal was a soup or stew of some kind. Mutti had a soup pot on the gas stove and made a different soup out of the leftover one from the day before with the addition of whatever she was able to get that day.

We rarely used the living room. Breakfast, lunch and dinner were eaten in the kitchen. Mutti acquired a third chair somewhere and we could sit down together at the kitchen table. When we were not eating I was always sitting at the kitchen table watching Mutti at her chores.

Slowly we became familiar with our new surroundings. Quickly we learned who lived on what floor.

We were not allowed to go outside. Because of the nearby railroad station the neighborhood was not a safe one for children, especially in the early years after the war. Men were always standing around in groups at the entrance of the rail yard looking for work. Many times, after they worked and got paid, they would go to the Pub at the corner and drink away, even in the middle of the day. Then, drunk and unruly, they would bum around the street. It just was not a place for children.

Waldstrasse - The Village that Raised Us

Waldstrasse 32. Pappa bought the property in 1935, which used to be a building complex with three five-story apartment buildings. One building was facing the street and two additional buildings had entrances off the back courtyard. In back of the courtyard also was a small two-story building with an apartment and an office where Pappa used to run his business. The office and apartment were on the second floor with stables for the horses that pulled the delivery trailers below. Next to it was a big hangar for trucks, cars and trailers. Beneath everything was a cavernous basement used for storing potatoes.

The house in all its glory no longer existed when I was growing up. For me Waldstrasse started as a building with the fifth and sixth floor 'as burned out caverns' and a tarpaper patched roof. Our apartment was on the fourth floor with the living room ceiling partially open to the floor above. When it rained the patched roof did not give much protection. Water dripped from the hole and we had a couple of buckets underneath to catch it.

Including the ground floor shop there were ten rental units. The janitor on the second floor, the former owner on the third floor and our unit were rent free, leaving seven for rental income. Built in 1910, the house needed ongoing repairs, and plumbing was a constant issue.

Mutti kept the property manager Pappa had hired, because "I don't have the stamina anymore that business requires." She continued "I feel real bad when I have to tell a tenant that repairs have to wait. I know they are not asking for much. It bothers me and I can't deal with it."

Mrs. Marquard came on the first of every month when the tenants paid their rent. One at a time they came to our apartment to pay. It was also the time to report any repairs needed in their apartment.

The majority of our growing years played out within four blocks of the house. Across the street was a grocery store, right next to the police station. A bakery was three houses up on our side of the street. Within those blocks we had three additional bakeries, two other grocers, two florists, a paint store, a hardware store, a hobby shop and a movie theater.

All tenants in the building and neighborhood had been there for a long time and those were the people who watched us grow up. Those families knew Pappa. Some we came to call aunt or uncle. They were our extended family.

A huge wooden double door, wide and high enough to let trucks drive through to the business yard, was the main entrance. Just inside the door was a light switch for evenings. In the early years the staircase lights were on timers set for two minutes and then shut off. Since we lived on the fourth floor, the lights would go off before we reached our door often. It became a game to race up the stairs, trying to make it without getting caught in the dark. Even in later years when the lights stayed on from 8 pm to 10 pm and only were on the timer after that, we still raced up the stairs, high heels and all.

There was another reason we tried setting records getting to our apartment. The odor in the stairwell could be 'gaggingly' strong. Coming home from school at lunchtime was quite interesting 'smell wise.' Passing each apartment I would know what was being cooked for lunch there. Sometimes it was mouth watering. Fridays though, fish day, was different. Every kitchen produced a fish dish and the stale odor could be overwhelming. Another reason to race to the safety of our apartment on the fourth floor. Those times we added the challenge of racing upstairs while holding our breath!

Then there is the fact that, except for one apartment on the third floor with indoor plumbing, all toilets were off the landing between floors. Although there were windows at all landings, the lack of fresh air mixed with odors from the toilets could be challenging at times.

Waldstrasse
1956
With Margot and Uncle Alfred
Our house is towards the back on the left.
The freight yard entrance is at the center.

Our Neighbors

Herr und Frau Schenck

Mr. and Mrs. Schenk owned the coal and potato store on the ground floor. They arrived early from their nearby apartment every day but Sundays, and stayed late. One could buy coal and carry it home or have larger amounts delivered.

Mrs. Schenck was in the store all the time, looking up and giving a wave if she saw us pass. As we got older and were allowed to play on the sidewalk, she always let us keep the toy of the moment, maybe a ball or jump rope or chalk, under the store counter.

Schencks had a German shepherd guard dog that was friendly with people he knew, both of us included. We would come into the store and 'Albo' would greet us and then go back to his usual spot behind the counter.

One day Margot rushed into the store and behind the counter to pick up our red ball. Albo was napping on his mat. Margot picked up the ball and as she was leaving the store Albo ran up behind her and bit her in the thigh! He obviously did not have enough time to identify Margot as 'friend.' From then on we both were extremely conscious of making noise and identifying ourselves as we walked in the store.

Schencks didn't have any children. Mrs. Schenck always liked to hear what we were doing, where we were going or what was happening in school.

Herr und Frau Ulbricht

Mr. and Mrs. Ulbricht also had no children. Mr. Ulbricht was the janitor and maintenance man of the building. He was the one who found Pappa's body in the storage cellar and alerted the police. Mr. Ulbricht never, ever smiled. He did talk to Mutti, not to us.

Mrs. Ulbricht was always friendly, although reserved. She had a job at the Berlin Opera. She worked every night at the concession stand before the performances and during intermission. She always looked dressed up in her all black 'uniform' when she went to work in the late afternoon. We did not talk much, but sometimes she would relay a particular busy night and how the staff handled it all in detail.

She described how they set out all the appetizers and sweets and poured many glasses of wine in anticipation of a rush. Then, at her designated post, she worked fast to serve as many people as possible within the 15-minute intermission. Cleaning up did not take nearly as long and she was home in the early evening. I thought it sounded very glamorous. I have recalled her focus on organization and planning often.

When we went door to door to show our grades at the end of a semester, as was customary, we always hoped that the Mrs. would be home and answer the door. She would look over the paper, ask about a subject and give us a quarter each. Margot always had better grades than I did.

Herr und Frau Fülster

Mr. and Mrs. Fülster and their son Jürgen kept to themselves pretty much like everyone else. I guess it was a remnant of the war years and before when everyone had to be careful and couldn't trust anybody, even friends and family. But when we met there were always the pleasantries about where we were going and what we were up to. Greetings remained formal - that was the German way. No first names, we didn't even know people's first names.

Although Jürgen was close to my age, we never played. We went to the same elementary school, but he was 'older,' a couple of years ahead of me.

Fülster's had a little garden in a section of Berlin where one could lease a small plot of land for 20 or 30 years at a time. Those neighborhoods were known as *Schrebergarten Kolonie* – leased garden plots – a green oasis in the city. The land was maybe an eighth of an acre and people were very industrious, growing vegetables and fruit trees on almost every inch of the land. A small structure was also allowed as long as it was not 'permanent,' Outside looks were very deceiving. The little huts were extremely well finished and equipped, often probably more comfortable than their small apartments. No wonder people spent weekends and often weeks there.

From early spring through late summer Fülster's regularly brought "something fresh from the garden" for Mutti.

One summer they invited Margot to come and visit there for the afternoon. Jürgen gave her a ride on his bicycle. In the early evening our doorbell rang. Jürgen was standing outside carrying a crying Margot. Apparently she dozed off during the ride home and one foot got caught in the spokes of the back wheel. Her ankle was bleeding and hurt. He felt really bad although it wasn't his fault. Mutti checked the leg. The skin was cut badly. Mutti bandaged up the ankle and for a couple of days Margot was propped up on Mutti's bed – the official 'sick bed.' She started walking again when the skin was sufficiently healed. It was Margot's only visit to Fülster's garden.

Herr und Frau Büll

Mr. and Mrs. Büll were in the small apartment on the third floor. The third floor traditionally had the fanciest apartments in all buildings in Berlin. Here the ceilings were higher and one of the apartments had a bathroom!

Mr. Büll was a retired clown from a big circus. He and his wife traveled the world until the start of the war.

Theirs was a fun place to stop. Mr. Büll always practiced old magic tricks on us. Sometimes it would be a new one and when it worked we would all laugh and laugh. When he laughed his eyes were sparkly and dancing and his tiny 4 foot 8 inch frame was shaking. Mrs. Büll, on the other hand, was a foot taller and weighed at least twice as much. When she laughed her body was jiggling like pudding. Sometimes Mr. Büll greeted us at the door with his red clown nose on and we were giggling the minute we stepped inside.

When I didn't know what to do with myself, Mutti often suggested, "Why don't you go and visit Uncle and Aunt Büll." When they were home I was always welcome.

Uncle Büll owned a little newspaper stand at the end of the block. He had to get up early to be at the kiosk for the paper deliveries around 4:30. Then he would be busy selling the daily papers to people going to work. After this first rush, Aunt Büll would go there so he could go home and have breakfast. They took turns throughout the day.

Coming home from school I always stopped to say hello at the kiosk. During the winter months he huddled inside the 5x8 wooden kiosk, a blanket wrapped around him, a kerosene lamp at his feet and wearing gloves with the fingertips cut off. The tiny window was only open enough to slide a paper through. When the season was milder he would be outside greeting people from afar.

Mutti helped out if one of the two was under the weather. On those days she would bring home Mickey Mouse and other cartoon magazines for us to read until she had to take them back in the morning.

I was probably eight or so when Uncle Büll asked once in a while if I could stay at the kiosk for as spell while he went home, probably going to the bathroom.

Of course, I loved it and was very proud to take his place. During our many chats I watched how he would get a customer's request without looking. So, when I was the salesperson, the first thing I did was to memorize the paper and magazine locations, hoping to get as good as he. Once I was familiar with all spots I crammed a lot of reading into that hour, or so, I was there.

Frau Schneider

Aunt Schneider was the former owner of the building and a war widow like Mutti. Her apartment on the third floor was the only one with a full interior bathroom. Pappa bought the building from Professor Schneider in 1935. Aunt Schneider, and her son Lutz and daughter Suzie lived rent-free in the apartment as part of the purchase deal.

Lutz was a high school teacher and Suzie studied at the university to become a teacher also. They both helped me with homework if needed and were great sounding boards. Suzie tutored English and French and Lutz helped me with algebra. Lutz often asked what was going on in school. His public demeanor was very serious but he took the time to have a little lighthearted banter going with me and I usually was not sure if he was fooling or not. He joked a lot and generally spread good-hearted teasing around. Aunt Schneider would just roll her eyes at his jokes.

I had to be at my absolute best behavior and minding my manners, because Aunt Schneider would report every minute variation to Mutti. It was Mutti's aim to raise children who were at least equal, if not more accomplished, than Aunt Schneider's.

Aunt Suzie was engaged. She was the first bride to be I knew, and it was very exciting to keep up with the planning. She was marrying Horst Kloss, a postal employee.

Word usually got around when, and at what address, there was an impending wedding. People gathered on the street and waited for the bride and groom. On Aunt Suzie's wedding, day Margot and I waited at the entrance door of our house very early to be sure we would get a good look at the bride. It was so exciting. Aunt Suzie saw us right away and winked as she walked to the waiting white horse-drawn carriage taking her to the church.

Then we waited for the whole bridal party to return for the wedding celebration. We were invited for cake and coffee and got to sit next to the bride. Well, that was the most exciting event for a while! The married couple lived with Aunt Schneider for several years before moving to a neighborhood near the Grunewald Forest.

Frau Broczinzki

Mrs. Broczinzki, her sister and mother lived in a small one-bedroom apartment. Aunt Broczinzki, a widow, was very tall and skinny and had white hair, just like her mother. After her husband died her mother and sister, who were evacuated from the eastern part of Germany, moved in. The two sisters took care of the elderly mother who was not well and mostly in bed. They were all old by my standards.

Aunt Broczinzki worked as a part-time housekeeper in addition to taking care of her mother. Whenever I visited their apartment, everything was virtually sparkling. The linoleum kitchen floor was as shiny as the windows.

One day, after coming home from school, I saw a hearse in front of the building. I asked Mrs. Schenck in

the store, "Why is the hearse here?" "*Kindchen* – little one"
she said, "Mrs. Broczinski's mother's cold got worse and
she died this morning."

I quickly went upstairs, hoping not to meet the
people carrying down the coffin. Mutti must have heard
me because she opened the door as I reached our landing.

A little later we heard the heavy footsteps going
past our door. We were very quiet and Mutti said, "The
mother was very old and sick for a long time. This is better
for her...and also for Mrs. Broczinzki. She had been taking
care of her for years."

Musgangs

In the summer of 1952, the house was renovated through
the Marshall Plan. The burned out fifth floor was restored
with brand new apartments. The attic and roof also were
new when all was completed. Tenants moved around. Mrs.
Broczinzki moved into the fifth floor apartment on the left.
The right side held a double apartment. Other tenants,
Mr. and Mrs. Heumann, living in a one-room apartment
with two children, applied for the two-room apartment,
but refugees from the East were given preference.

Mr. and Mrs. Musgang and their five children
moved into the apartment above us. The adjoining
apartment was rented to a single woman, their adult
daughter, Miss Musgang.

As far as we could see, Musgangs, as we called the
family, moved in with very little. Soon new furniture was
brought up the stairs. "Bought with their refugee
allowance," Mutti commented. Mr. Musgang did go to
work every day. Mutti thought he was a construction
worker.

It is the weekends I remember the most. Mr.
Musgang always came home late and very drunk on
Fridays. We could tell when he came home. He talked very
loud to himself as he slowly made his way upstairs. Then
we heard the bang of the apartment door slamming,
followed by lots of yelling by both Mr. and Mrs. They were
obviously fighting.

We had never experienced anything like it and
followed the happenings awestruck. Until now, the most
noteworthy noise among the mostly older tenants was the

slamming of a door. Sometimes it was followed by a "Sorry, the wind ripped the door right out of my hand" yelled to no one but directed at everyone into the stairwell.

Sometimes the children would leave the apartment and sit on the stairway until the parents quieted down.

When he overturned the furniture during the ruckus the noise was something else. We could tell what kind of furniture was being tossed. Chairs only made a light thump, the sofa was a dull thud, and the table was a hollow thud. The kitchen cabinet with the dishes made the most ruckus. Sometimes there was a long silence after a big thump. We waited quietly for the next noise wondering what we'd hear next. And so it went.

Once in a while the Mrs. sent one of the children across the street to the police station. Then the patrol car came and escorted a handcuffed Mr. Musgang to jail and all was quiet in the neighborhood again. Mrs. Musgang never pressed charges and he would be back by the following afternoon. After a big ruckus like that, it was quiet for two or three weeks and then the circus started all over again.

Mutti often sarcastically remarked how people behaving like that had lots of rights because they were refugees and solid hardworking Germans just could not get any help. Mutti went to the housing department once to see if she could evict the family because all tenants feared a confrontation with Mr. Musgang. Even sober he was very temperamental and surly. But that, and the many arrests, was not a reason for eviction.

Our weekend 'by-stander' adventures continued. We were very aware not to be in the stairwell at the same time as Mr. Musgang on Friday nights.

Miss Musgang

Miss Musgang left the house early every morning and came back very late at night, if at all. We could tell because of the lack of activity above us. Mutti was not sure if she was working or not. She dressed very strangely for a woman, stranger than Aunt Ruth, who was also always wearing slacks, a 'no no' for women at the time. She also had very short cropped, slicked back hair. Tsk, tsk, lots of whispering.

A couple of years later Miss Musgang moved out. During many chuckling and tsk-tsk adult conversations, I overheard that Miss Musgang moved in with a girl friend and Miss Musgang was the boyfriend!

Minna and Herr Heuman

The only person new in the complex was Mrs. Jüngling. She lived in a small one-room apartment behind the store with her daughter Jutta, Margot's age and infant son Lutz. We had very little contact with her at first. Mr. Jüngling was never around; he had been in jail for robbery for several years. The baby was not his and was talked about when everyone thought I couldn't hear. Because of some legal loophole she had to wait for Mr. Jüngling to finish his jail sentence before she could divorce him.

Mrs. Jüngling met Mr. Heumann, Lutz's father, while she was on a work detail re-claiming bricks from the rubble.

Mrs. Jüngling worked as a part-time housekeeper. She also helped Mutti here and there. Sometimes doing an errand, sometimes looking after us. They often had long conversations in the kitchen about the years passed and 'the state of the state' today. Soon she had the nickname 'Minna' short version for 'maid' and became a member of our small family.

Minna was not a 'city girl'; she grew up in Schlesien – Silesia – and missed the country. She was in a heavily bombed area during the war, her nerves were shot, and she couldn't stand any noise or uncertainty. Now she just wanted peace and quiet.

After her baby was born, Social Services paid her weekly visits to assure she was a fit mother, although she already raised Jutta. It seemed to her that they harassed her. She would get very nervous before the impending weekly visits and worried that they would take away the baby, whom she loved. She was close to a nervous breakdown many times; she went to a doctor often for counseling and medication.

Once though, she did have a breakdown. Mutti saw an ambulance coming while looking out the window. She quickly sent us downstairs to check on Minna. Margot and I got there the same time as the ambulance drivers with the cot. Apparently she had a complete breakdown while a social worker was asking questions. They called the ambulance.

Minna was crying, "They are taking me to a sanitarium. They are taking Jutta and Lutz to a home. I can't stand it. What will happen to me?" over and over. I remember holding Minna's hand while the ambulance personnel strapped her onto the cot and then all the way to the ambulance. Margot walked on the other side. We told her we would be here when she came back, "Yes, you'll come back. And you'll get Jutta and Lutz back also. Mutti said so." She was reassured but was softly sobbing as the ambulance door closed.

Mutti visited Minna a couple of weeks later and was able to reassure her that the children were only in a home while she was recuperating. Social Services told Mutti that Jutta and Lutz would be returned the day Minna got home. After several months of treatment in the sanitarium, Minna was released and the children came home the next day. Although Minna still got edgy before any special events or Social Services appointments, she always came through it without 'episodes,' as she called her breakdowns of the past.

Once divorced she and Mr. Heumann married and Social Services ceased visiting.

Everybody liked Minna. She always listened patiently, was sympathetic and understanding, and generously handed out humorous advice. Next to Mutti we were closer to Minna than any other member of our family.

Minna was good for Mutti also. Since Minna was a single mother until she married Mr. Heumann, she understood perfectly what Mutti was up against. She also understood the sarcasm Mutti had developed as self-defense, living with her brothers and now used it again when she was upset. Minna found a way not to take it personally, even when it was directed towards her. "Oh, she'll get over it. I bet she's feeling better already," she used to say.

When Miss Musgang moved out, Minna and Mr. Heumann applied for the apartment and moved there from their ground-level room. Now Minna lived just one flight up from us.

Our Berlin Relatives

Oma

At first Oma lived a few blocks away at Emdener Strasse. After she was finished with the mandated work of cleaning up and reclaiming useable bricks from the rubble, she began working on an assembly line at a machine factory six days a week and we rarely saw her. Sometimes, on Sundays, Margot and I visited her for a little while and then went back home. Our greetings were always very formal, a handshake and curtsey.

I'm not sure if it was 1947 or 48 when Mutti quietly mentioned, "Oma is going to court today to get the divorce."

"What is divorce?" I asked. I had not heard it mentioned before.

Mutti explained, "When people marry, they usually stay together. Divorce is frowned upon and people simply do not talk about it, and when they do, it is with disdain for the people involved."

She continued, "Oma will no longer be married to Opa. After the war was over he did not come back to the West. Because of his Nazi Party affiliation he felt safer in East Germany. He didn't rank high in the Nazi Party but he was very visible in the Emdener Strasse neighborhood and everybody knew that he reported anything and everything to the higher ranking officials. He knew that if he came back to Berlin he would be arrested. No one will go after him there. Many Nazis are In East Germany or in South America. Because of this circumstance, Oma could start proceedings for a divorce without Opa's consent. Oma will be all right, she has lived alone for several years now."

We never had any contact with my grandfather. Many years later Mutti learned that he had moved in with her sister who lived in the Spreewald Region in East Germany, not far from Berlin.

After living at her Emdener Strasse apartment for forty years, Oma moved into an apartment in our building in 1952. Luckily the move did not really take her out of familiar territory. She could still visit many of the same stores.

We saw her more often then, even if it was just to say *"Guten Tag,"* hello. She kept her own household but often joined us for Sunday afternoon coffee.

After she retired and Mutti started working, she helped Mutti keep the apartment neat. She also started to visit her sister, Aunt Anni, in Tempelhof once a week.

Uncle Alfred

From our kitchen window we could see the backyard where Pappa's business used to be. Uncle Alfred lived there now and was building the same potato wholesale/retail business for himself. During the war he was shot in the thigh and was now walking with a stiff leg.

Severe TB ravaged one of his lungs and he was waiting for surgery. In 1946, he agreed to an experimental procedure where one lung was replaced with a balloon-like rubber bladder. It would keep the chest cavity from collapsing and enable the other lung to function more easily.

Aunt Elfriede had moved in and took care of the house and business as she had done for Pappa before he married. They lived together in the apartment above the garage in the backyard

Mutti did not like Uncle Alfred. She was angry because she had to pay full price for potatoes like all other customers. He did not give us any extra. As a result, Mutti looked for other stores. Margot and I did not go there often in the early days.

Aunt Hilda and Werner

Aunt Hilda and Uncle Alfred were divorced right after the war. She and their son Werner lived in Weissensee, East Berlin, with her mother who was widowed. We spent a lot of time with Aunt Hilda and Werner on the farm in Sudentenland during evacuations from Berlin.

Werner visited his father on weekends and during school vacations. He came by city train and I knew the times he usually arrived. That's when I went to the backyard and we spent a lot of time together.

I don't remember seeing Aunt Hilda again until the early 50's. From then on we made regular visits to Weissensee on holidays and her birthday at the end of August.

Aunt Elfriede

When Uncle Alfred married in the summer of 1950, Aunt Elfriede moved out promptly. She found a little studio apartment in the borough of Kreuzberg. It was kind of a rough neighborhood.

She kept to herself and was considered 'odd.' She was very attractive, slim and often with a gentle smile on her face, but never married. By this time she was in her mid-thirties and an old maid by the standards of the time. Mutti said that she had lots of suitors as a young woman. "I guess nobody measured up to her taste," Mutti would finish up one of those conversations. We only visited her a couple of times and later lost all contact.

But before that happened she invited me to visit and spend the night during one summer vacation. Telephones were still rare, all arrangements were done per postcard, so it took several weeks until a date was set.

One morning Mutti walked me to the city tram heading for Kreuzberg, a half hour ride. Aunt Elfriede was waiting at the station.

We walked to her apartment building close to a very big and picturesque park. The apartment was in the cellar in the rear of the complex. Many buildings renovated unused cellars and created apartments. Aunt Elfriede's was one of those.

We walked down dimly lit stairs into the cellar and then along a narrow hallway to her door. It was damp in the hallway and the air almost not breathable. Only the light from the stairs made anything barely visible.

Once inside it was still dark. The room only had one very tiny window near the ceiling at the far end. There was one ceiling light with a low light bulb. Aunt Elfriede lit a couple of candles and everything looked cheerier already.

There really was not much to do. We talked about what Margot and I were doing while she cooked *Mittagessen*, the mid-day meal, on a one burner cook top.

The apartment was tiny. A twin bed was tucked into an alcove. A kitchen table and a couple of chairs were in the middle of the room. The rest of the furniture was a dresser where the radio was and an armoire. On the wall over the cook top were a few shelves for the dishes.

After lunch we walked around her neighborhood, looking at all the stores and windows where she went shopping. Then we went to the park. It was huge, terraced into a hillside of the Kreuzberg with small ponds and fountains at almost every level. It was so different from other more traditional parks that I knew. We spent the rest of the afternoon there. I really enjoyed it.

Then we went back to the small apartment. What stands out is the darkness of the hallway and also in her apartment. We went to bed early. I remember being very restless and having a hard time falling asleep. But then suddenly it was morning and time to get up. Again a very creepy walk to the toilet room in the dark hallway.

And after breakfast it was time to get to the tram and my ride back home. I must have been nine or ten, I remember thinking that Aunt Elfriede was lonely and I felt sorry for her. I also had the feeling that the time spent together didn't cheer her up.

After my visit we met her in a park a couple of times. I don't know if it was coincidence or not. Although Mutti always invited her for birthdays, she never came.

She came along to Opa Sieg's funeral in 1952 and I think that was the last time I saw her.

Occasionally we heard from acquaintances who had seen her. Years later we heard that she moved to West Germany. She never made contact again.

Uncle Helmut, Aunt Elschen, Ingrid and Dorit

Uncle Helmut and Aunt Elschen lived with her parents, Mr. and Mrs. Freier, in their one-bedroom apartment since they married in 1939. Mr. Freier was killed during the battle for Stalingrad, Russia, in 1943. Mrs. Freier worked in a factory and Aunt Elschen took care of the children and the household. Uncle Helmut was in a prisoner of war camp in Siberia, Russia.

Ingrid and Dorit were our closest cousins. Although they lived only two short blocks from us, we did not see them very often in the early years. Families were busy coping with recovering from the war and surviving everyday life. We occasionally played in the summer months, and we always got along.

Uncle Helmut finally came back in the fall of 1949. He was 'skin and bones,' there was no better way to describe him, but he survived the labor camps he'd been in. (More about his life in 'Soldiers', page 173).

Mutti's side of the family basically stopped getting together after the war. Aunt Elschen had separated herself somewhat from us. After Helmut returned the tradition of birthday and holiday gatherings was slowly re-established. I think Uncle Helmut expected life to continue as he had known it before the war and that included visiting on birthdays. Oma's birthday in August became the largest gathering of the year. (Oma's Birthday, page 169).

Aunt Hille and Uncle Erich

Aunt Hille, Hilde Bahr, was not really related. She dated Uncle Werner for many years and they were engaged at the time of his death. Everybody loved her cheerful disposition and she stayed close to the family.

She stayed in touch throughout the war. She was crazy about children and married Erich Piatzina in 1943. Erich was a soldier and also was in a Russian prison camp. While a prisoner, he contracted TB and was released right after the war was over. He recuperated at a medical facility. One of his lungs was removed, but he did not have the restoring surgery that Uncle Alfred received. He was considered 100% disabled and couldn't work.

Aunt Hille was very sad to have no children of her own. When she mentioned it, it was followed by a deep sigh and silence.

Once the family gatherings resumed, we saw them two or three times a year at birthdays and more often when there was a special occasion like Confirmation (Protestant 'coming of age' ceremony – see Religion page 202) or a wedding.

Aunt Hille was my absolute favorite! She always hugged me close and asked lots of questions about what I was doing during school vacation, what book I was reading, and so forth. She also came to my defense, or Ingrid's, when we were 'picked on' by the other adults. Margot and Dorit, being younger, usually were left alone by the other grown-ups. So, of course I loved her.

Aunt Anni and Uncle Emil

Aunt Anni was Oma's sister. Anni and Emil Warnke lived in Tempelhof, a very nice residential section of Berlin. They had quite a large apartment that also had a balcony, a very prized amenity. Although they were very close to the airport, there was no bombing damage in the neighborhood.

We usually visited twice a year, during the summer for Uncle Emil's birthday and in December for Aunt Anni's. When it was Aunt Anni's birthday we also knew that Christmas was really close.

Uncle Emil worked at a bank. Because of his poor eyesight, he wore very thick glasses, he did not qualify for the Army. Aunt Anni worked as a seamstress from the apartment. They did not have any children.

Aunt Anni always had a treat waiting for us when we arrived. During the summer visit we played on the balcony after we had our piece of cake. From the balcony we could glimpse some of the nearby Tempelhof Airport. Sometimes we were allowed to walk from the apartment to the fence surrounding the airport.

When we were a little older we were allowed to walk to the airport. It took a couple of hours. It was fascinating to watch the planes take off and land as we walked around the fencing until we reached the entrance. As soon as we arrived at the entrance, we had to turn around to be back at the apartment in time for supper. It always seemed like a real adventure.

Always Hungry

I remember very clearly being hungry all the time when I was little. Everything had been rationed since before the war started in 1939. Food was scarce during the war. Once the war was over it was even more difficult. At first you could barter for additional food by going to farmers in the surrounding countryside. As the years stretched on, less and less was to be had.

Hungry and obsessed with food, Margot and I managed to find what was there. I discovered liverwurst in the kitchen cabinet when less than two years old. Mutti found me sitting on the kitchen floor with liverwurst all over my face having eaten the whole thing.

My memory is hazy of the times during the war when we spent several months at farms in Schlesien – Silesia, and Pommern. Food was plentiful there, but I was a very finicky eater; no eggs, no chicken, no milk. Mutti was often beside herself with my lack of appreciation, knowing how hard it was to get anything in Berlin.

From daily routines to special events, everything was dominated by the thought of food. Food was stored and saved months in advance of upcoming birthdays and holidays.

It was very normal for children to be home alone. Just after we moved, Mutti always went by herself to hunt down food supplies. Margot and I spent many hours alone in the apartment. When we couldn't think of anything else to do, we searched for hidden food in all possible hiding places.

We knew that Mutti bought chocolate on the black market and, naturally, we found it. When she attempted to get it out for a special family occasion, only the empty wrappers were there.

We knew that Mutti bought sugar on the black market in small increments. She saved it for making *Marzipankartoffeln*, a traditional Christmas holiday candy made of sugar and ground almonds. It was to be a special treat.

One day, having wondered for a while where she was hiding the sugar, we went through her closet thoroughly. It meant bringing a chair from the kitchen so that we could reach the top shelf. We found it way in the back covered up with a towel. There were several small bags. First we stuck our fingers into the granules to get a taste. Yes, it was sugar! After a while of using our fingers we each got a spoon from the kitchen and started eating seriously. We stopped when it was all gone. Carefully we replaced the towel and tried to leave no traces. We must have done a real good job because Mutti did not suspect a thing. She discovered our deed a couple of weeks before Christmas when it was time to make the candy. Mutti went to her closet - no sugar!

Mutti was so hurt and disappointed. She sent us to our room. "I don't want to see you again for the rest of the day," she said. Then we listened to her sobbing in the kitchen, "Oh God, what have I done to deserve such bad children!?" She said it over and over again. That was our punishment, having to listen to Mutti. I know I felt really bad for days.

The candy was supposed to be our main present. I know we did not get anything else except a generous Christmas dinner, a present in itself.

We regularly stole food from Uncle Alfred. He had four horses to pull the flatbed trailers for sales and deliveries. The horses were stabled in our backyard. Every late afternoon a fire was built in the outdoor stove and a huge metal barrel, full of potatoes was cooked for the horses' evening meal. The potatoes were the rejects that could not be sold. As the potatoes cooked, the aroma would waft through the yard and to our apartment on the fourth floor. Being hungry, that smell was torture. With Mutti's permission, we would sneak into the yard.

Constantly checking to see if anybody was around, we inched towards the open pot. Uncle Alfred and his workers were busy with the horses in the stables.

Standing by the pot, we'd poke the potatoes, checking to see if they were ready. Then we started eating right there, one potato at a time. If there were blemishes or foul areas, we didn't notice. We burned our fingers and mouths every time, but those were the best tasting spuds that I can remember.

First Visit to the Zoo

At first we had the most contact with Aunt Schneider in the apartment below us. She had many bolts of fabric left over from her earlier sewing projects and soon gave Mutti some, "I no longer sew and have no use for these." The first material was white linen-like fabric with a beige loose-checker pattern.

Mutti was a good seamstress. She had learned the fine points of tailoring from the woman she rented a room from until she got married. She planned to use the white stuff to make summer coats for Margot and me.

When she was done cooking and cleaning, she would head to the living room where the cut pieces of fabric were on the table. All sewing was done by hand, of course, as we did not own a sewing machine. As usual, Margot and I stood by watching. As time went by the pieces of fabric Mutti had cut were starting to look like something we could wear. She told us of a free day at the zoo that was coming up, "I hope I can finish these coats for you to wear to the zoo."

Berlin's zoo was one of the largest in Europe before the war. It was heavily bombed and many animals lost. The zoo planned a big re-opening in the summer of 1946 and Berliners were invited free for one day. We could not imagine what kind of wild animals we would see. Mutti wasn't sure how many had survived.

The day arrived. We got up early! Washing, dressing and breakfast were done very quickly. Our coats fit perfectly. Mutti gave us the white knee socks to wear, which we usually only wore on some Sundays. Normally we wore our wooden sandals without socks.

The excitement started even before we left the apartment. Mutti said, "We will be riding in the *Stadtbahn*, street trolley, today. The zoo is too far for us to walk." We had seen the trolley many times as it was making its way along Turmstrasse, one of the major thoroughfares in our borough of Tiergarten. Today we could go on it. It was the first time that we would be riding somewhere.

Before we headed out, Mutti repeated what seemed like the hundredth time, "You must behave! No running or jumping or loud talking, keep your coat clean and make sure not to get holes in your socks. You only have one pair." We promised to be good.

The trolley stop was three blocks from our house. We did not have to wait long. "Watch the horizon, you should see it coming soon," Mutti said. When the yellow wagon appeared in the distance it got larger and larger quickly until it reached our trolley stop.

The train was pretty full; it seemed that everyone was going to the zoo. We could not get any seats. Mutti showed us how to hold on to a vertical metal bar so that we would not tumble as the train jerked when it started and stopped, and also when it went around corners.

The ride was over very quickly. The trolley stop was right in front of *Bahnhof Zoo*, the main train station for long distance trains. It was also the trading place for the black market. Mutti explained, "As you know, food along with everything else is hard to come by. Grocery stores have a very limited supply. But if people have anything to trade money, jewelry, a camera, just as an example, they can probably get what they need, like butter, sugar, cigarettes, etc." We didn't really care; we just wanted to get to the zoo.

The zoo was across the street. We joined the quick moving line of people to the entrance. Mutti just said, "Three" to the attendant counting every person, and we were through.

We roamed the wide walkways and stopped at every animal display. Mutti read all the descriptions to us and then we moved to the next cage. She remarked over and over how small the zoo was. "There used to be ten lions, four polar bears, ten giraffes and I don't remember how many chimpanzees."

To us, though, it was amazing and exciting so see one 'king of the jungle,' a big beast showing us his scary looking teeth as he yawned; one delicate looking giraffe; a couple of zebras playing tag; and one lonely polar bear lounging on the rocks of his huge outdoor den and every so often jumping into a pool in the middle and a moat around everything, and many more. I think the fun-loving bear made the biggest impression.

I remember that it was a very warm day with lots of walking. At lunchtime Mutti bought lemonade from a vendor and found a bench for us. Sitting on the bench we shared a couple of rye sandwiches for lunch that Mutti brought in her purse.

A man carrying a big camera on a tri-pod stopped and asked "Wouldn't you like to have a photo of this occasion?" Mutti nodded and after he quoted a price she agreed. He took the picture of the three of us and we cherished it for a long time, always reminding us of one of the few outings with Mutti. (See cover photo).

We cruised the trails a little longer, revisiting the polar bear and the chimpanzees. I was getting tired and when Mutti said, "It's time to get back to the trolley stop to get home," and we didn't complain.

Unexpected Diagnosis

Late in 1946 a letter arrived from the manager of the Tiergarten District. Mutti was assigned a clerk position in the district's recordkeeping department. Margot and I would be in a day-care facility while she worked. We thought this was exciting; we would have playmates every day. First we had to go for a health check-up on behalf of the Health Department, a standard procedure. We both had a thorough exam at a designated doctor's office a few blocks from our house and also a chest x-ray at the nearby hospital.

Within days another letter arrived for Mutti to come back to the doctor's office with Margot. I went along because Mutti didn't want to leave me home alone.

I stayed in the waiting room when Mutti and Margot went into the doctor's office. I waited. When they came back out Mutti looked very serious. She just said, "Heidi, let's go." During the short walk home she told me, "the x-rays showed that Margot has tuberculosis, and has to go to a sanitarium." (The state run facility for treating tuberculosis patients in Heckeshorn was generally referred to as 'sanitarium,' we just called it Heckeshorn for short.)

I heard of tuberculosis before. That's what Uncle Alfred had. She continued, "It is in the early stages and the doctor thinks that staying at the sanitarium will give her a good chance to get completely cured." "When does she have to go?" I asked. "Tomorrow morning," Margot chimed in with a smile. She thought it was an adventure to go away.

Mutti was busy the minute we arrived home. The doctor had given her a list of items Margot would need at Heckeshorn. Mutti had a long list of 'two of everything' to provide for Margot. Mutti started packing. In the morning we would take Margot to Heckeshorn, an area in the lake and forest region on the outer rim of Berlin.

Mutti told us that Margot would be having strict bed rest for however long it took to get better. Well, we both could not imagine staying in bed all day, and for many months yet!

Later, alone in our room when we were in bed and supposed to be going to sleep, we tried to figure out how Margot got TB. We were told that there were many ways one could get it. Having contact with an infected person or drinking contaminated water was one of the most common causes. We did not have any contact with Uncle Alfred, the only person we knew of with TB, until after his surgery when he was considered TB free. So, that was not it.

Then we recalled the many times we both drank water from the old well pump in the backyard even though we were told very firmly not do drink that water. The summer had been very hot and the few times we were allowed to play in the backyard we got water at the pump. The pump was rarely used. It seemed that we pumped endlessly before any water trickled out of the faucet. I cannot remember what we played or what we played with, we did not have any toys, but I remember getting water at the pump.

Taking Margot to the Sanitarium

The next morning we were very quiet. Margot's small suitcase was already standing by the door. Many items that Margot was supposed to have 'two of' were mine. Nightie, sweater, socks, etc. we only each had one of. Now I had none. Mutti said "I'll get you some soon," while grabbing the suitcase as we headed out the door. Margot and I wore our new coats, ready for the adventure.

Getting to Heckeshorn would be a long trip. First we walked a couple of blocks to the S-Bahn station, the city train, were Mutti got tickets for us with a voucher from the Health Department. The train came as promptly as Mutti had promised. It only had a few passengers and we quickly found seats. Margot and I had a window seat each.

After several stops we had to change trains to catch the one that goes to Wannsee in the Lake District. That train does not run very often and we had to wait a long time. When it finally pulled into the station we could see that even fewer passengers were on it.

Again we had window seats and I remember looking out the whole time. The train went through fields and forests. All I could see were trees, narrow roads and paths.

Finally we arrived at 'Wannsee,' the train's *Endstation*, last stop and turn-around. We thought we had arrived, "No, we're not there yet. We have to take a bus to the other side of the lake," Mutti told us.

On the bus we were able to get window seats again. Soon after it got going we could see the lake. It seemed very big. We drove over a long bridge and saw the shoreline on either side, but we could not see any end. Mutti told us that she went swimming there before the war and that we probably would swim there also some day. We nodded. The bus ride was a lot bumpier than the one on the train. Finally the bus driver yelled "Heckeshorn," our signal to get off.

We could see the sanitarium from the bus stop. It was a big structure, several floors high. A few steps and we were there. Mutti said, "Say good-bye to Margot. Children are not allowed inside, so wait here for me." I gave Margot a hug and then they both disappeared inside the big red brick building.

I waited a long time. The sanitarium was at the edge of the lake and surrounded by woods. It was not cold but I was getting tired of standing around. For a while I was sitting on the front steps. I was getting hungry and also had to go to the bathroom. There was no place for me to go. I started to walk around, back and forth, back and forth, not too far from the building in case Mutti came out. After a while I went into the woods but wet my pants before I could find a suitable spot to pee. I felt yucky and started to cry. Slowly I went back to the front of the building and continued to wait. I stopped sobbing; the need to cry was gone, now I just wanted to go home.

After what seemed like forever to me, Mutti came down the steps. *"Ich habe hunger,"* I'm hungry, was my greeting. "I'm sorry, but I don't have any food," was Mutti's reply that I had heard many times before.

Then I continued on to relay my trip into the woods. Mutti said, *"Ist schon gut, das kann schon mal passieren,"* it's ok, those things can happen. "I'll wash everything when we get home, but first we have to make the trip back."

It took the better part of two hours to get home. This time I kept standing during all rides; I did not dare sit down with my damp underwear.

I wanted to know what Margot was doing now and Mutti relayed the checking-in in minute detail during the train ride. "Margot is in a ward with nineteen other children of all ages. She will have strict bed rest; she will not be allowed to get up, not even to the bathroom. She will probably be there for about a year, a long time."

I did not know what a year meant, but "a long time" was impressive.

"Where will she eat? Do they have enough food for 20?" I asked. Mutti said, "There are many more people there, probably 400 or so. Yes, they have food for every one of them for breakfast, lunch and dinner," and she continued to say that "the nurses will bring food on a tray to Margot's bed. She will have enough to eat."

I remember being very impressed. I asked Mutti what nurses do. When she explained their job, I decided that that was what I wanted to do when I grew up, be a nurse in a pediatric ward to help children get well so that they could go home again.

Visiting Heckeshorn

When we talked about 'Heckeshorn,' it always meant sanitarium. Sunday was visiting day in Heckeshorn. All treatment and recovery hospitals were called 'sanitarium' in Germany. At first Mutti was allowed to visit once a month. Then the schedule was every two weeks and after six months it was every Sunday.

I remember those trips to Heckeshorn very well. Although children were not allowed inside, I went with Mutti because she did not want to leave me alone for the day. Visits at Heckeshorn took up most of the day. A few times she asked Oma, Aunt Schneider or Minna, if I could stay there while she visited Margot.

Aunt Schneider had a tea party with me during the afternoons I was there. She had a fancy, glass-enclosed rolling cart with a china tea set. She brought the china onto a table in the living room and we had tea and a small piece of pound cake each. I remember well how careful I was not to drop any crumbs onto her rug. Aunt Schneider was a very gentle person, careful and measured in speech and actions at all times. She spoke in a very low voice and

I had to pay attention not miss a word. Time went by very fast.

A couple of times I stayed with Oma for the afternoon. Mutti and I would leave the apartment together and on the street she walked towards the train station and I went to Oma's by myself. At Oma's, I liked to look at her lead-crystal collection. Several bowls were displayed on a mantle above the sofa. Oma took them off the shelf for me to hold. They were very heavy and always seemed to sparkle. I never saw them being used. I think they were wedding presents. Oma also had a coffee table book about Japan. The houses and way of dressing of the Japanese was very intriguing to me and the many photos of the fat Sumo wrestlers were just plain weird. I looked at the book from beginning to end every time and because I was not there very often, it always seemed like I saw it for the first time.

When I stayed with Minna, Mutti took me to her apartment. Her son Lutz was a baby and her daughter Jutta was several years older than I. Those afternoons were the only time I really had contact with Jutta. We played hopscotch on the sidewalk for a little while and later she read some stories to me. I don't think we ever played anything together again. I only heard through Minna what Jutta was doing as we were growing up. Rarely did we pass each other on the stairs.

Aunt Elschen let me stay once. "I have enough on my hands with Ingrid and Dorit and my brother's children," she said other times. When I was there Ingrid and I quickly went to play outside so that we would not make any noise or any kind of dirt in the apartment.

Mutti often did not have enough money for the extra bus fare, so after arriving by train at Wannsee, we walked around the lake to Heckeshorn instead. During the summer months Mutti always had migraines and the journey was very arduous for her. I remember walking along the road holding Mutti's hand while she was crying because she felt so bad.

Mutti was always glad to be able to see Margot for however brief a time was allowed. She told me about the big visiting room with a glass wall in the middle, one side for the patients and the other for visitors. The glass did not quite reach the ceiling and Margot and Mutti could

hear each other and talk through the glass wall while I
waited outside. It seemed to me that I always waited a
long time but it probably was no more than 15 or 20
minutes. I usually sat on the bottom step of the entrance.
There was absolutely nothing for me to do.

Sometimes Mutti brought along a small treat for
me. I remember the time when she gave me a wonderful
ripe tomato. A little while after Mutti disappeared in the
building I bit into the luscious red fruit, sucked all the
juices heartily and realized that I had a big gap along my
upper front teeth when I was done. One front tooth had
been loose and now it was gone. "That is the best way to
lose a tooth," Mutti laughed after she came down the
stairs and we headed home.

Once I was told to watch a certain window on the
second floor. Shortly after Mutti went inside the building,
Margot was at the window and waved vigorously. She was
also talking to me but, of course, I couldn't hear anything.
We waved and waved. That was the only time I saw my
sister during her stay there.

Mutti was usually down after visiting. On the way
home I listened to Mutti as she told me all she heard from
Margot. Margot had some wild stories from the ward to
tell, mostly how they made fun of the nurses. Margot was
three and a half years old and some others were almost
fifteen, the older girls leading on the young ones. Margot
happily went along with whatever was hatched. Mutti said
she wouldn't want to be one of the nurses.

During the winter the children were fully clothed in
bed to stay warm. Mutti took socks and sweaters that the
aunts in Bochum knitted to Margot... After one of our
visits Mutti came out of the building with a couple of balls
of wool yarn in her hands.

Margot told her that they had a strictly enforced
naptime after lunch. All children were supposed to sleep
or rest, and no talking. Children were expected to do
exactly as they were told in those days. That's how we
grew up. The nurses expected nothing less and did not
patrol the wards after lunch. The kids had long afternoons
without interruptions. One day when the nurses came to
get everyone ready for supper they were confronted with a
mess of yarn on every bed.

Margot said, "One girl was lying on top of her
blanket and playing with her socks. She found a loose

thread and pulled it." "Look everybody", the girl whispered. "We all sat up and watched her pulling the thread at the toe of her wool sock." "It comes off real fast" the girl said as row after row of knitting unraveled. Margot continued "I looked carefully at my socks and saw a little thread sticking out where my big toe is and pulled. It was easy, just like she said."

All the kids in the ward unraveled their socks, sweaters or vests - whatever they were wearing. The nurses made each child roll their wool into balls, one for each color. Margot's socks, sweater and jacket of natural colored wool turned into two big balls of yarn! Mutti brought the yarn home and started knitting socks and a sweater for Margot again.

Mutti dreaded those Heckeshorn visits. As time went by she started to think about the Sunday trip mid-week and I heard her sighing a lot. When I asked what was the matter she said, "I wonder what going on in Heckeshorn and what I'm going to hear about on Sunday." As young as I was I never asked to stay home. I knew that I had to go along and keep her company, as she needed somebody to talk to.

After twenty-one months, Margot was free of tuberculosis.

Getting By

Not much happened during the two years Margot was away. People in general were keeping to themselves, exhausted from the war and coping with ongoing hardships.

I remember spending almost all my time with Mutti - shopping, watching her cook, cleaning, and talking. I was the one Mutti talked to about everything.

We had more contact with the neighbors than our relatives. Oma worked six days a week. I seldom saw Ingrid and Dorit. Uncle Helmut was still a prisoner of war in Russia with no word of when he would return.

Winters were very cold. Mutti did not have enough money to buy coal for all the ovens. In the beginning, she usually just bought what we needed for the day and night. Our days were spent in the kitchen where the coal oven was used for cooking and heating at the same time.

Later, when she could afford it, coal was delivered to our basement storage shed. What were built as bomb shelters were now storage sheds from where we would fetch coal as needed. Getting coal was a very creepy experience to me.

I always went to the cellar with Mutti, because being left behind alone, waiting in the gloomy hallway, seemed even worse. She unlocked the heavy steel basement door and I promptly asked her to leave it wide open. She lit the candle we brought and went down the narrow staircase, the buckets we carried clanged against the stonewall. We had to make several turns in the narrow walkways until we came to our shed. The creaky door left ajar, we quickly dumped coal into the buckets with the candle flickering wildly as we hurried. At that point I was stiff from fright and just kept my eye on the barely visible coal. With buckets full we retraced our steps. I moved ahead, hoping not to make a wrong turn and prolonging this trip to the basement. I would not feel relieved until the basement door was locked again.

Our small radio was in the kitchen and we listend to music until the power was turned off. Then it was time for bed. Mutti started the ritual of heating a brick on top of the oven, then wrapped it in a towel and put it in my bed. After a little while I put on my nightie and dashed to bed.

For once it was in our favor to live at the train depot. When coal was loaded from train cars onto trucks, it was piled high on the trucks. As the trucks pulled out of the depot's gate onto Waldstrasse we would watch the coal slide off onto the street. On those days I was standing at the curb in front of the house and dashed onto the street to pick up bricks of coal. It was not dangerous because there were very few cars on the roads. Sometimes I could get as many as twenty to twenty-five bricks. That was quite a haul, considering three or four bricks would heat the kitchen from lunch until evening.

The first couple of winters I did not have shoes, just my wooden sandals. When it was really cold I wore long wool stockings, an extra pair of socks and double underwear. The aunts in Bochum were sending regular packages with socks and sweaters that they knitted for us with sheep's wool. I remember those very scratchy woolen socks, sweaters and also underwear.

The Blockade and Beyond

Life did not seem different to me during the Blockade of Berlin. Food was already scarce, we did not have any money and Mutti was often lamenting that she didn't know how she could make it through another day. Margot was taken care of at Heckeshorn, a small consolation.

After the end of the war, the Allies agreed to co-exist in Berlin after they carved up all of Germany into Allied zones. Berlin, in the middle of the Russian zone was divided into American, British, French and Russian sectors and all agreed to co-operate. They all did, except Russia, of course.

From May 1948 to June 1949, the Russian blockaded all roads and train tracks to cut off the food and fuel supplies to the city. The Russians were sure the Allies would give up and they could capture Berlin for good.

The initiative of some pilots got the Berlin Airlift started. Everything from butter to coal was brought into the city of over 2 million by air. Pretty soon C-47s and other French, British and American planes were landing every 90 seconds around the clock at Tempelhof Airport. Trucks were lined up for distribution throughout the city.

Rationing was stricter than ever, and fewer allocations were given out. For Mutti it meant many hours of waiting in line and she did not always get our rations. Often supplies ran out before it was her turn. When I said, *"Ich habe hunger, Mutti"* (I'm hungry), many times she'd say, *"Aber Kind, ich hab' doch nichts für Dich"* (Child, I don't have anything to give you) with a deep sigh. When Mutti recalled those days in later years she said, "When you were hungry and there was nothing I could give you, that was the hardest to live with." We existed on very little.

Supplies were more plentiful during the war, even though it was not much. But after the war, everything was used up. The farmers had nothing left to share. All trees in the Tiergarten Park were chopped down for firewood.

The winter was extremely cold. I remember trying to melt the solid ice on the bedroom window with my breath in the morning. Slowly a peephole would form on the opaque surface and I could get a glimpse of the sky. Then I quickly ran to the kitchen and leaned against the stove to get warm.

Officially the blockade lasted from June 24, 1948 to May 11, 1949, but the planes continued flying until September to restock and to get all supply lines re-established and running. Recovery was very slow. To this day I can feel the hunger pain in the pit of my stomach.

I think it took about another two years until we slowly noticed changes in the food supply. That is everywhere except in the Russian zone. The Russians kept what would be known as East Berlin separate from the rest of the city. There were a lot of 'word-of mouth' reports of how life did not seem to change there after the war.

We could see it ourselves on our twice-yearly visits to Aunt Hilda, Werners' mother, starting in 1950. She lived in Weissensee (East Berlin) with her mother, about an hour away from our house. She worked as a secretary.

We took the S-Bahn (city train) and after a while changed over to a tram. As soon as the train entered the Eastern sector we could see the difference. Soldiers carrying machine guns were standing on the platforms at every stop. People inside became eerily silent, stopped talking, making no eye contact, and everybody just staring at what was in front of them.

In the other sections of Berlin, one hardly felt the presence of the Allies, except for large signs like 'You are entering the British sector.'

Mutti instructed us not to talk about anything at all because, "We don't know who is listening and how things could be misunderstood," and she continued, "It was just like that before and during the war for all of us, but we don't have to worry about things like that now, only when we visit Aunt Hilda."

Life in the Eastern sector seemed to stand still. That was the reason why Werner came to live with Uncle Alfred, his father, in 1952 when it was time to enter high school. Aunt Hilda wanted Werner to have a good all around education without the Eastern propaganda that glorified Communism that made the Western governments into ogres.

Our aunt was always expecting us, watching out of her living room window until we appeared. As soon as we reached her fourth floor apartment, she would close all windows and turn up the radio quite high to cover up our conversations, "I don't know if the neighbors are home." Even with that, only general topics were discussed.

When things started to get a little better for us, Mutti took items to Aunt Hilda that she could not get in East Berlin. Mutti always brought several pounds of good coffee because she would lament, "I can't get any real coffee here, only the awful tasting *Kaffee Ersatz* (the chicory coffee substitute). Oh how I miss a real good cup of coffee! "

We did not have a telephone and Aunt Hilda could not write what she wanted. Mail going to the West was checked and labor camps or other punishments would be the repercussions of a letter implying that there was anything lacking in the East.

Mutti guessed at what to take and generally she was right on. "Well, I just have to remember what was hard to come by before and during the war years." Sometimes it was a good bar of soap, a pair of stockings, colorful thread, light bulbs, and so on. We each carried something so that we did not have to carry a big bag and arouse suspicion.

After the traditional afternoon coffee, brewed carefully with the coffee we just brought, we went for a walk around Lake Weissensee, a lake a block away. Margot, Werner and I, if he was also there, walked ahead and Mutti and Hilda could talk without having to worry about being overheard.

Aunt Hilda's elderly mother did not want to leave her home and move West, which many people did before the Berlin Wall was built. So Aunt Hilda stayed in the East.

Many years later, Aunt Hilda followed Werner to West Germany. She was allowed to leave with two suitcases and sign a paper not to make any claims against the Eastern government – translation 'forfeit her pension/social security.'

The Allies peacefully coexisted in Berlin with the exception of the Russians. They continually tested the nerves of the Berliners. For instance, Russian planes broke the sound barrier at least a couple times daily, which made a big noise, sometimes even broke windows, and was totally against the Allies' agreement. The Allies protest was duly noted on the radio and in the newspaper, but the Russians continued with that nuisance.

They started posting soldiers at points where their zone started and conducted ID, bag and body searches of Berliners entering the Russian zone. They would confiscate all Western goods including magazines and books. One of the sarcastic running jokes was "...and after they confiscated books and newspapers they run into the guard house and read them all!"

East Berliners could not go to the other zones without applying for a pass. That's why we always visited Aunt Hilda, it was simpler for us to go into the Russian zone than the other way around. By 1956, virtually all travel to the West was restricted.

People started to abandon the Eastern government and fled to the West all along the East-West border. The eastern government started to come down on their citizens and strengthened the border patrols. Any shimmer of disobedience from anyone would land them and often their family in jail. But more and more people fled from the East to the West. Soldiers controlled over 100 miles of the East-West border. Berlin offered a few loopholes: the subway and street crossings.

By 1961, 3.5 million East Germans had defected, twenty percent of the total population. The East German Government took action. August 13th, 1961, was the beginning of the Wall.

In the middle of the night the East German Army started a barbed wire fence along its entire border with the West. The wire fence was swiftly followed with the construction of the twelve feet high wall of cement. Next to the wall was 100 feet wide strip of 'no-man's land' on the eastern side that was fenced with barbed wire.

Eventually the cement wall marked 27 miles of the east-west border through the city of Berlin. The remaining miles, mostly in wooded and rural sections, were marked by double barbed wire fences and patrolled by armed soldiers. In very rural areas, where controlling the border was more difficult, minefields were installed.

School Years

First Day of School

In the spring of 1948, Mutti started to make my 'first day of school dress' from one of Oma's summer dresses. The German school year went from early April to the following March. My first day of school was supposed to be that spring but it was put off until fall because many schools were still closed. Bombings made them unusable; many children could not go to school.

In the fall the city started a 'shift school year.' Available schools would be used morning and afternoons so that all children would have schooling. School usually just went from 8 am to 1 pm. Now half of the students would go to school from 8 am to 12 Noon and the other group from 1 pm to 5 pm. I was in the 8 to 12 group.

My school year started in September of 1948. On the big day Mutti woke me up very early because she was going to curl my very straight long hair with a curling iron. This was new to me, until recently my hair was not long enough. The curling iron was heated over a low gas flame on the cook top. One by one the strands of hair were transformed into something I had seen in newspaper pictures. Of course, I had to sit very still to avoid getting some skin burned by accident. When I was ready with my new hair and dress and super white knee socks and very shiny shoes, Mutti walked the three blocks to school with me. I remember walking very carefully, trying not to move my head so that the curls would not come undone.

During the few hours of school, a classroom and a seat were assigned, and our teacher was introduced to us. I remember having been told by Mutti "Listen to the teacher and don't talk if you weren't asked," many times.

The teacher told us to sit up straight in our seat with hands folded on top of the desk if we were not assigned some kind of duty. "Raise your hand when you ask a question and wait your turn," she said. Teachers did not have to put up with any bad behavior or interruptions. We just didn't dare. Being sent to the principal was the threat hanging over our heads. As far as I can remember only a couple of pupils were sent to the principal's office during the elementary school years.

The first day of school was a big event, equally important as Confirmation. First day of school marks the transition from small youngster to student and Confirmation is the stepping-stone to young adulthood.

On the first day of school, everyone paid attention to the small children. When school let out, the parents, and sometimes many relatives, waited in the schoolyard with the traditional *Schultüte* for the new student (see my 'first day of school' photo). The *Schultüte* would be filled with extra school supplies and treats like chocolate and other assorted candies. Mutti was there with a *Schultüte* stuffed with paper and an apple on top. Mutti apologized, "I just don't have anything to fill the bag." Berlin was in the middle of the blockade and everything was scarce. Then we went to the photographer's studio nearby for the official 'first day of school' photo. Mutti had made an appointment there but we still had to stay in line and wait.

On the way home we stopped at all the stores where we usually go shopping and I was congratulated on having survived the first day of school. At the house our neighbors must have set their alarms because every single one, starting with Schenck's at the store, opened their door and asked me how I liked my school day. I felt happy and very special that day. I must be all right, everybody was smiling. That was better than all the birthdays I had so far. Although it was a weekday, Oma was visiting in the early evening to mark this special occasion.

We crammed a whole school year into the September to March stretch. After that I was on the regular school year schedule. Enough buildings were functioning again with room for all students.

1948
First Day of School

Elementary School

I don't remember any difficulty learning. But I do remember the fear my first grade teacher managed to instill in all of us.

She was a very stern, older person and I dreaded her cleanliness inspection. She picked a time at random and started with, "Let's see if you cleaned behind your ears." Sitting at our desks we had to stretch our arms in front of us. She slowly walked along the isles of the thirty or so desks. She'd stop here and there, "Stand up please." The student stood up, "Turn over your hands." They did and then she would inspect fingernails, push up a sleeve to look for dirt, and she would look behind the ears. If she found dirty fingernails, she sent the pupil home with instructions to scrub and come back

She also checked for head lice - a very common condition at the time. Lice could spread just by contact with our heads; for instance if we were looking at a map together, we tried not to stick our heads too close to our neighbor's for that reason.

Once it was my turn to stand up. I wore something with short sleeves. I held my breath and followed her eyes as they traveled over my hands and wrists. Then they moved up my arms. She stopped at a dark blotch on my right upper arm. "You haven't washed there in a long time!" she scolded.

"Yes, I did. This is a birthmark I've always had," I countered.

She rubbed the spot, "You're lying."

"No, I'm not," I cried.

She shook her head, "Go home and wash."

Of course, every single student was looking at me. How I hated that moment! I did not ever like to have attention focused on me and this was so embarrassing, especially since I knew she was wrong.

It was mid-morning; I did not meet anyone I knew as I walked the three blocks from school. I knocked and knocked on our door. Mutti was not home. Of course, she was out getting groceries. I sat on the step by our apartment and waited. Finally I heard footsteps coming up the stairs. I called "Mutti?"

"Yes, Heidi. What are you doing here? You are supposed to be in school!"

I relayed my teacher's decision.

"That's ridiculous! Doesn't she know anything?" Mutti wrote a note stating that I had this faint large 'liver spot' since birth and sent me back to school. The teacher did not apologize, but she also never inspected me again.

Still very memorable to this day is the really awful free mid-morning food that was ladled out in first and second grade (1948/49). Of course, we should have been thankful to get this free food donated by the Allies. For some it was the only food they had all day I'm sure. Food was scarcer than ever during the Blockade.

Food for all the schools was prepared in several commercial kitchens somewhere in the city. After being transferred into insulated barrels, it was trucked to the schools. Everything was still steaming hot as the barrels were opened. It was either a soup or a rice dish. I brought Pappa's army-issue food canteen and spoon from home for my portion. We lined up with our canteens and were guessing what it might be. The soup was manageable.

When it was rice day, I approached the steaming food barrel with hesitation. Rice was not part of our standard foods. Mutti never cooked rice at all. The rice dish, probably a version of rice pudding, was pretty bad, even when you are starving. What was ladled into our canteens looked something like Elmer's glue with some dark nuggets floating in it. The rice was cooked until it fell apart and sweetened with dried apricots and raisins. The apricots were cut into tiny slivers and the raisins ballooned to at least four times their size and were all slimy. The dish was so sweet, it was hard to swallow.

I could not finish the rice and closed the lid tightly. Throwing away the leftover food was unthinkable. Nobody threw food away ever during these hard times. I carried the food home for Mutti. She could not stomach the rice either and gave it to Oma.

Our head classroom teacher taught German, math and reading. We stayed in the same room throughout the day, except for gym, of course. Teachers for subjects like handwriting, geography, music and art came to our classroom. The break between classes was five minutes, enough time for the teachers to get to their class room and for us time to go to the bathroom. Mid-morning we had a twenty minute break when everyone had to go into the yard, no matter the weather. We walked the perimeter within the walled schoolyard, round and round until the 'twenty-minutes' bell rang. This routine did not change until high school.

I made my first friends during elementary years - Anke, Barbara and Maria. Our friendship consisted of walking together during the long break and sometimes going home the long way after school so that we had more time to chat. We stayed together throughout the school years, having managed to be assigned to the same high school.

Every two years a new head teacher was assigned to our class. So, in third grade a lovely, tall young woman was introduced. She was as nice as she looked and she had thirty eager students trying to please her. I remember working very diligently in class and also with homework for that smile of approval.

English was introduced in fourth grade and it seemed easy to learn.

For fifth and sixth grade we were lucky again. This time a more mature woman but equally as likable and fair to all students, entered our lives. Biology was added to our curriculum but I liked geography better.

Late in fifth grade all students took an aptitude test to determine their talents and which high school path would best suit them.

The 'Practical Branch' graduated after ninth grade and students then went onto apprenticeships in shops, offices, building trades etc., along with three years of trade school.

The 'Technical Branch' graduated after tenth grade, going to more advanced education for careers like nursing, surveying, mapping and others. Four years of advanced schooling along with apprenticeships were required.

The 'The Scientific Branch' graduated after twelfth grade and students qualified for the university and the path of their chosen career.

Being sent to an R&R retreat during the fifth grade caused me to fall behind in English and math. R&R retreats were part of the German Health Care System's recovery and prevention program. (Read details in 'R&R Retreats', page 141). The retreats always lasted four to six weeks without any homework assignments. Naturally, I fell behind. Mutti and Aunt Schneider arranged tutoring with Aunt Suzie.

Tutoring definitely helped to improve my grades so I might qualify for the 'Technical Branch' of high school, which I needed to reach my goal of becoming a nurse.

1951 School photo

High School

The teaching routine changed in high school. We had our head-teacher and homeroom base where we studied German, German creative writing, math, algebra, French, English and geography. For biology, chemistry, art, music and gym, we moved to the other designated rooms. Chemistry was especially exciting to me. We went to a lab and experiments were part of the lessons.

One other change was that gym was now after all other classes were finished. I would walk the three blocks home for lunch and then back to school for gym.

In seventh grade, I had a very good English teacher, Herr Meier, who recently escaped from the East. But this first year in high school was marked by his arrest for molesting students, some from my class.

Herr Meier made English very exciting and a fun class. Unfortunately, as I watched him interact with the other students in class, stroking and grabbing and lots of blushing on part of the girls, I became very uncomfortable and did not look forward to class. Several of the girls, all very well developed, had regular tutoring sessions at his home

After weeks and weeks I finally relayed it all to Uncle Lutz from the apartment below, who was teaching at my school. He asked me many times, "How do you like your teachers?" He listened and nodded. Over the next few weeks he kept asking me, "How are things?" and I would relay whatever I observed.

Just before the end of the first half of the school year Herr Meier was suspended and taken to court. The students, all girls, had to testify. He was convicted for indecent liberties with minors, taking advantage of his position, etc. He went to prison for several years. School was a lot better place after that.

Although during those weeks we did not talk about it at all, almost everyone must have noticed something and, in turn, was very uncomfortable, not knowing how to handle what they saw. Once it was over, it was like a heavy blanket was taken away. We could look at one another again and have normal chit-chat.

Art and music continued to be in our curriculum. I particularly liked music. I never learned to read notes, but I had a good voice and was part of the chorus. The chorus performed at every occasion that took place in the auditorium. We all learned to sing harmony. So, even at other occasions wherever there was singing, someone quickly asked "who sings harmony?"

French came easy until a four-week R&R retreat in eighth grade really found me behind with French and algebra. This time I went twice a week for tutoring with Aunt Suzie. I struggled but was determined to bring my grades up. It was a lot of work, the afternoon babysitting job and evenings spent either studying or with Aunt Suzie. Slowly I could see my grades move up.

A memorable time during high school was the Hungarian Revolution in the fall of 1956. It was a very tense time. Most of our teachers were refugees from the East and started a new life in Berlin.

In late October, Russian troops were hovering just outside of East Berlin, ready to move into Hungary if so ordered. The general belief was that if they were moving into Hungary they would roll right through Berlin and we would be occupied.

I remember Herr Vogel, our main teacher, explaining, "One of these mornings I may not show up. I will have decided to stay one step ahead of the Russians. If I get captured by the Russians in occupied Berlin, it will be jail or worse for me. Because I escaped once, punishment could be very severe."

We listened to the news very closely. During breaks between classes the latest news bulletins were passed to the teachers and they started every class with an update.

We never knew if our teachers would be in class the next day. Several did not want to wait until the last minute and left for West Germany, as did many families throughout Berlin. I remember Mutti and actually all other adults, being very solemn all the time. Nobody wanted to live in a Berlin occupied by the Russians. World War II memories were still very fresh.

This tension-filled period lasted about four weeks while the International community tried to intervene. It didn't work. The Russians invaded Hungary to squash their revolution and they would occupy the country for about 30 years.

The troops went around Berlin and we escaped Russian oppression. All but one teacher came back to Berlin and our school and our life was back to normal.

History, geography and German creative writing were my favorite classes. History and geography classes often covered similar areas. Events like the Hungarian Revolution reminded us that we were watching history. Any current event was usually dissected and discussed even if it had nothing to do with our current studies.

It didn't have to be dramatic. When the American Grace Kelly married Prince Rainier of Monaco, we had a lively discussion about Monaco's history and debated the 'royalty' of Prince Rainier. Our history teacher gave them "Well, maybe they'll last five years...."

Creative writing was pretty dry at first. We had to write about subjects that were difficult to get creative about, like 'How I spent Sunday.' Then our very enthusiastic teacher, Herr Klein, came up with assignments like 'A creepy experience,' 'On the way home from school I....,' followed by 'This is my room' "your real one or make one up," was his comment. Now finally I could give my imagination free reign.

Assignments were given Mondays and the finished piece had to be handed in Thursday or Friday. The papers were graded over the weekend and handed back to us on Monday, always with lots of comments in the margins and a grade.

Before the papers were given back to us, Herr Klein singled out one or two pieces, made a few comments and read them to the class without saying whose it was.

The first time one of my papers was read I was totally caught off guard. Herr Klein started with "To my surprise I didn't yawn once. I wanted to know more after every paragraph." As soon as he began reading 'This is my room' I knew that it was mine about a totally imaginary room.

I smiled when I read "Well done, you have a very easy-to-read style," in the margin. The '1' below, an A+, was my first in German. Margot was usually the one who got '1s.' This gave me a deep down confidence that I did not have before.

Change of Plans—Change for Life

During ninth grade in the fall, Mutti asked me into the living room one day after school. "I need to talk to you."

This was very unusual; everything was always hashed over in the kitchen. I was wondering what was up and quickly searched my memory for any bad deeds Mutti might have discovered. Nothing came to mind.

Mutti looked very serious, "*Setz Dich doch bitte* – please sit down," she motioned to the two easy chairs by the small round table in the corner where we normally have our evening cup of tea. "This is very difficult for me," she started. "You are working very hard and I respect that very much, but I'm afraid this will not help you go to nursing school."

'What?' I was thinking. I didn't know what she was talking about. My plan was clear, graduate and go to nursing school. I wanted to be a pediatric nurse ever since Margot was hospitalized with tuberculosis. Mutti and I talked about it for years.

"I have been to the various agencies that determine your half–orphan benefits. Under the rules only one in the household qualifies for free education; the one with the better grades. We both know it is Margot."

I was stunned. "No matter how hard you work and study, your grades will not get better than hers. And you know very well that I do not have any money to pay the thousands it takes to pay for your additional schooling."

I was shocked. Up to this day, all I did was supposed to get me admitted to nursing school.

During the following weeks there was only one subject at home - 'What shall I do?' My motivation for study was gone. I knew I had to decide on something. Quitting school was not an option. By law, everybody had to go to school until they turned eighteen.

Going the 'Practical Branch' way seemed to be the only solution. Graduate and go to a trade school. After a few weeks of debating back and forth of 'What to do? What to do?' I said, "Why bother struggling through tenth grade? Why not graduate after ninth grade and go on?"

Mutti and I met with the school principal and she confirmed that it was a viable option. Once I decided to graduate early I had to find an apprenticeship. As an apprentice I would go to a trade school for three years, get minimum wage and two weeks paid vacation.

But where to go? Being a secretary did not appeal to me. I couldn't imagine myself sitting down most of the day, no matter how interesting. Working in a store was left, but which branch? Ingrid apprenticed at a china and cutlery shop, she liked it but said it was always cold in the shop. A drugstore did not appeal either.

Mutti and I walked down fashionable Kurfürsten Damm, Berlin's version of New York's Fifth Avenue, and scrutinized the stores: furniture, antiques, galleries, ladies' clothing, record shops and more. We made a list of stores to apply to. The Wegena Company, specializing in lingerie, offered an apprenticeship and I accepted. I was enrolled in the Retail and Wholesale School for Textiles.

Then I had to break the news to the few classmate friends I had - Maria, Barbara and Anke. I left high school with the ninth grade diploma. I kept in touch with my friends and the teacher and the class invited me to their tenth grade graduation ceremony and evening party.

I remember very clearly that one day during class I was thinking 'I can't wait for my school years to be over.' I wanted to be eighteen. I didn't look forward to three years of business school and sales clerking. I wanted it to be over with. But I also knew that I didn't have a choice in the matter and didn't think about it anymore.

Business School

On April 1, 1957, I reported to Wegena's company head-quarters. There were about forty of us, all starting an apprenticeship. We were welcomed by the president, Mr. Bartels, and then we were given the address of the branch shop we were assigned to.

I was assigned to a small branch in Tempelhof, near the airport. It was a short tram ride and I was wondering what lay ahead.

Once I arrived, it became clear very quickly. Wegena carried all lingerie items including nightgowns and bathrobes. All merchandise was either in glass display cases, on storage shelves or in large closets with glass sliding doors. I was not allowed to approach customers.

The shop manager assigned sales clerks as the customers came in. I was supposed to make myself look busy and observe the activities. Once a clerk was finished with a customer I had to put the merchandise back to the assigned spots. If it was nightgowns or robes they needed to go back into the closet and lined up evenly with all others, like soldiers on parade. I was constantly rearranging merchandise and cleaning glass.

My workweek was Monday through Saturday. On Sundays all stores were closed. Monday, Tuesday and Thursday mornings I had classes at the 'Retail and Wholesale School for Textiles'. In the afternoon I went to the shop. In addition to basic German and math my classes included textiles, accounting, window decorating and English.

In textiles we learned all about fabrics, where they originated and the production process to the final product. Cotton, linen, silk and many others were studied in depth.

In accounting we studied many business modules, how they worked or why they failed. We were given endless examples and also had to complete many business plans. To my surprise I had a very good head for accounting.

Window decorating included art. It was a class that I really enjoyed. During the first year we studied the theories of shop window decorating. In the second year we had to decorate windows in school, always according to a given theme. In the third year we 'graduated to real windows. Once a month I decorated one of the windows of the shop where I currently was. I always was looking forward to it.

During my first year I also had to spend a month at Wegena's main office. The company manufactured many items at the Berlin headquarters. They had huge sewing rooms with probably forty seamstresses in each.

I learned to use a sewing machine. First, I was sewing simple, straightforward seams. Then I had to construct a bra, which was a lot more complicated than the straight sewing of a hem. At the end of the month I had to produce a bra from scratch. I picked the material, designed the pattern cut and produced the bra. I passed the test. And now, in addition to keeping all glass spotless, I also was the in-house alteration and repairs 'expert.'

Customer service was a big part of this business. If something did not fit exactly, the client would be fitted and alterations made while they waited in the dressing room. If it took longer, we delivered the merchandise to their homes.

I was the delivery person of course. I never minded that part of the job. It was a chance to explore the neighborhood. I was assigned to several different branches of the chain during the three years, all of them in more rural, upscale sections of the city. I got to know many suburban areas well.

In the second year, I moved into the line-up with the other clerks. I knew someone was always watching to make sure I didn't make any mistakes or mishandle a customer. The year in the background prepared me well to be comfortable with clients.

Throughout the three years I had to write a monthly essay about something related to this particular business. Sometimes it was a real stretch to come up with a subject that I could fill two pages. I wanted to make it good so that the shop manager would approve and headquarters as well. I did not want someone to send it back, asking for a revision.

In the spring of 1960, I graduated from business school with a merchandising degree. I was now eligible to work anywhere, even open my own shop if I chose. To get a business license in Germany you needed a business degree.

There was no party or celebration. The diplomas were handed out in a large meeting hall. I said good-bye to my classmates whom I would never see again and went to the shop.

Wegena offered me a start-up sales clerk position with a monthly salary and two- weeks paid vacation, standard business practice. I stayed with the company.

In the Kitchen with Mutti

Every day started and ended in the kitchen. Since the kitchen also doubled as our bathroom, it was the first stop for brushing my teeth after a dash to the toilet a half-flight down the staircase. We only had running cold water and while I was brushing my teeth, Mutti heated water on the burner for the sponge bath.

Everything was done under Mutti's watchful eyes. Tips regarding healthy teeth, "Don't forget the wisdom teeth area, food easily gets stuck there," to cleaning the face, "Do not use soap on your face. It is too harsh. Only use buttermilk and then rinse with water," were disbursed generously.

Eventually Mutti bought a dressing table for our bedroom. It was a place to sit down and leisurely get ready for the day with a bit more privacy while Margot was having her turn at the kitchen sink.

Make-up was not allowed at school and until one turned 15, it was frowned upon everywhere. As we grew up we experimented often but wiped everything off before we left our room.

Mutti was always in the kitchen. She was either preparing food, or reading the paper with her second cup of coffee, or writing a postcard, or doing some light laundry, etc.

As far back as I can remember I was sitting on 'my' chair in the kitchen talking, listening, and watching Mutti. There was not much else to do. We didn't have any toys or games and the only radio, until much later, was in the kitchen also.

Most of the day was devoted to cooking. Breakfast was always the same: a soft-boiled egg and some rye bread with butter. Mutti believed in eggs as a 'whole food and brain food,' and she made sure of our daily ration. Rarely did we have jam. In the early years I would have a glass of water with breakfast and later a cup of coffee. I did not drink milk.

The largest meal of the day, *Mittagessen*, was at lunchtime, the equivalent of American dinner. Right after breakfast, Mutti went shopping for the day's groceries and hurried home to start cooking. We did not have a refrigerator, so all foods were bought in small amounts, just enough for that day.

In the early years, *Mittagessen* could be a variation of potato dishes: mashed potatoes with flour gravy, maybe spiced with mustard, sometimes with a little bacon added for flavor; refried potatoes with onions and a bit of bacon finished with freshly chopped parsley; boiled potatoes with butter and lots of chopped parsley.

I was never encouraged to cook. "The kitchen is too small for more than one," Mutti would say and she was right. There was barely enough room for her to negotiate.

Sitting in my chair I was safely out of the way. Mutti usually commented about what she was doing and where she learned it. The month spent at the French farm was her cooking boot camp. She said, "Everything I do, I learned at the farm. I try to duplicate the taste all the time. I can't stand the watery and skimpy German cooking."

Of course she was referring to her youth in the 1920s and 1930s, the month helping on a farm in France as part of Hitler Youth duty, and the World War II years. Food was not as tasty then, austerity measures had been in place for about twenty years.

During the weeks on the French farm she was working in the kitchen because of her migraines, instead of helping on the fields, which was this program's purpose.

I was watching every move Mutti made. I knew how to prep any vegetable properly even though I rarely was asked, or allowed, to help. In my mind I could chop onions and peel and precisely cut vegetables with record speeds. Vegetables and potatoes were the bases for vegetable stews, which was one of our standard meals. Mutti often gave me a taste of whatever she was preparing, a chunk of carrot or cucumber or maybe cauliflower. I loved the taste of fresh veggies!

Later seasonal dishes had a special buzz about them. White asparagus, a German specialty, was only available for about three to four weeks in May. Mutti guessed when the first might be for sale at the vegetable grocers. At home she checked and peeled them carefully.

"You don't want to cut away any of the tender part." Once they arrived she prepared many versions: asparagus with Hollandaise; or topped with browned breadcrumbs and butter; or topped with browned butter and chopped hard-boiled eggs.

Other much anticipated foods were Chanterelle and Boletus mushrooms. They arrived midsummer into the fall. When she was prepping the mushrooms for cooking, she recalled going mushroom hunting during the war when we were evacuated to the countryside. Mushroom hunting is a national ritual in Germany. Mutti explained, "We would only get the ones we could recognize; all varieties have a poisonous look-a-like, so we were careful. I never went alone, but always with several neighbors. First, it was safer not to be alone in the woods and, secondly, I could let someone else double check what I was about to pick if I wasn't sure." Her mushroom dish was always the same and I never tired of it.

First she chopped some lean bacon and an onion and sautéed them in a deep pot. Then she added the picked-over and cut-up mushrooms. She sautéed them for about ten minutes or so, while the aroma started to fill the kitchen. It was mouthwatering. Then she dusted everything with a bit of flour. "To give the sauce a little body, I don't want to burn the flour, just get it lightly brown", as she was stirring things in the pot that I could not see but visualize. She put a lid on and let the dish simmer for about twenty long minutes.

I was getting hungrier by the minute. While the Chanterelles simmered, she also boiled potatoes. Once they were done, poked with a sharp knife for doneness, she drained and tossed them in the pot over low heat to let any excess moisture evaporate. She quickly chopped a handful of parsley, tossed them into the mushroom pot, dipped a spoon into the sauce and pronounced it "Hmmmm, ready!"

As soon as I had my first bite, my expectation was satisfied, absolutely yummy! Silence blanketed the kitchen while we savored every last morsel. Today, 'Chanterelles' are still one of my favorite foods.

When food became more plentiful, in the early 1950s, the standard meals were vegetables – always fresh. I cannot remember having anything canned. Mutti could not stand the taste, "I'd rather have a small portion of fresh green beans over a bowl full of canned." Potatoes were the traditional main meal or side dish, we never had rice or pasta, and very little meat. Sometimes Mutti would buy a beef bone with some meat left on it to use as a base for the vegetable stew.

Mutti prepared many dishes with green beans, carrots and peas, asparagus, cauliflower, parsnips, beets and kale in the fall. "Kale is better if it had been through a good frost, as it takes the bitter taste away."

As the recovery continued meat dishes were based around ground beef, or a mixture of ground veal, pork and beef. *Königsberger Klopse*, meatballs in a spicy white sauce, was and is one of my favorites. *Falscher Hase –* fake rabbit, the name for meat loaf, was a Sunday specialty. Chicken was very expensive and was served only on very special occasions, like my Confirmation in 1957.

A very special treat always was *Tartar*. Mutti usually told us, "We're having *Tartar* tonight," in the morning before we left. This was a dish Margot always was home for. We went to the table with great anticipation. The *Tartar*, already mixed in a bowl, was divided into three equal portions. Sliced pickles and dark bread spread with sweet butter accompanied this supper. I remember that we always ate as slowly as possible to make it last.

Kartoffelpuffer, potato pancakes, was another favorite. It was Mutti's version of a fast food meal. She most often made it Saturdays. Saturday was a bigger grocery shopping day because she had to buy food for two days. All stores closed Saturday at 2 pm and didn't open again until Monday morning. This often did not leave much time for cooking the mid-day meal. They are so simple to make; grated raw potatoes mixed with eggs, a little flour and salt and pepper. That's all.

Walking home from school on Saturdays I was looking forward to *Puffers*. We never said *Kartoffelpuffer*. As usual, Mutti already fried the first batch by the time I reached the kitchen. She continued making *Puffers* in batches until they were all done. Applesauce is the classic pairing. Sometimes I experimented with spreading a thin film of hot mustard over the top. I loved to eat them plain, straight from the frying pan, best!

We rarely had sweets. Between meal snacks were rare. If we had one it was an apple or a pear and, when in season, a juicy peach or a handful of cherries, my favorites. Desserts were not part of our regular meals. On some Sundays or special occasions we had a fruit dessert like poached pears, applesauce or stewed plums.

In later years we would have pastry at Sunday afternoon coffee time, around three or four. Often we went to the *Konditorei*, pastry shop, on the next block together to choose our piece. The pastry display made it hard to decide. I often chose an éclair, filled with light vanilla pastry cream or a *Windbeutel*, a big round puff pastry cut in half, heaped in the middle with whipped cream and dusted with powdered sugar. In the summer a slice of fruit pastry topped with whipped cream was my favorite.

With our selections carefully wrapped we rushed home where the coffee was never ready soon enough for us to be able to enjoy our Sunday treat.

When I came home from school around one o'clock, lunch was ready and Mutti had read the newspaper in the kitchen. She would make a comment or two about events that she read about.

After lunch I read the paper and sometimes asked her for some enlightenment: about prisoners of war, about a World War II event, comments from foreign governments, etc. Her comments would be highlighted by a reference to the past. For instance, if someone in Switzerland made a strong comment about Germans and the Nazi era, she would say, "Yes, it was very difficult for many Jews to survive or escape. But many other governments could have done more, especially Switzerland. Many Jews fled there and if they did not have enough funds to pay the government fees, they lingered in camps or worse, were sent back to Germany, which was a death sentence and they knew it. Those foreign governments should get off their high horse!"

On the last day of the month, Mutti bought the monthly Mickey Mouse magazine for us. On that day Margot and I had a race competition. She who was home first and finished *Mittagessen* in a reasonable good manner would get to read the magazine first. It was extremely important to Margot to be first. We were sitting on our chairs in the kitchen waiting for the other to be finished. After a while I told myself that it was not that

important and stopped asking Margot "'Are you done yet?"
When I happened to be home first, I knew Margot was not
far behind and I read all Mickey Mouse stories very
quickly. I guess I learned speed reading then.

If anyone came to our door, the conversation often
took place in the stairwell. Sometimes neighbors were
invited into the kitchen. They often came to report a
problem in their apartment that needed attention. Mutti
was always polite but hated these visits. "Don't be a
landlord and live nearby. One just doesn't get any peace.
They really should go to Mr. Ulbricht, the Super, but
because I'm here they don't."

Mrs. Brocinzki rang the doorbell regularly on her
way to the apartment one floor above. A chat with Mutti
provided relief from climbing the stairs and carrying the
groceries. She brought along neighborhood news she'd
heard in the stores: about new people moving into the
building next door; an older resident being hospitalized; a
woman across the street having committed suicide "She
turned on the gas burner without lighting and just sat on
her chair. The whole building could have blown up! You
wonder what made her do it?" A long silence followed her
report.

Most often it was Minna who visited. People never
bothered to whisper or try to conceal anything from me.
When they finished talking about the children and
reviewing and opining about Berlin and the rest of the
world, the most talked about subject were Musgangs, the
tenants upstairs, or goings on at Uncle Alfred's.

My First Cooking Experience

I was five or six when the first tasty morsel I prepared
myself was toast. Not the 'put-it-in-the-toaster-and-wait-
for-it-to-pop-up' kind we are used to today. First, I had to
beg for a piece of bread from Mutti. She would always say,
"I don't have any extra." Everything in the cupboard was
rationed. Every inch of the loaf of the dark rye bread was
allocated to last until we were due for another loaf. One
day when Mutti was talking to Minna in the staircase, a
loaf of bread was sitting on the cutting board on the
kitchen table. I was alone.

It was winter, and we lived in the kitchen because it was the only heated room in the apartment. The tile oven, heated with coal, used for cooking, heated the 7' by 14' kitchen at the same time. The sides of the oven were tile and the top was iron, and when it was heated, it served as a cook top.

So, the oven was hot, there was a loaf of bread on the table and Mutti was nowhere in sight. With a long bladed kitchen knife, I chopped off a slice. I quickly put it on the hottest part of the oven's top. A delicious aroma of warm bread developed almost immediately. I checked the bottom of the slice to make sure it was not getting too dark, just like I had watched Mutti doing many times. The bread needs to be a very dark brown, but not black. It seemed to take a long time until the color looked just right. Then I flipped the slice over to darken the other side. The second side darkened much faster. When it looked ready, I flipped the slice to expose the hot side. I sprinkled the crusty top with white sugar from Mutti's reserves and then quickly drizzled water over everything. Some spilled sugar started to burn and the smell permeated the kitchen. Sugar and water created a light crust on the very hot piece of bread. My masterpiece was ready! The first bite into the crunchy concoction was absolutely divine, and the whole piece was devoured in a minute. I don't remember the trail of evidence at all.

Upon Mutti's return, a look at the smoke, a glance at the leftover bread and a quick one at me, was all it took. "Go to your room, Heidi, I don't want to see you for a long, long time. And don't wait for dinner, because you just ate your share!"

Grocery Shopping

As long as I lived at home, we did not have a refrigerator. Mutti went to market every day, sometimes even twice because nothing would keep very long. In the winter she could buy butter and things like that in larger amounts. We had a very wide windowsill outside the kitchen window that doubled as food storage in the winter.

Before I started elementary school, I went shopping with Mutti every day. Our school week was Monday through Saturday. So after school started I could only go along during vacations. I loved going with her. Sometimes we just shopped in the stores on Waldstrasse. There was always a plan. With arms entwined, we went to the furthest store and started buying there, having checked availability and prices at the others along the way. The vegetable and fruit store was one block up and around the corner. The owners knew Mutti from the pre-war days. Pappa, of course, used to be their supplier of potatoes and vegetables.

First, Mutti walked along the vegetable display from one end to the other to see what the choices were that day. After waiting her turn came the usual: „Wie geht es denn Frau Sieg" (How are you?) and "Na, Heidi, bist Du brav und machst der Mutti keine Sorgen?" (I hope you are staying out of trouble and not giving your mother a hard time), while Mutti made her selections. She would buy a pound of carrots, "The little ones please, they are sweeter", two onions, a small Savoy cabbage, "They are milder than the other kind", a half pound green beans, "They look good and fresh", a half pound peas in their shell, "Oh, I can smell them, they were just picked", a bunch of parsley, and two apples, "Those with a little blush."

I knew that the apples were not for the soup, and they would be a treat for later. I loved apples, my favorite fruit. To me, the best tasting varieties were 'Cox-Orange' and 'Boskopp.'

Once everything was placed in our shopping bags, we continued on to the bakery. Our standard purchase was a half loaf of rye bread, still warm from the oven, "I would like the blunt end, not the pointy one, please." Wrapped in parchment paper, it now added to the weight of the bag. The grocery store was straight across the street from our building, the next to the last stop on a typical outing. Mutti asked for a quarter pound of butter and three eggs "from today's delivery, please."

Sometimes, if it was towards the end of the month, she would ask the owner to "write it up", instead of paying. That meant she was low on cash and had to wait for her widow's pension to arrive at the end of the month before she could pay her bill.

Frau Schenck, in the potato and coal store, on the ground floor of our building, was another store where she could do that. Frau Schenck gave her extensive credit, knowing that she would get paid. That store usually was our last stop. One pound of potatoes was the final item she needed that day.

Wednesdays and Saturdays were *Markthalle* days, the indoor farmer's market near City Hall. We had to walk a few additional blocks and I always looked forward to it.

Farmers from around the region came with their goods. From live chickens and fish to spun yarn and everything in between, all would show up at the farmer's market. That's also where the seasonal items would be available first: asparagus, strawberries, Chanterelle mushrooms. All fruits and vegetables were only available for a short time while the harvest lasted.

Mutti bought the first bananas at the farmer's market. I think I was eight or nine. This was an exotic fruit. I thought bananas did not have much of a taste and preferred apples anytime.

The Big Lie

Margot and I were sitting on the deep windowsill in the kitchen. It was getting dark outside and very shadowy in the room. We were waiting for supper. It was late Fall 1948, during the Russian's blockade of Berlin. We knew that there would not be much food on our plate. A few days earlier Margot returned home after two years of recovering and being cured from tuberculosis.

While we were waiting for Mutti to come into the kitchen to turn on the light and fix our sandwich, Margot was talking about some of her experiences at sanitarium Heckeshorn. Complete bed rest is one of the mainstays for recuperating from TB.

She was in a dorm for twenty children. It was fully occupied. Try to keep children down 24 hours a day! There would be long stretches during the day when no nurse would look in on them. So, one at a time they would get out of bed and start to tickle a designated friend. The challenge was to last as long as possible without giggling.

Margot told me that she was not ticklish anymore and dared me to test her. When I tickled her belly she started to squirm pretty quickly. She tried to evade my tickling fingers and turned this way and that way and finally laughed out loud! We were both laughing and she was still squirming. Suddenly, the curtains and the curtain bar came crashing down on us!

We stopped. Mutti would be very angry with us. What should we do?! We knew we could not put the bar and curtain back up. The window was too high, almost all the way up to the eight-foot ceiling. We thought perhaps we also broke off the supporting hooks. If it were broken, we knew Mutti would not be able to have it repaired. There simply was no money. Mutti was a widow, raising us by herself. We just got by.

We both were very afraid of what Mutti might do to us. We did not want to get spanked! We nervously watched the clock. Mutti sure would be here any second.

Then Margot said, "Well, Mutti knows I have to be treated very carefully. I need rest and should not be upset or stressed." I nodded in acknowledgement. Mutti had explained everything to me before Margot came back home. She continued, "When Mutti comes I'll tell her I was leaning against the curtain while looking out the window and all of a sudden the curtains came down" "Good," said, "but I don't think she'll believe it." "Why not?" Margot finished as we heard Mutti approaching.

Mutti opened the door and stopped. We were still sitting on the sill. She stayed in the doorway and demanded, "What happened here?" Silence.

She turned the light switch. "My curtains! How did they come down?" Silence.

"Tell me, Heidi!"

I murmured, "Margotwaslookingoutthewindowandallofasuddenthecurtai ncamedownallbyitself."

"What?" she came toward me. "I can't hear you." I repeated a little louder and slower while looking straight down on the floor, "Margot was looking out the window and all of a sudden the curtains came down all by itself."

Silence.

"Really!" she said and turned to Margot who was also staring at the floor. "Look at me, Margot," she continued. "Is that how it happened?" Margot looked straight at Mutti and nodded vigorously.

Mutti looked from one to the other and stormed out of the kitchen slamming the door, into the living room and slamming that door shut also. And then she was yelling to no one in particular about the bad girls she had and she did not know how she could raise us to become responsible adults. "I don't know what to do with them!"

And then it got very quiet. We did not speak or even whisper. It seems to me now that we held our breath for long periods of time.

Finally we heard the living room door open. Mutti walked through the short hall and came into the kitchen. "I don't want to see you for the rest of the day," she started our reprimand. "There will be no supper for you two. Go to bed now!" she ordered.

Very cautiously we walked past her out of the kitchen, through the hall and into the bedroom we shared. Without turning on the light because we did not want to be scolded for wasting electricity, we shed our clothes and crawled into bed. Mutti did not come to say "*Gute Nacht.*"

After a while Margot whispered "Are you asleep?"

"No," I said and continued, "Mutti is really mad at us, and I hope she is not still angry tomorrow."

"Oh, she will be ok," Margot said and started to giggle softly. "The nurses got mad at us a lot and the next day everybody always was back to normal."

I was not that confident and felt pretty bad for having lied so boldly. For two years, while Margot was getting treatments, Mutti and I had lived alone and I tried to be 'a good girl,' very consciously not wanting her be upset and never lied. I did not have to. Life was very simple and straightforward.

The following morning we approached the kitchen very cautiously. The curtains were back up. Mutti was slicing bread from a fresh loaf. "Good morning," she greeted us like all other mornings, except her smile was missing. We were almost back to normal and the day went on.

Our conspiracy worked! We practiced the united front against Mutti many times. When we found ourselves in trouble, it always turned out that "Margot did it."

A New Atmosphere

Margot returned home after almost two years in the sanitarium. I happily shared the bedroom again with my sister. Before falling asleep at night she recited stories from the wards at the sanitarium and the island of Sylt. Sometimes they were funny but mostly they were scary stories about people getting grabbed in the dark by a monster or being pulled into the stormy sea.

On the island of Sylt, she was mostly with children her own age. In the sanitarium in Berlin the children in the ward were all ages between three and 15; the older ones had some rough war experiences. They not only told many horror stories but they also set a pretty combative tone with the nurses. Not that Margot did much talking there; she mostly listened and soaked up a lot of that attitude.

She was not the sister I remembered. The conspiracies against Mutti seemed funny and adventurous at first. Soon, though, I realized that it was not just a one-time event for Margot. I became a less and less willing participant. Mutti was always saying "be careful" or "don't do this or that." I listened and tried to follow the rules.

I remember the first time Margot talked back to Mutti. We were grocery shopping in the morning. Margot was skipping ahead, scraping the tips of her shoes on the pavement with each step. Mutti cautioned "Margot, don't scrape the tops of your shoes."

Margot looked back and said, "why not?" Mutti explained, "Your shoes will get worn out too soon. I'm not getting a coupon for shoes for you for another two months!" Margot kept on skipping, scraping her shoes.

"Margot! Walk normal and stop scraping your shoes!"

"Why should I?!" she yelled back. She sounded just like the girls talking back to the nurses in the stories she relayed from the sanitarium.

I was holding my breath wondering what Mutti would do or say. Mutti just got very red in the face. "Wait till we get home," and we continued walking. Mutti was very quiet the rest of the outing. Arriving home she sent Margot to the bedroom.

After a while I followed Margot. She was very indignant and questioned what got Mutti so upset. We talked for a while about how to behave, how the tone that she observed in the sanitarium should not be used with Mutti, that she was being disrespectful and rude.

Then I went to see Mutti in the kitchen. While she prepared our lunch, she got her disappointment off her chest. I hoped that this would not happen again. But it did. Over and over. Margot was ornery and I tried to achieve peace.

Sometimes it was a little thing that fully charged the atmosphere in the house. "Margot, could you please hop over to the grocery store and get some bread?"

"Do I have to?"

"Yes, I'm busy cooking." Grocery stores close at 6:30 pm with German precision. Mutti would ask around 5:45 for her to go. Getting several reminders from Mutti, Margot put it off and put it off. At 6:25 pm, Mutti lost it and yelled at Margot, "Go NOW!"

Margot would slowly leave the apartment to fetch the bread just in time. Later, at the dinner table, Margot ate heartily. I had lost my appetite and Mutti was very quiet.

It was a scenario that became part of our home life - Margot being stubborn and confrontational and I the mediator, especially when they stopped talking to each other.

I couldn't understand why Margot kept on upsetting Mutti. Mutti tried very hard to make life as good as she could. She spent the last pennies on us. There often was nothing left for her.

I tried to do as was expected and not to upset her in any way. I did not upset her often, if I don't count the young years when we really didn't know any better. I was more of a concern to Mutti because of I spent so much time alone and had my recurring panic attacks. I think that's why she did not object when I went to Uncle Alfred's almost every day.

My panic attacks started right after Margot went to the sanitarium. It usually happened at night when I was alone and it was dark in the bedroom. The fact that Pappa was shot while sleeping was going round and round in my mind. I also heard a lot of stories and conversations about people dying in the war, dying young. Those images stuck in my mind, I guess. I didn't want to die young or in my sleep.

Sometimes the thought went away. Other times I couldn't think about anything else. It seemed as if I were disappearing into a deep, dark hole and couldn't breathe. I quickly got out of bed and ran to find Mutti.

She was still awake and I already felt better with the light on. I would tell her what happened and then stayed with her until I got sleepy and went back to my bed. Keeping the light on while going to sleep was not an option.

Mutti mentioned the attacks whenever we had a doctor's appointment. I was told that the panic attacks were war and trauma related, not unusual at all. I would outgrow them when I found a purpose in life.

Once in elementary school, in the early 1950s, Margot spent more and more time at a friend's house, leaving right after lunch and often coming home late for supper. Mutti would wait a certain amount of time and then gave up and would give the go ahead to eat. If they had an argument before Margot left, then it would be finished when she returned. It got worse in our teen years.

Margot and I quickly got over these disagreements and returned to normal conversations. It took Mutti several days, sometimes longer, to recover. She just did not know what to do with Margot. Whatever she tried, it was not good enough from Margot's point of view and it bothered her.

Margot was angry deep down that we were without a father and that other families had much more than we did. She thought if Mutti remarried and we had a father, our lives would be better financially. She also believed that a man would understand her better than Mutti. Margot always demanded to get something and ended up upset because Mutti could not provide.

Having spent so much time with Mutti alone I knew exactly how much our meager income from the house and the widow's pension was and what our living expenses were. Mutti tried to stretch what she had. Before the end of a month, she often ran out of money and the neighborhood stores gave her credit. But no matter how often I explained this to Margot, her attitude stayed the same, "Spare me the details, I really don't care. She can do something."

I can't say that I didn't notice the world around me, especially when my cousins could show off new outfits at their birthday and every holiday and we could only dream of such things. I was content with what I had. But I also remember sometimes thinking, 'when I grow up it'll be different.'

Saturdays and Sundays were quieter. Sunday was family day, and everybody spent time with their parents and siblings. Margot stayed home and run-ins did not happen often, unless she came to the table late or forgot to dust, for example. We always went out together on weekends; hiking, window shopping, to a movie and later to nightclubs and rarely had disagreements then.

When I started business school I took the same bus going and coming back every day. Margot was often waiting at the bus station at the end of the day. She relayed the latest spat with Mutti, maybe it was about a hairdo, maybe about music, maybe it was about needing money and Mutti said 'no.' Whatever it happened to be at the time, Margot would say, "I didn't give in and I left. I'm not coming home for supper. I have my house key and will be home around 10. Can you talk to her?"

At home Mutti had supper ready. While I ate, she told me her side of the story. Then when Margot got home I would explain that Mutti was upset because she added bangs to her hairdo without consulting her (in the Germany of the 1950s one just did not do such a thing without parental agreement), or I counted out why Mutti didn't have any extra money. Peace returned for a few days.

Years later Margot told me, "I was so angry when you moved to Switzerland. You abandoned me." She still had two years of high school to get through and was alone with Mutti.

Uncle Alfred

With Margot at the sanitarium I visited Uncle Alfred more often. For lack of anything else to do I would ask Mutti if I could go and visit.

I would go in the afternoon. First, I saw Aunt Elfriede to say "*Guten Tag*" and then go on to Uncle Alfred. He was always lying on the couch in his living room obeying doctor's orders, "two hours resting every afternoon." He was always happy to see me and after asking "What's new Heidi?" he would talk non-stop. "The doctor didn't say I can't talk."

I was sitting on a chair next to the sofa and listened. He talked about his plans for the business, how he would build it up with Aunt Elfriede's help. "Just like August did," he said often.

Sometimes he talked about soldiering and being wounded. "When I was shot in the upper thigh during a battle, I didn't know it. I walked on it normal- like until it was over. Then I noticed the holes and wet spots on my trouser leg. Suddenly it hurt and I knew I was shot." He was sent to the infirmary tent. "The doctors inserted a pin to reconnect the bones, somehow managed to damage the knee in the process. I haven't been able to walk normal-like ever since." His left knee was permanently stiff.

Uncle Alfred had a VW. If he had to drive anywhere while I was there he always asked if I wanted to come along. Of course I did. I had to let Mutti know first that I would be home a little later than usual. Sometimes they were short drives in the neighborhood. Other times he would drive all over Berlin to visit somebody he wanted to do work for him or maybe he wanted to do some 'horse trading,' literally. Horses pulled the flatbeds and he often bought or traded them. He would maybe buy a horse or was interested in a trade. He just loved the process of making a deal.

Uncle Alfred would talk about what the plan of this particular trip was, what he meant to accomplish. If I had to wait in the car while he kept his appointment, he relayed the chain of events to me on the drive back home. I was always fascinated by the goings on and by being 'the fly-on-the-wall' learned about business that I had no idea I was learning.

One of his favorite stops was at car dealers. He traded his car every year for a current model. First it was VWs, then an Opel and then a Mercedes. Before he traded the car, he stopped at all the car dealers for his "car talk," me in tow, starting in late spring. At first I listened in on the conversations that always ended with price negotiations. After several weeks I quickly wandered off, examining the new cars while he was doing his dance. By fall he had made his deal and we didn't go on those trips until the following year when he started all over again.

When Werner was visiting on weekends, I tagged along with whatever he was doing.

From early on I also remember Walter, Uncle Alfred's friend from the war. He lived in East Berlin, working as a stonemason. He came every weekend and sometimes every day after work. Walter repaired all the damage to the apartment building where Mutti and Pappa used to live. When the repair work was done, he proceeded to expand the floor plan by building a room over the garage that would become an office and above, on the third floor, he built a big bathroom and laundry room, part of which later became Werner's room.

I was welcome to keep Walter company. I watched as he built brick walls, mixed cement, cut wood for window frames, all the while explaining to me what he did and how it is done right. "Do it right the first time and you won't have to do it over. It may seem slow going but it's faster in the long run," was his favorite saying as he moved along. When he was done with the apartment, he tackled the cellars. There he had the help of whatever crew Uncle Alfred had working for him at the time.

At suppertime I relayed my busy afternoon to Mutti.

My first Job

It was September, or maybe October, 1949 in Berlin, and I was seven. The Berlin Blockade ended a few months ago. All goods, especially foods, were still rationed and scarce.

"Heidi, there is a job to be done and I believe you are the only one who can do it!" Uncle Alfred looked at me with a smile. I could not imagine what he had in mind.

In the back of the five-story apartment building, Uncle Alfred operated his potato business; the retail outlet was in the courtyard. Potatoes were stored in a large hangar next to a smaller apartment building. Vast storage cellars were below. During the war those cellars were used as bomb shelters. On the ground level of the apartment building were a couple of horse stalls. I would often visit the potato yard after school in the afternoon; there always were people coming and going. It was much more fun being there than to watch from our kitchen window.

Uncle Alfred had two men who worked for him full-time, loading and selling potatoes and taking care of two horses. In the fall the number of men could be up to eight or ten. They were busy unloading sacks of harvest potatoes from freight cars onto to flatbed trailers at the nearby railway and then the horse drawn trailers arrived at the yard. The huge red wooden hangar door would slide open and the unloading started. Coarse brown hemp sacks filled with 100 pounds of potatoes were carried to the cellars and emptied into wooden bins. When those bins were full almost to the ceiling, bins in the hangar were next. Over the course of 4 to 6 weeks, the storage would be completely filled.

I stayed out of the way, mostly listening to the men's banter. Occasionally a sack would break and spill all over the cement floor. Quickly I helped picking up, starting with the ones in the men's way. My uncle nodded with smiling approval. Uncle Alfred could not do any physical work but was very good at organizing his crew and appreciating their work.

So, when my uncle had a job for me on that fall day, I was very willing. "See the sliding door?" I nodded. "You see where the door slides between the house and the hangar?" I nodded again. "There is so much dirt and dust in there that the door no longer opens enough for a trailer to get in. You are the only one skinny enough to fit into the gap and to scrape out that crud! What do you say?"

"Sure, I'll do it!" as I headed towards the hanger.

The gap between buildings was about 40 feet long. I slid sideways into the dark gap, the heel of my shoes scraping one wall and the toe the other. With a narrow shovel in my right hand I was reaching sideways and started to scrape the damp, musty dirt one bit at a time towards the front. Slowly I inched my way to the back. If I bent just a little my forehead would scrape the rough mortared wall, and my back was sliding against the other.

'Mutti will be upset when I come home all dirty' I was thinking. I could not see the back of my skirt but imagined that it was really bad from brushing against the wall. I only had two skirts, one for school and one for the rest of the time. Mutti will definitely be upset. Over and over I scraped and dragged the dirt to the front of the gap. My knees and elbows started to hurt from the scratches. I just could not avoid hitting the walls.

Finally I was done and I went to find my uncle in one of the cellars. He told the men to stop for a minute and "inspect Heidi's job." A big pile of sand, pebbles, old leaves and small branches greeted them at the hangar door. They all smiled and patted my shoulders.

"Well, I couldn't have done it better myself," he said. "I'll remember that and will ask you again when I have a job just for you. Go to the office and Elfriede (his sister) will give you 1 Mark and then come back and see how many potatoes you can carry home."

I was beaming. I had never been paid for anything before. I wanted to jump up and down and scream and yell, but I didn't. I picked up as many potatoes as I could fit into my gathered up skirt and skipped up the stairs to our apartment, two at a time. I was thinking that Mutti would be pleased to get the potatoes and hoped that she would not see my dirty backside for a while.

I worked with Uncle Alfred off and on. At the train depot I was taught the fine art of balancing a 100-pound sack of potatoes on a two-wheeled hand dolly so that it was basically weightless. That's how we transferred hundreds of tightly packed potato sacks from train cars to flatbed trucks.

After the cellars were filled with the fall harvest crop, potatoes needed to be shifted and sorted constantly. A rotten potato that's not spotted can spoil a large area quickly, smell awful and be a real pain to clean up. I became an expert at following the 'rotten potato smell' and finding those bad ones.

Aunt Ruth

Uncle Alfred married Ruth Brown in 1950. Ruth was working for his main competitor at the rail yard. When it became evident that they were dating, there was plenty of gossip. Uncle Alfred was about 5'6" and Ruth was over six feet tall, a very masculine looking woman. They definitely made an unconventional pair.

Mutti sent Margot and me with a bouquet of flowers to extend congratulation from our family. We were invited to sit next to the bride and groom. I relished the white cake with strawberry filling that was served. I tried to be very careful not to spill anything but dropped a section of strawberry. When I tried to casually peek under the table, I saw that it had landed on the brides dress. I carefully looked around to see if anyone had noticed. Everyone was talking and laughing and paying me no mind. I was glad when it was time to go home and someone else would get my seat next to the bride.

Aunt Ruth, as she was called from then on, stepped right into the role of being Alfred's right hand after the wedding. It was not common for a woman to work in this very blue-collar environment. Plenty of sarcastic remarks flew about whenever she was seen among the workmen, or even driving a tractor to the station. She was also wearing pants most of the time, totally unacceptable! The remarks were never stronger than when she was pregnant after several years of marriage.

I continued my visits and working for Uncle Alfred. Aunt Elfriede stopped working for her brother the minute it was known that he would marry, just as she did when Pappa married Mutti.

Werner moved in with Uncle Alfred in 1952 when he had to enter high school. He would get a better education in the West. Werner was put through the same young adulthood that Alfred and Pappa had experienced at their home. He got up early, rode his bicycle to school and when he got home he had to help with the business. Werner was involved in all phases of the wholesale business, which was especially busy in the fall. When business was slow, Alfred gave him busy work like washing all cars and sweeping the hangars so they were in tip-top shape.

Homework had to wait until he was done and that was often late. Werner, of course, was not happy with this routine and quite homesick. It certainly was different from home life with his mother. Mutti remarked often how Alfred seemed to act like the 'Old Sieg,' referring to Pappa's father.

After high school Werner went on to business school, living in the small room that was created for him in the attic. Although I was visiting almost daily, I saw him only briefly because he usually had to finish a job. He moved to West Germany shortly after graduation.

Very early on Sunday drives were established. I always went to visit right after our Sunday meal. Regardless of the season, Uncle Alfred was game for an outing. It was unthinkable to him to stay home on a Sunday afternoon. The Grunewald was a favorite destination. He'd drive and drive until he found a good spot to park and then we had a short walk. Because of his stiff leg the walks were very limited. This routine continued after he married also. Werner came along on Sunday drives if he was not visiting his mother.

In the winter Uncle Alfred put a sled in the trunk. Once we reached the woods he tied the sled to the bumper and gave us a long ride on the forest road. There were not many cars at that time, so it was really safe and I loved it!

In the summer he would drive around until he saw a nice restaurant where we could have a coffee outside.

A Real Job

Aunt Ruth hired a housekeeper, Mrs. Schlokowski, after Aunt Elfriede left to take care of the house and cooking while she was working. Before their first child was born, she called me into the office and said, "The baby will be here soon and I will continue working. Frau Schlokowski will take care of the baby in the mornings. Would you like to have the job of *Kindermädchen,* babysitter, in the afternoon after school? We will pay you five Marks a week."

I was feeling very happy. I would have a real job! I said, "Yes, I would love nothing better. But I'll have to talk to Mutti first."

I rushed home and Mutti agreed, of course. She thought it would be a very good diversion and learning experience for me. I was spending a lot of time there anyway and Margot was hardly ever home for company. Mutti said, "You can keep the money but you'll have to pay for some luxuries like movies from now on." A movie ticket cost a half German Mark at the time. I quickly added up in my head how much I could save even with paying for movies.

My cousin Helmut was born in July of 1954. Until I graduated from high school in 1957, I went to my new baby-sitting job every day after homework was done.

I woke Helmut from his nap. After he had his snack, I went for a long walk pushing Helmut in the baby carriage. When he was a little older, we went to a nearby playground. The main attraction was the huge sandbox. Helmut was happy there for hours. Back at home Mrs. Schlokowski made his supper and I fed Helmut and later taught him to feed himself. I usually read him a story before Mrs. Schlokowski put him to bed. On Sundays I went there after lunch.

My first proud purchase was an Agfa Brownie Camera for $14 Marks. I've been taking photos and recording our doings ever since. After that I saved and spent my money mostly on clothes and shoes, mainly shoes. I felt very good about myself when I liked the shoes I wore on any given day.

Helmut's sister Hannelore was born in the summer of 1956. My obligation stayed to take care of Helmut. Aunt Ruth's mother Mrs. Braun, who lived nearby, helped out with the new baby

After I started working I still went to visit Sunday afternoons. Uncle Alfred and Aunt Ruth kept up their Sunday afternoon outing routine. Everyone present at the time was invited along. Mrs. Braun was always there and if Werner didn't visit his mother he came along also. I don't know how we all squeezed into the car, but the large Mercedes made it possible: Uncle Alfred in front driving; Aunt Ruth and the baby next to him; Mrs. Braun, Werner and myself holding Helmut in the back; and sometimes Margot came along too.

1957
Typical outing with, left to right, Uncle Alfred,
Aunt Ruth with Hannelore, Heidi with Helmut,
Frau Braun.

All About Clothes

The monthly widow pension and child allowance Mutti received did not cover clothing. We were given a clothing allowance as needed.

As we outgrew major items like shoes or a winter coat, Mutti had to apply for additional funds from Social Services. If something was worn out or outgrown before its allocated 'life,' Mutti had to show proof. Margot grew at a much faster rate than I and as you read earlier, she also simply wore stuff out before its time.

The government agency Mutti needed to communicate with was a bus ride or an hour long walk from our house. We always went with Mutti because if something was outgrown, we had to model it. Mutti really dreaded these visits and being scrutinized like that. Before we left the house she took a pill, something like Valium today, to make sure she would not get upset should any of the clerks make snide remarks as they were sometimes known to do.

If Margot's shoes had a hole in the top leather, but the soles were still not worn out, Mutti was told to patch the hole so that Margot could still wear them. If the clerk agreed that a coat sleeve and hem were way too short for Margot, Mutti would get a coupon for a new coat.

Mutti was busy sewing and knitting all our clothing. Mostly Oma and Aunt Anni gave a dress or jacket they no longer were using to Mutti. She would carefully cut all seams and take them apart. After ironing the pieces flat she proceeded to cut pieces for a dress or skirt for me.

From the early 1950s on I remember that Aunt Elschen, Ingrid and Dorit were getting new outfits at Easter, Whit-Sunday and Christmas, and their hand-me-downs always went to Aunt Elschen's nieces and nephews.

We did get hand-me-down clothes from my cousin Werner, who is two years older. Out of his slacks Mutti would make a skirt. From one of his jackets she could make a top. I could wear his shoes; they were already too small for Margot. I never minded the hand-me-downs, except when I had to wear Werner's shoes. They were obviously boy's shoes and very clumsy looking and I was very conscious how they looked. But they were the only shoes I had. With my babysitting money I bought shoes after window-shopping for days and days. To this day I'm very particular about shoes.

Mutti continued to get wool from the relatives in Bochum and was knitting, tops, jackets and knee socks for us. Some jacket-sweaters she knitted in complicated patterns. I remember her sitting by the stove, the knitting in her lap and the pattern instructions on the table. She marked off every row that was completed before starting the next one. Sometimes I heard her swearing and cussing because she missed some turns. "I'll never try this pattern again!" she said. Of course, that never lasted long and when one sweater was done, she started another one with a similar pattern. People noticed the beautiful knitted things we were wearing and asked Mutti if she would knit a sweater for them. Throughout most of my school years Mutti knitted sweaters and had some welcome extra income.

After the house was renovated, Mutti found that it actually cost less paying off the Marshal Plan loan than she had spent on repairs all these years. She could keep a tad more from the rents and there was some extra money around. I was twelve when I had my first new winter coat. It sure felt good, and I was very proud wearing it.

Margot and I started sewing along with Mutti. I remember the first dress I made when I was fifteen. Before I could start I had to clean off the living room table. I cut the pattern and put all the pieces together with stickpins. Then the job of sewing started. All stitching was done by hand. I had to put everything away and set the table again when I was done for the day. The next day the routine started all over again.

It took over a month to finish the dress. It was a dark green long sleeved dress with a wide skirt that bounced a lot with layers of starched petticoats underneath. Years later I reworked the green dress into a new one. But then I could use a friend's sewing machine and it just took a couple evenings to complete.

I continued to sew my clothes because ready-made was very expensive and hardly ever fitted my small frame anyway. I would go to stores to get ideas though. When I could not find a pattern I liked in the catalogues, I learned to make my own.

I also knitted a few sweaters. Margot and I thought it would be unique to have similar outfits and knitted the same turtleneck sweater only in different colors, hers was purple and mine green. After homework and babysitting we would knit until it was absolutely time to go to sleep.

When our masterpieces were completed, we scoured all the good sporting good stores to buy our first pair of slacks. I must have been sixteen and Margot fifteen. We were very particular with what we wanted. We could wear these outfits when we went to sporting events and also hiking. Finally we found what we had in mind, green stretch pants for Margot and purple ones for me. We felt very stylish and cool!

Mutti was a very good fashion tutor. I never bought anything without her input. We scrutinized magazines and shop windows together deciding what would look good on a short person, which we both were. When I started babysitting I saved my money for sweaters, blouses and of course, shoes.

1954
Margot and Heidi
1959

German Health Care System

I rarely went to a doctor's office. General health, dental check-ups and shots were done at school twice a year, part of the German Health Care system. The school gave me a note to take home for Mutti to sign when a check-up was scheduled.

Nurses did the check-ups and if they found a cavity, which did not happen often, I got a voucher to go to the dentist. We were weighed and our height measured and if they found anything to suggest further checking, we were given a voucher to see a doctor. I was always underweight and regularly had to see a doctor. If the doctor's thorough check-up didn't detect anything else, I was sent home with a reminder to eat more. For being chronically underweight, I qualified for the doctor recommended *Verschickung* – a get well R&R spa retreat children routinely were sent on. (Read about R&R retreats, page 141).

Although I had measles, whooping cough, chicken pox and typhoid fever when very young, once in school I had to have shots for those, TB and Polio vaccinations followed.

We had colds and earaches but cough syrup or warm oil dripped into the hurting ear would take of it. Mutti took us to see a doctor only when we had a high, persistent fever.

In the winters of 1949, '50 and '51, both Margot and I were prescribed sunlight. Three times a week we walked to the doctor's office for our appointment with the sunlamp. Naked from the waist up and protective goggles over our eyes, we stood in front of the sunlamp for twenty minutes with four or five others. Of course, we stood still and were absolutely quiet, just as we were told.

Throughout the years our scrapes and bruises were never treated by a doctor:

Margot being bitten by 'Albo' the coal shop watchdog – Mutti cleaned the wound and if no infection showed, that was it.

When Margot's foot got caught in bicycle wheel spokes, Mutti cleaned it, applied bandages and watched as it healed.

Dorit hit the back of her head sledding with Margot in the rubble near her house. It was bleeding pretty hard when she came inside. Cold compresses and band-aids took care of that.

I remember falling off a swing onto my chin on a playground near Ingrid's house. Blood was dripping all over my shirt. Mutti covered the cut with a couple criss-cross band-aids.

The four of us went sledding in the Rehberge, a woodsy park about four miles from our apartment. Rehberge had a favorite sledding hill bustling with people all times of the day. It must have been during school vacation. Ingrid and Dorit stopped at our house as planned and we walked to Rehberge together, two sleds in tow. It was cold so we wore extra layers of everything, especially double stockings and underwear.

We had been to Rehberge once before and remembered how to get there. Finally we arrived at the sledding hill. It looked very steep. We walked to the top next to the tree-lined slope that seemed to take forever and then, skirts tucked safely under us, we whizzed down the hill in no time. Margot and Dorit on one sled and Ingrid and I on the other.

The afternoon went by quickly. The light started to dim and it was getting hard to see. Ingrid and I were making our last run when we missed a slight angle on the slope and crashed into a tree. I was sitting in front. I bumped my forehead, bit my tongue and through my lower lip. It began bleeding badly and it hurt! I didn't have anything to put over the bleeding except a handkerchief and it was soaked through quickly. I couldn't help but cry. There was nothing for us to do but to make the long walk home. The bleeding stopped by the time we got home. My tongue and lower lip were swollen for days.

The 1950 Flu Epidemic

Mutti did not get colds very often, but when she did she would just carry on doing as little work as possible and stay in the kitchen to be warm. I remember huddling next to her in front of the warm stove wishing for her to get better fast. The coughing always worried me.

Margot and I were very afraid of Mutti not getting better and maybe even dying. We were half-orphans, and without Mutti, who would take care of us? "What would happen to us?" I asked her. "The State would take care of you," Mutti answered. I knew that meant an orphanage. I had never heard any good stories about an orphanage.

I asked Oma once if we could live with her if something happened to Mutti. "No, I couldn't do that. I'm too old and I have to work. I couldn't have you around." She finished our conversation, "I probably would visit you some Sundays."

Margot and I went through our short list of relatives considering who might take us in. Uncle Helmut and Aunt Elschen? Of course not! Uncle Alfred and Aunt Ruth? Too busy. Aunt Hille and Uncle Erich? No room in their small apartment. Aunt Anni and Uncle Emil? They did not know anything about children!

1950 found Germany with a wide spread flu epidemic. Mutti's winter cold was eventually diagnosed as flu by the doctor who made the house call. Doctors made house calls regularly then. She was weak and had to go by ambulance to the hospital. When we came home from school one day, Minna told us that Mutti was already in the hospital.

It was January 1950, we were eight and seven and had to fend for ourselves. Minna kept an eye on us and boosted our morale. In the mornings Erich, her husband, sent Jutta and Lutz off to school and Minna came to check on us. She made sure we were dressed right and had some bread before we went off.

After school Margot and I met in front of the building and walked a couple of blocks to a little wine shop that also served a hot soup every day. The owners had known Pappa, and Mutti sometimes visited them.

Mutti asked Minna to arrange for our meal there. The soup was our warm meal of the day. Afterwards we went home to do our homework. Minna came again in the evening to see if we needed anything. We went to Oma's apartment on Sundays for supper.

Children under sixteen were not allowed to visit hospitals. Minna went to see Mutti a couple of times. Afterwards she reassured us, "She is doing much better and will be home soon."

While Mutti was gone, Margot and I stuck close together, being children with model behavior. We did not want to give anybody reason to complain to social services. Mutti was in the hospital for six weeks and we were very relieved when she was home again.

It's the Appendix

Aunt Schneider, Aunt Suzie and Uncle Lutz and family invited me to go on a picnic at the beginning of our summer vacation in 1952. First we went on a big cruising boat on Lake Wannsee to the Grunewald Forest. We had a picnic there and I played games with Suzie's and Lutz's daughters. For game playing we simply took off the dresses and played in our underwear. It was really a lot of fun.

On the way back I started to have long stomach cramps that just didn't want to stop. I had trouble walking from the train station to the house. When Mutti saw me she just took her purse and we went to the doctor's office. Luckily we only had to walk a couple of blocks. The doctor determined that I had appendicitis and sent me straight to the hospital. Another walk. I just wanted to curl up somewhere and sleep to get away from the pain.

A bed in a children's ward was assigned and I could finally lie down. It all happened very fast. That same evening I was prepped for surgery the next morning. My appendix was taken out and then I spent two weeks in the ward recovering. Mutti came to visit a few times.

The hospital on Turmstrasse was also a teaching hospital and the group for morning rounds was always large. At each patient's bed, the lead doctor recited the patient's history and treatment. The stop at my bedside was usually short, appendicitis being rather straightforward.

One morning, though, the group was larger than ever, over forty doctors. As it turned out, the chief surgeon for the hospital and Berlin's Medical University was leading the round. Prof. Dr. Gorbrand was very well-known throughout Europe. The group's murmur came closer and closer to my bed.

Finally it was my turn. Instead of the normal short stop and ho-hum description, Dr. Gorbrand asked detailed questions about the surgery and progression of recovery.

Then he pointed to my full first name, Heidemarie. "Do you know the popular soldier's march "Heidemarie"?" he asked me. I shook my head; I didn't want to admit that I knew the first few words and nothing more. "Well, gentlemen, how about it? Do you know the song? Let's sing it for Heidemarie."

With a huge smile he led the whole group in a very loud and complete rendition. It was the kind of fuss I always tried to avoid. I bet my face was beet red! I didn't know what to do with myself. But I joined their laughter before they moved on to the next patient.

The day to go home finally arrived. It had been two weeks since the surgery and I was told to stay in bed for another week. School was starting again in two weeks and I should be completely recovered by then. Mutti was very mysterious while we were walking home. "I have a surprise for you. You'll never guess!" she kept teasing me.

When we turned the corner onto Waldstrasse, I saw several big trucks parked in front of our house. "Our house is getting re-built with funds from The Marshall Plan," Mutti explained. "The fifth floor, the attic and the roof are going to be new. Our ceiling will be renovated. No more leaky hole! The side façade will get a layer of mortar; your room will be better insulated with that. Your room will also get a new window facing south, so you'll get more light into the room", she finished.

Wow! That was a surprise. I knew that we applied to The Marshall Plan several years ago. "The work started yesterday and should be done in a couple of months," Mutti said.

Laying on Mutti's sofa while recovering, I watched the charred wood around the hole in the ceiling being cut away and replaced with fresh lath. A few weeks later the plaster was patched and the whole ceiling painted. All interior reminders of the war damage had disappeared.

Recurring Pneumonia

I developed a high fever sometimes every year. My back and chest would hurt and the fever would go up very quickly. Mutti went to the doctor's office and he came to the apartment after office hours. The diagnosis always was pneumonia.

Mutti told me that this was happening regularly since I was a baby. I was always considered sickly. I would get a shot of penicillin and get better really fast, but then I had to have four weeks bed rest. What a way to spend summer days. The good part was that I could be in Mutti's bed in the living room where Mutti and Margot would stop by once in a while. When it was very hot, a special treat was a bottle of Coca Cola that I didn't have to share.

I remember those long days in bed very well. Time went by slowly. A large oil painting of Der Königssee, Kings Lake, in the Bavarian Alps, was hanging on the wall behind the sofa. I studied it for hours, every path, tree and cloud. I could paint it from memory today.

My pneumonia kept returning. Sometimes it just interrupted my summer. One time it happened the day before my final exam at business school. I could not take the test. My doctor's statement allowed me to take the test a couple weeks later. To my relief, I passed and graduated with my class.

I always knew when a certain pain in my back started that pneumonia was coming on.

P.S.

Many years later, I was in my Forties, it was determined that I never had pneumonia. It was a kidney infection, but never diagnosed as such.

My doctor explained, "You were born with a part of a third kidney. That third kidney never functioned but would get infected regularly. The kidney was near the lower lobe of the lung and the lung showed a sympathetic infection, that's why the conclusion always was pneumonia."

Over the years the infection spread to my left kidney. Because it was never treated, the kidney was totally diseased and needed to be removed. The doctor continued, "If your other kidney is not affected, you'll be just fine. We only need one kidney." During surgery the doctor found my right kidney to be in perfect health.

I remember being angry and sad at the same time for all the years I was sick and the summers that I had to spend in bed. It was so unnecessary! But my anger did not last more than a few minutes. It was just life that happened to me.

R&R Retreats

Aside from vacations with our Bochum relatives, my only vacations were the Health Care System sponsored R&R retreats. These R&R retreats were available to anyone ten years old and up. An application needed to be filed, accompanied by a doctor's recommendation. Often these were recovery as well as prevention retreats. I went on several retreats because I was extremely underweight. The stays in Bad Salzdetfurth and in Bavaria were my favorites.

Bad Salzdetfurth

In the fall of 1952, I was accepted for a four-week stay at Bad Salzdetfurth, one of the many spas that Germany is known for. All Europeans have taken regular spa retreats as prevention for hundreds of years. My chronic underweight could be helped with lots of R&R and hefty food. Except for my hospital stay this year I had not been away from home and had no clue what to expect. Mutti said, "Just do whatever the chaperone tell you to and you'll be just fine!"

    With the acceptance for a trip came sheets and sheets of regulations: what to bring, where to sew in the name tags, how to pack. A week before departure I had to go to the health department for a final check to assure I was not ill and also to make sure I did not have head lice, a very common condition for many years after the war.

    Mutti checked our hair regularly for signs of lice. I don't remember ever having any. If she thought she saw something resembling lice or their eggs, she gave us the 'radical treatment.' It meant a regular shampoo and then kerosene getting massaged into the hair. That would kill any lice and eggs, but it also hurt. A few days later the hair was combed with a special 'lice comb' with extremely fine teeth to remove any residue. I smelled of kerosene for days and the combing yanked out a lot of hair. But the nurse did not find any signs of lice during the check-up and I was good to go.

With a nametag around my neck and small suitcase to take along, Mutti brought me to the bus station early in the morning. Two chaperones took over the care of forty children. They herded us to assigned seats on the bus. Everything always was very orderly. Seats, beds, table places, all were assigned, no need for rushing or pushing.

Bad Salzdetfurth was in the middle of Germany in a very picturesque foothill area. At the spa I was in a double room. I can't remember who my roommate was or where in Berlin she was from. We did very little talking.

In the morning we dressed and went to breakfast together. Afterward we had to get our towels and go to the bath session. Every morning, six days a week we had to sit in big tubs with healing salt-mineral water. Then we had to go straight to our room for a long rest before lunch. After lunch came another rest period.

At three in the afternoon we gathered in the entry hall dressed for walking. We walked behind the chaperones in pairs to the nearby woods. I don't remember any rainy days and we could walk every day. I loved the walks. The smell of damp earth and fallen leaves in the woods reminded me of some hikes in the Grunewald and felt very comfortable. The best part of those walks was the singing. As soon as we reached the woods we started singing folk and hiking songs, songs we all knew very well.

I remember the night hikes especially. Whenever there was moonlight we repeated our hiking routines after supper. When we gathered in the lobby, it was dark already. We walked two or three abreast and were reminded not to dawdle and to keep contact with the line in front of us. We didn't have to be told twice, and we stuck close together. It was a little eerie as we entered the forest. Our singing seemed extra loud and echoed through the woods. Between songs the rustle of our feet on the fallen leaves was the only sound. I loved it!

Some children were crying often because they were homesick. I don't remember being homesick at all. I was not worried; Mutti would be there when I got back. I certainly did not miss school.

We kept the same routine for four weeks and then it was back on the bus for the trip to Berlin. Mutti received a post card announcing the day and time of my return. Everything that required a timetable was punctual. The transportation system was no exception. Our bus arrived promptly on time. Mutti was waving as we pulled into the station.

Abtsee in Bavaria

In the early fall of 1956 my R&R was going to be in Bavaria. If I had twinges of uncertainty before the first spa stay, this time there were none. I was looking forward to the trip. It turned out to be my favorite vacation of all.

Again Mutti delivered me to the meeting place at the bus station in the early evening. I had enough sandwiches and fruit to last until we arrived there the following morning. I had hardly eaten all day. After coming home from school, I helped with the last bit of packing.

By the time I was sitting in the bus I was starving and had one of those sandwiches right away. By the time we were on the Autobahn – Interstate – it was dark and I could not see anything. Everybody seemed to be asleep; it was a long night in the quiet bus. Curiosity kept me awake.

We were already in Bavaria when daylight broke. I couldn't wait to see the big mountains that so far I had only seen in movies. We were still driving in the foothills of the Alps and mountains were often hidden by trees. When we were rolling past open areas I could see some distant mountain peaks and was eager for us to arrive.

The retreat center was on the shore of Abtsee, a small lake and town near Laufen, close to the Austrian border. From the lake I had an unobstructed view of the Alps. Finally! I felt very lucky to be there and stay for a whole month!

We were a small group of twenty along with two chaperones who filled the one-level house. The house, with wooden floors, was comfortably furnished and felt very homey. This time, except for mealtimes, the days were largely unstructured. We could go for a swim before breakfast if we wanted, and I did. It felt utterly luxurious to walk down the short grassy slope and jump into the frigid lake. A warm hearty breakfast was especially welcome after that.

The chaperones presented us with options for the day at breakfast. We often hiked in the nearby woods, walked to the small town of Laufen or walked along the nearby Salzach River. This major German river is snaking through the Bavarian landscape. We made many treks into the surrounding area that I clearly remember.

One outing was to Berchtesgaden and the Königssee. This is very picturesque and often painted lake surrounded by alpine peaks including the famous Watzmann, the highest in that region. We had a painting of the Königssee in our living room at home. I thought the lake was as impressive in real life as it was in the painting, I paused and admired it as long as I could. We hiked on some mountain trails and ate the sandwiches we packed in a high meadow. I could have gone on and on, but we had to hike back to town and our waiting van.

Another side trip took us to Salzburg, Austria, only an hour away. The Trapp Family story was already well known in Germany and I was excited to see the city. It was as beautiful as the photos I had seen. We took the tram up to the Salzburg Castle with an expansive view over the city and the Alps beyond. We made a game out of identifying the individual mountains.

One adventure within this trip was visiting the underground salt mines. At the entrance we had to slip on protective pants, tops and hats for the journey underground. An open cage elevator took us below where a train with small open cars was waiting. We rode the train through dimly lit mine tunnels just wide and high enough to get us through. The air smelled of salt and it was very cold. After a few minutes, it seemed longer than that, the tunnel opened into a huge brightly lit area. We had arrived at one of many underground salt lakes. Except for this public lake, all lakes were used for salt production. We walked through an exhibit highlighting the steps from water to saltshaker.

After that our group filled two flat bottom boats, attached to iron cables. Slowly and silently we were pulled across the water. The stone ceiling was especially low over the lake and I remember being very relieved when we arrived on the other side and another elevator brought us back to the surface and daylight.

Then there was another castle with elaborate gardens and fountains that moved in sync with waltzes. We had a lot of fun dashing under the water arches without getting wet.

Another memorable outing was a visit to the Stille Nacht Kapelle, Silent Night Chapel, in Oberndorf, also in Austria. Franz Gruber first played his composition "Silent Night" for this congregation on his guitar in 1818. The small chapel felt very cozy, not like the big churches I had been in so far. The song of course became famous and is sung around the world at Christmas time. It was not Christmas but we sang "Stille Nacht" on the way back to our lakefront home.

When the retreat came to an end I would have liked to stay, not because I did not want to go home but because it was so beautiful there. I loved the mountain area. But, of course, we all had to go back home.

Mutti's R&R

Women could apply for R&Rs at Mütterheims - Homes for Mothers. The theory was that mothers need R&R just like everybody else. Women with five or six children were given preference. After many tries Mutti finally got a well-deserved vacation in the summer of 1955.

Mütterheims were usually in country settings. Sometimes they were large estates that were converted; some retreat homes were built just for that purpose.

The women did not have any responsibilities or duties, a true vacation from the every day. Mutti sent a postcard letting us know how she enjoyed the vacation and company of women like herself. She was with forty other women. They went hiking, played card games, watched movies and did a lot of reading.

Margot and I were on our own for four weeks when I was thirteen, and Margot not quite twelve. We took care of ourselves and knowing that if anyone reported anything to Social Services we could be in trouble. We strived to be model children. Until we were sixteen there was the threat that we could be sent to a home for juveniles if Mutti appeared to be unfit.

We hand-washed our laundry to be sure we appeared spotless. Mutti left grocery money with us and we shopped and fed ourselves. Although neither of us had experience with cooking, we cooked stews on weekends. We followed recipes from a magazine and it was quite tasty. The rest of the times we made boiled, fried and scrambled eggs and lots of sandwiches and always cleaned up right away.

We stopped at Minna's after school to say hello. She also came to the apartment ever so often to be sure we did not let the dishes pile up. Oma checked on us after she got home from work.

Margot always came home early from her friends' house and I was home around 6:30 after my babysitting job. We did not go out, not even to a movie to be sure there was no doubt about what we were doing. Sunday afternoons we visited Uncle Alfred and usually stayed until suppertime.

Time went by quickly and we were glad when Mutti was home again.

Fun Times

It was not common at all to go out and play. We were only allowed to connect with children and people we knew. We didn't even play with the few other children living in our apartment building. Margot and I generally stayed in the apartment and found things to play with when not hovering around Mutti.

Because of the close proximity to the railroad station's entrance we didn't play outside on the street. Besides, for many years there was rubble leftover from the war on both sides of our house. It just was not safe or conducive to playing.

On some very warm days in the summer we went to play in the courtyard behind the apartment building. If we played hopscotch or games like that, we had to be sure to remove all traces from the pavement before heading back to the apartment. If any marks were left, a neighbor surely would ring the doorbell and tell Mutti.

Cousins Ingrid and Dorit, and later Werner, were our most frequent playmates. We did not play together very often but the times were often memorable.

Cooking with Ingrid

The first toy that I remember was a dollhouse given to me while Margot was in the sanitarium in Heckeshorn. One afternoon Aunt Schneider rang the doorbell and was waiting on the landing carrying the two-story dollhouse. It had been stored away since her daughter, Aunt Suzie, had outgrown it. It was a complete surprise, I didn't have a doll or anything else toy-like. When I played with dolls, a curled up towel usually played the part of a doll.

While Margot was in Heckeshorn, Ingrid was the one to come and play. Ingrid and I always got along and looked forward to those rare times when we were allowed to visit. She lived two city blocks away, a major distance when you are not allowed to venture alone past the front door of your house. She usually came to our house. Aunt Elschen always was 'too busy' to let me come and visit there.

Ingrid was a year older than I, old enough to be allowed to maneuver the blocks and crossing two streets by herself. Aunt Elschen would watch from their front door on Wiclefstrasse until she came to the corner of Waldstrasse. The corner lot was rubble and watching from our fourth story window, Mutti and I could see her before she reached the actual corner. We started to wave wildly until she noticed us. She waved back, then turned around and waved back to Aunt Elschen. It was the signal that we were watching, and rounded the corner. Ingrid then started to run and only stopped for crossing the street.

Waldstrasse is divided by green space, traffic on each side was one-way, and so it was pretty safe, besides there were very few cars. If it was not family, then there was always a neighbor who kept an eye on us to make sure we arrived safely. This was a ritual that we kept for many years, someone was always watching.

During one of those visits, the dollhouse was set up on the bed and the little aluminum stove, the centerpiece, on a low table by the window. We played house all afternoon in my room with the most part spent in the kitchen. We wanted to cook and decided to make pancakes; we figured we could do that. Mutti happily supplied all we needed: the stub of a candle, flour and water.

The stove had a smooth flat top and in the front it featured a movable door for baking. That's where the candle stub went. It slowly started heating the doll house's stove top while we carefully mixed water, flour and a touch of salt to just the right consistency, very thick, something like Elmer's Glue.

When the candle finally heated the stove enough we poured a silver dollar-size batter round onto the top. Again we waited patiently until the edges seemed dry, then it was time to turn the pancake over. The light brown hue let us know that the candle made the stove good and hot. It was not long after that the pancake was deemed ready. We moved it off and quickly poured another. It started to cook while we shared the first one.

We each took a half, popped it into our mouths and delighted at the warm treat. We chewed long and slow to make the taste last and last. We were not talking; we just smiled, savoring that tasty morsel.

Soaking in the Big Tub

Our apartment didn't have a bathroom when I was growing up. The apartment building dated back to 1905 when bathrooms were still a novelty. We had running cold water in the kitchen where we heated it for pouring into a bowl for sponge baths. About every other week we had the luxury of a soak in a big tub.

Although the sixth floor was partially burned out and had a temporary tarpaper roof, the laundry room was usable. Tenants of the building could reserve the room once a month for a couple of days to launder. Any Saturday that was not reserved we could use if we wanted to. In the years right after the end of the war, it was rarely used because nobody had enough coal or wood for the built in oven underneath the huge cauldron to heat the water. I think it was toward the end of the forties when we first used the laundry room more regularly.

So, when the room was not used Mutti would fill the cauldron, the size of a small hot tub, and heat the water. She made a fire in the built-in oven under the cauldron. Every twenty minutes or so she checked on the fire and added more wood. On laundry day, the laundry was boiled with soap in the cauldron and then transferred to the large, oblong zinc washtub for scrubbing. It took several hours for the water to get really hot. The heat from the cauldron also heated the small room and it was always toasty when the water was ready.

At the bottom of the cauldron was a faucet for drainage. We filled buckets with water and filled the long washtub that was standing in the middle of the room. Margot and I could be in the tub at the same time. It was long enough for us to slide down. We slipped into the water, the moment of utter delight had arrived. We were submerged up to our necks and lay still, enjoying being engulfed by the warm water. When it was starting to feel just a tad on the cool side, we quickly lathered, rinsed by pouring a bucket of warm water over us and got out.

Of course, if Margot was not home I could have the tub to myself. Although it felt a little creepy when I was in the laundry room all alone. The room had just one small window and if it was getting dark outside, the single light bulb was giving off a dim glow. The makeshift door was put together with odd boards and didn't have a lock.

During school vacation I asked Ingrid to share the tub. It was always a special time. The preparation was more than half the fun. We knew the routine of lugging the water buckets in preparation and cleaning up afterwards and could do it ourselves. If Margot was around, she would ask Dorit to come also and we had to stretch the water to fill the tub twice for their turn.

When the building was renovated in 1952, the attic and laundry room were included. The small window in the room was replaced with a larger one, another light was added and instead of the rickety wooden door the room now had a lockable metal door.

The attic, across the landing from the laundry room, also had a new metal door. Due to the new roof, the attic now had a higher ceiling, more convenient for hanging the laundry, and wall-to-wall windows on two opposite walls for cross ventilation.

Those windows offered a birds-eye view of Waldstrasse. I could also overlook the train depot and the Westhafen, west harbor, beyond. At the time it was the largest inland harbor in Germany. Container ships brought goods and food supplies to the harbor through the many canals criss-crossing Germany. They were unloaded to train cars and shuttled to the depot where wholesalers unloaded the wares onto their own trucks. It was breathtaking to have this almost endless view after being surrounded by tall buildings at all times.

I went up to the attic many times just to look out one of the windows for a while.

Scaredy Cats

The late 1940s and early 1950s were scary times in Berlin. It seemed as if not a day went by without a crime involving children was news. Most often it was a child found dead in the rubble of a burned out building or in a cellar of an apartment building. The theory was that children were lured with food or candy either with, "I know where there is a bag of chocolate", or perhaps by an elderly woman or man, "Would you please help me with this bag or groceries upstairs."

We were instructed not to accept anything from anybody that we did not know well and also, against our drilled-in manners to be helpful, not to go and help anyone we did not know.

One afternoon, I think it was 1950, Ingrid and I were strolling home from a Saturday matinee at the neighborhood movie theater. It was a summer day and the street was busy with people. We were just giggling about something and found ourselves near a doorway. Suddenly a voice from behind asked "Would you be so kind to help me with these two bags. I live on the fourth floor?" We turned and were in front of an elderly woman. We looked at her and her bags and started running as fast as we could around the corner to Waldstrasse. We didn't stop until we reached Schenck's store.

Mrs. Schenck was at the door and asked, "My, you're running as if chased by the devil! What happened?"

After we calmed down we relayed what happened and described the woman. "I don't know her from your description. Maybe she does not shop here or she just moved into the neighborhood. Maybe she really needed help. But you did the right thing. Sadly you shouldn't trust anybody you don't know."

Mutti said the same thing after we recounted the event upstairs. After we both calmed down, Mutti and I walked Ingrid home.

A couple of years later, when both Ingrid and Dorit were visiting, Margot and Dorit played outside the apartment and Ingrid and I stayed put.

This one time Mutti had to go somewhere and Ingrid and I were alone in the apartment. We played movie star all afternoon in my bedroom. We recreated scenes from a movie we had seen or we pretended to be movie stars out in the public. We'd sign endless autographs, we'd go to restaurants and, of course, everything was served free because we were stars, or we went on plane trips to an exotic place and, of course, because we were stars, we did not have to pay. We reveled in our fame!

Suddenly there was heavy and repeated knocking at the apartment door. Who would be knocking instead of ringing the door bell? We looked through the peephole and couldn't see anybody. We looked at each other "Who would be hiding from the peephole?" we both wondered.

I asked, "Who's there?" After a pause a very deep voice said, "The murderer!" Ingrid and I ran back to the bedroom. Ingrid slid under the bed to hide.

My goodness, how to get help? I certainly could not run to our neighbors. The murderer was waiting outside!

I opened the bedroom window, leaned out as far as I could and at the top of my lungs screamed "Help! Help! A murderer is outside my door!" I screamed and screamed.

After what seemed like hours Uncle Lutz, in the apartment below, looked out of his window and up at me, "Heidi, get back inside! I went upstairs. It is Margot and your cousin Dorit. Open the door and let them in. I'm coming up too."

Well, what a relief! We opened the door. Margot and Dorit were mad at us for letting them wait. Hungry and thirsty, they wanted to come inside. Uncle Lutz chided, "You silly ones. Do you really think a murderer would announce himself?" He continued, "Heidi, the whole neighborhood was worried that you would fall out the window!"

Margot and Dorit had been practicing this prank all afternoon, knowing they could scare us. Dorit with the lowest growl was chosen to do the talking.

Ingrid and I were the butt of jokes for years.

Kinderfest

Kinderfest simply translated means children's party. It is one the first recurring events that I looked forward to.

In 1946, neighborhoods resurrected this tradition from earlier years. *Kinderfest* was really for everyone. During the summer months many apartment complex associations organized one. It was a Sunday of amateur performances by children, games and dancing for all. It brought a bit of color in the otherwise very dull existence.

Our apartment building was not large enough for this kind of event, but we were invited to participate at Oma's and also at Uncle Helmut's association. There was an early meeting with all children present to decide who could do what. Then costumes were made. Depending on what part we had we brought what we had from home and the rest was designed and made. The costumes were always made of crepe paper and we had to be very careful to make sure they lasted through our performances and picture taking afterwards. It was really amazing what crepe paper could turn into.

I remember being a trapeze artist dressed in pink crepe paper and my hair tied back with a shiny white ribbon. I was carefully balancing my way to the middle of a chalk line on the floor. At the center I met the girl who started from the other end. We curtsied, trying not to fall off the trapeze, turned around and continued to the starting point. Another time I was part of a folklore doll duo. We were wind up dolls, dressed in imaginary Bavarian costumes. As soon as our imaginary key was wound up, we started to dance to a folksong (doll-like-stiff) until the song was over.

Announcements of an upcoming *Kinderfest* were plastered all over the neighborhood. The party started at 2 pm. People paid a very small entry fee to cover expenses and everybody brought their own snacks and drinks.

After the performances, dance music played until late - sometimes a band sometimes a record player. Social games were sprinkled in for fun. I remember those Sundays only as fun – no drama. As years passed there were fewer *Kinderfests*, as the need for these fun events had run its course.

In the mid 1950s the associations for *Schrebergärten* (the allotment gardens in the city's green spaces) revived those Sunday entertainments as *Laubenfest*, or summer cottage party.

I think I was fifteen when Margot and I started to seek out those events. We walked quite a few miles in our high heels until we reached the *Laubenfest*. It usually was all about dancing and food. We paid a small entry fee. There always was a band playing and we could dance all afternoon and often way into the night until it was time to go home.

It was dark when it was time to head home - dark as in no lights in the narrow alleys between garden plots. It was a little spooky and we made sure we stayed together. We were relieved when we reached the highway and could see again.

1947
Wind-up Dolls: Ingrid, Dorit and Heidi

Kinderfest

1950
Everyone is dancing

The Radio

Every day started with the radio, our window to the world. We listened to the radio while Mutti did chores in the kitchen. In the evenings we huddled around the kitchen table again until it was time for bed.

Unlike today, there were no commercials. Types of music were mixed and changed every hour. There was an hour of opera followed by classical music, then maybe current hits, then folksongs, some jazz, and so on.

Five minutes of news were broadcast on the hour, every hour and an hourly program of expanded news and commentary at noon. On Sundays and holidays only classical music was played. Soccer games by national teams took precedent over everything, and they were always broadcast live.

On some very solemn holidays, like *Allerseelen* (All Souls Day, also referred to as Memorial Day) the music was very serious and heavy. Lots of Wagner was played and sometimes it sounded just awful and we actually turned it off.

At first we had a small radio in the kitchen and Saturday afternoons were best. After lunch from two until five, the main station broadcast its popular *Wunschkonzert*, (by public request) music program.

Every request was accompanied by a special message for someone's birthday, or in memory of a fallen soldier, or perhaps sent from a daughter in America to her mother in Berlin. So we listened with fascination and imagined the accompanying message or story. Mutti answered many questions like, "What is immigrating?"or "Where is Canada?"

From folk songs to opera, anything was played. We often hummed or sang along with a folk song. I learned the lyrics to hundred of songs, singing along with Mutti.

Some more modern tunes reminded Mutti of her younger, dancing days. One song *"Es wird in hunderd Jahren wieder so ein Frühling sein"* (A spring like this happens only once in a hundred years), a romantic tango, always made Mutti smile and remember dancing with Pappa. It was their song.

If an opera excerpt or aria was played, Mutti relayed the story of the opera. Usually the request was for a specific performer and I learned who the revered artists in all genres were.

As years went by Mutti added a second radio in the living room that was later replaced by a combination radio and record player. Margot and I inherited the old radio and had non-stop music in our bedroom.

Margot discovered the AFN – American Forces Network – in 1952 or so. We turned to that station the minute we got home. It was an all English-speaking station, of course. Sometimes it was difficult to follow the fast speaking disc jockeys. They would relay little stories from their home state once in a while and it was always fascinating.

Stick-buddy Jamboree, a country music hour, was in the afternoon before pop and rock. We listened to Jim Reeves and many other stars in this all- American line-up.

Thursday afternoons was the weekly Hit Parade, "Fresh from the States." After I started baby-sitting I had to miss that program, but Margot filled me in after dinner when we listened to AFN some more.

Although the music was new to Mutti and she could not understand any of the lyrics, she never objected. When we tried to dance to this modern music she experimented right along with us.

Dancing would sometimes be shown in the newsreels from around the world when we went to the movies. That's when we watched in fascination the Jive and Rock and Roll, and tried to re-enact the moves at home. I remember lively evenings when we danced with Mutti around the living room to Bill Haley's Rock Around the Clock during hit parade. The Twist was the next strange dance we tried to master. I liked all types of music and cannot imagine a world without music.

Another ritual was listening to 'Who Done It?' Thursdays after supper. We made sure all homework and kitchen clean-up was done so that we could listen to the police show. It always started with a long silence, then footsteps hurrying, a creaky door opening and a very deep voice saying, "*Guten Abend* (good evening) we are on the trail of..." This half hour show had us glued to our seats. It often took several episodes to finish the story line. Plenty of time to discuss 'Who Done It?'

Sports

When I was growing up, sports were only done in school, especially if you were a girl. Girls were not supposed to sweat. Only if you had a special talent, say swimming, gymnastics or tennis, sports were encouraged through clubs.

During the school year we had gym twice a week. In the spring, the class walked the mile to the public indoor pool for swimming. We carried swimsuits and towels with us. After the mandatory shower, we learned the different strokes during our 45 minutes of pool time. After our sessions we walked back to school for the next class. At the end of the school year we were tested for the different levels of swimming proficiency in the different strokes. During sixth grade we all practiced for the 'First Aid swimming certificate'. For the test we swam non-stop for twenty minutes and after that went through some lifesaving techniques. Everyone passed.

In the summer we went to a nearby track. It was the only time we were allowed to wear pants, sweatpants that is. We changed into shorts at school, pulled the sweatpants over and walked to the track for running and jumping.

Fall and winter we were in the gym playing volleyball, testing our indoor track talents and practicing gymnastics. Most of the time was spent with the different elements of gymnastics: uneven bars, pommel horse, rings, parallel bars and floor exercises. Of all the sports, I liked swimming and gymnastics best.

Our gym teacher must have spotted some speed. In sixth grade all elementary schools had a meet at the Olympic Stadium. The schools entered their best prospects in the different disciplines. I was in the 100-meter dash and also the 4x100 relay.

This friendly competition had been planned for months and was really a big event. Our day started early with getting to the bus. We didn't have school buses. For special events, like this one, excursion buses were leased. It took a while to get parked outside the stadium and then to find our assigned spot inside. It was very exciting to be inside the big Olympic Stadium. I had heard a lot about the Olympic Games that took place there in 1936. The stadium was much bigger than I imagined. It was huge! We had to stick close to our gym teacher and chaperones while waiting for our turns. The competition was over for me very quickly. Our school must not have scored very high or I would have remembered.

During high school the schedule was pretty much the same except we had gym after lunch. After regular classes were over, around 12:30, I went home for lunch and then straight back to school for gym.

Unless walking and dancing counts, I did not do any sports outside of school. Of course, I walked everywhere, no matter how far. I had to figure out how long it would take and then allow the time for walking. Going up and down to our fourth floor apartment was plenty of exercise for anybody.

And dancing surely was great exercise. From waltzes to the Cha-cha, Mutti was teaching us the different dances to music on the radio. Two or three times a year we danced at family occasions. After supper, tables were moved along the walls and the middle of the room was taken over for dancing. Everybody took turns dancing with one another. It really was a must to know how to dance if you didn't want to sit and watch. We usually danced non-stop for two to three hours. As we got older, fourteen or fifteen or so, Margot and I started to go to nightclubs to dance.

Although soccer is the national sport in Germany, I didn't follow soccer much. I kept tabs on which teams were best but no more. I did keep up with the big bicycle races. We watched bicycle races when the route led them through Waldstrasse. I remember wondering how racers could stay so close together. What if one made a mistake? They all would fall like dominoes! I was very impressed, and it always fascinated me. Margot and I went to the *Sechstagerennen*, a very popular six-day race, a couple of times. It is a team event where the competitors rode 24-hours a day for six days in an indoor arena.

Most teams had at least one well-known rider and it was interesting to follow their progress, or not, during the night. Between sprints, they often showed off just for fun, and the crowd loved it. We went on a Saturday afternoon and tried to watch until Sunday. Sometimes we made it until noon and felt totally grown up to be able to do that. Then we went home and straight to bed.

For a few years Ingrid and I went swimming at the public indoor pool every Thursday after school. We had a standing time to meet in front of her house and then walked the mile to the pool house on Turmstrasse.

Margot and I went swimming at Wannsee beach a couple of times every summer during our four-week school break. Because of Mutti's migraines, we had to go alone. It was a long trip to get there. I remember the distance and time well from Margot's sanitarium stay.

Mutti usually cooked our lunch to take the day before: a sautéed pork cutlet, several tomatoes, pickles and pieces of fruit. In the morning she wrapped it up, carefully making two packages for us to carry. Mutti gave us the fee for the train and the beach entry, along with enough to buy a Coca Cola each.

She also made two demands: no accepting anything from anybody, no matter how tempting, and "Eat a tomato every time you were in the water and maybe swallowed some water. Tomatoes are anti-bacterial, and I don't want you to catch something."

Loaded up with food, a blanket and towels we set out. Once there we spent as much time in the water as we could. After lunch we waited impatiently until the mandatory twenty minutes to allow for digestion had passed. We stayed most of the day, wanting to get as much out of our entry fee as we could. We were always really tired by the time we were back home. We did not have a real curfew, "Just be home before dark," was Mutti's rule.

A few times we went to nearby Plötzensee and met up with Ingrid and Dorit. We walked about three miles, carrying a small blanket and our provisions. Because Plötzensee was so close, we had an early lunch and just carried a snack.

Movies

I saw my first movie in 1950 and I loved it! I was fascinated and would have liked to see that movie over and over again. Sitting in the dark, I got completely wrapped up in the story. At first, I could go maybe once a month to a Saturday afternoon matinee, and later I went every Saturday.

The movie theater was a block away, close to Ingrid and Dorit's house. The program always consisted of a newsreel, a Mickey Mouse cartoon and then Abbot & Costello or Zorro or a cowboy movie as the main feature. A couple of years of that and then we graduated to other matinee materials, maybe a German musical, or a western or an Esther Williams movie! Ingrid and I had similar tastes and went to the movies regularly for years.

First, we watched a newsreel, with news from around the world. It lasted about fifteen minutes and included sports news. They covered everything from gymnastics to car and motorcycle racing. I loved the car racing clips and was intrigued by skiing and tennis, never thinking for a minute that this is something that I could do.

Ingrid and I were Esther Williams fans! We wanted to swim and smile like Esther. Going to our weekly pool outing we practiced swimming under water, smiling while we were at it, of course! We did this for hours. Occasionally we impersonated other stars but Esther Williams was the favorite.

I was ten or eleven when I first saw a movie scene being filmed. It was summer and we had to walk a few blocks from our school to the outdoor track for gym class. As we rounded a corner close to the track the usually deserted street was jammed with trucks, cars and people. Men were unloading many tall lamps on wheels, large trees in buckets and lots and lots of big boxes. We stopped and watched. Soon we figured out they were getting ready to film some scenes for a movie. We didn't dare ask anyone what was going on, afraid to get sent on our way. So we waited and watched everything being set up.

Then we saw Heinz Rühman, a very popular German movie star at the time, coming out of one of the cars. Forget track! We stayed.

We watched as the actor was being filmed coming out of a house, talking very loudly and agitated with a little girl. Again, and again, and again. We couldn't believe our good fortune to be able to watch.

It was late afternoon when one of the crew reminded us of the time, "You better go home before you get into trouble. Your parents must be wondering where you are!"

Oops! I rushed home. Mutti was looking out the living room window, waiting for me to come home no doubt. Yes, she was worried. Then I relayed my exiting afternoon and I didn't even get a reprimand.

Of course, I wanted to become a movie star. Who didn't? Mutti humored me and went along with the fantasy. But later she squashed my talk about becoming an actress very swiftly and said "You have to either be born into an acting family or sleep your way into the roles." This was food for thought for a long time.

Many years later, on my bus ride to work, I watched students leave the bus and walk towards the Acting Academy. They looked like regular people to me. By that time, of course, I had already been told that I needed to earn a living and acting school definitely was not in the budget. I was extremely shy and by then had to admit to myself that there was no way I could possibly perform, never mind be able to talk in front of a bunch of strangers.

Routines

Visiting the cemetery and a weekly gin rummy evening became routines like the evening walk, if weather permitted, or the cup of tea before bed.

It is a German tradition to go for the digestive walk. It mostly happens from spring to early fall. After Margot came back from Heckeshorn, we joined the many walkers outside for the evening stroll. As soon as supper was finished we walked a few blocks to Turmstrasse, where most of the larger stores were. We were walking up and down the street, stopping at every shop window. We carefully examined the wares and expressing our firm opinions. It was also a time to stop and chat with people we knew.

In the mid fifties, an Italian ice cream store opened on Turmstrasse. Through the store window we could watch the ice cream being made. This was very unique, something we didn't know before. It was the most popular shop on the street. There were always people waiting to get their ice cream. When it was really, really hot, we also stopped for our real Italian ice cream cone. Then we tried to eat it as slowly as we dared to make it last without dripping all over ourselves.

When we were home again, it was time for our cup of tea before bed. I always liked my tea black. Sometimes in winter when it was really cold, Oma would join us. She brought a bottle of rum along and put some in her tea, and then she would pour some for Mutti. We could have some too if we wanted. I always asked for some. Tea tasted even better with rum to me.

Visits to the Cemetery

In Germany, anyone who had a relative at a cemetery made regular visits there. Graves are marked by elevated dirt about one foot high, five feet long and a foot and a half across. It is a tradition to maintain the grave like a mini-garden and that takes maintenance.

Pappa was in a cemetery in Plötzensee, near the lake where we went swimming. From spring to fall, we went there once and sometimes twice week to take care of the grave. Ivy was planted around the bank of the grave; on top were the annuals that needed care. Mutti always planted pansies there, different colors every year. Behind the headstone was a hardy rhododendron that grew quite large over the years.

After taking care of the flowers, we often went between the rows to look at other graves. Some people had very elaborate settings; some with a wrought- iron fence surrounding the plot, some had a little bench next to the grave, and some had huge and ornate headstones.

During the week it was fairly quiet. On weekends we could watch people streaming there from all directions. We joined Uncle Helmut and his family on Sunday afternoons for the walk to the cemetery. They had to come by our house where we met them. Mutti only made it once in a while when it was not too warm. Mrs. Freier, Ingrid and Dorit were also in the group. They were going to Mr. Freier's grave, their grandfather. During those months we saw our cousins regularly.

It was a two-mile walk and we carried a little rake and a watering can. We watered and weeded the grave and then raked the dirt around it to have it look fresh. Aunt Schneider often asked us to water her husband's grave because she had trouble walking so far. We were home in time for the Sunday afternoon cup of coffee.

Gin Rummy

Thursday evenings were gin rummy evenings except at Easter and Christmas, but those were the only exceptions. This custom started soon after Oma moved to an apartment next to ours in 1952.

Thursdays we had an early supper because by 7pm we had to be at Oma's apartment for game night. The lacey tablecloth that normally covered her large wooden table was removed and the table was game-ready.

At first Mutti, Oma, along with Uncle Helmut, Aunt Elschen and her mother Mrs. Freier were the players. The wager was pennies and they took turns keeping score. We learned the game by watching. Soon Ingrid could join in and not long after I was playing also.

At the end of the night we all gave Oma some money on our account. They were small amounts. I gave maybe a quarter, sometimes less. It was our Christmas fund. Oma kept track of our donations and the week before Christmas we could get our money to get presents.

I kept asking Oma regularly how much I had saved. I spent many months window-shopping and planning what presents to buy for Mutti, Oma and Margot. One year it was a fancy handkerchief for Oma, a scarf for Mutti and a sausage for Margot

The radio was always on and if they broadcast a soccer game, we had to be absolutely quiet so that Uncle Helmut could listen while he played. The evening's conversations and opinionated comments covered everything from sports to politics in Germany and around the world.

During those evenings it became quite apparent that Dorit and Margot could do and say just about anything and the adults chuckled indulgently. They often went outside to play. More often than that they came back hurt. They played among the rubble of the ruin next door, slipped and got hurt; or they balanced on top of the benches on Waldstrasse's park and fell, etc. To my knowledge, they were never scolded.

Now, if Ingrid and I just mentioned something taboo for us at the time, like lipstick, the adults, all at the same time, gave us a rebuke. After several years of this, Ingrid once spoke up, "Why is it that Dorit and Margot can get into all kinds of scrapes and you just humor them? Why are you always harping at us? We can't do anything right?" "You are older. You should know better. It is expected of you," was the instant reply. End of speaking up.

I did not like the constant harping. Especially Aunt Elschen was very vocal. "Oh, look at your hair! You're not old enough to wear it like this." Or "You should get better grades than this. You'll never amount to anything this way. Your mother can't support you forever!" Uncle Helmut sometimes seconded those comments. Oma and Mrs. Freier usually just smiled and didn't say anything.

I remember generally saying very little, keeping my head down mostly. Even when walking on the streets, I was so shy that I did not look at people. My eyes were glued to the pavement, hoping nobody would talk to me or at me.

I think I was thirteen when I felt the need to change. "Why should I always look down?" I thought. I remember the first time I made a conscious effort to always look ahead and at people's faces. Of course, nothing earth-shaking happened, because people were busy with their own lives. But I felt relief from some unseen burden that seemed to keep me looking down; it sure was a great boost to my morale. I felt more a part of my environment rather than looking from the outside in.

Mrs. Freier was quick to laugh and it was nice to have her around. She always defended Dorit no matter what. Dorit was her favorite and we all accepted that. But she also had kind words here and there for the rest of us.

Mrs. Freier was a heavy smoker, like many people in those years. She had emphysema. One evening in October 1957, she had trouble breathing and went to the hospital to get oxygen. Her lungs were so congested that she was beyond help and suffocated. Everyone was shocked. Dorit hurt the most.

Our gaming evenings stopped.

Let Loose as Teenagers

Before World War II, Berlin was the capital of Germany and culturally it was the capital of Europe. In the post-war years, Berlin worked hard to earn that place again as a matter of pride.

There was never a shortage of events from hard-edged satires to comedy to opera. Mutti let us go to concerts, sporting events and bars if we went together. Margot and I saved our money to see Louis Armstrong, the Chris Barber Jazz Band from England, Caterina Valente, singing superstar in Germany at the time, and others.

Die Eierschale, presenting live jazz and Eden Saloon, with sometimes live Rock and Roll, were the most popular event bars. They allowed under-age customers and served what we called *Sportsmolle*, an alcohol-free drink. It looked just like beer including foam on top. I was fifteen when we were allowed to go there as often as we wanted as long as we stayed together.

The Eden Saloon was our favorite. It had a big dance floor and we danced endlessly to the most recent hits from America on the largest jukebox in Berlin. *Sportsmolle* was served free for girls every evening. Sometimes Margot's classmate, Renate, and her older brother were there also. Through her brother we met many boys from other Berlin boroughs, all older than we were.

At ten all underage patrons had to leave. Bright lights were turned on and a thorough ID check conducted to make sure no one under sixteen remained. I always had to show my ID, Margot looked more mature and was never asked.

On weekends we sometimes went on to private parties with friends from the Eden. We had to come home with the last train, which was at 1 am. Mutti did not worry, as long as we stayed together.

Margot and I were not looking for a boyfriend, we just wanted to dance and have fun. At the nightclubs, our nickname was 'the ice maidens.'

We met some interesting characters. Some were like us, still going to school and just socializing for the evening.

We spent the most time with a group of three young men on the wrong path. They were what we considered harmless crooks. We didn't know this at first. After they didn't show up for several weeks, we asked why? We found out that they were in jail.

They were high school buddies from a poor section in Berlin, who broke into apartments, taking valuables and fencing them for much needed cash. They must have been known by the police. After a rash of break-ins, the police came to their homes, found a connecting thread to a robbery and off to jail they went. It didn't bother us, as they didn't hurt anyone and were a lot of fun.

We couldn't quite understand why they didn't learn and stop. Once in a while we tried to adjust their morals and remorse factor but that proved pretty useless. So we just enjoyed them when they were around, because they were like big brothers. We did go on many late evening parties with them, feeling very safe.

The other friends we spent many weekends with we met through Margot's friend's older brother Wolfgang. We were a large mixed group filling three cars when we went out together, but we also often took the train. Whatever was interesting that weekend, a party, a bar, a live band; we sometimes pulled straws and went with the decision. From early on, everything was Dutch. I was free to do as I pleased.

Any occasion would be the start of a party at someone's house; a soccer win, a birthday or snowy roads. Again we pooled our funds, bought some beer and the party was on. During all those years we had two parties at our apartment. My sixteenth birthday and Carnival were the occasions.

My birthday party involved food, beer and a lot of music. Our bedroom was the party room. My Murphy bed, with a four foot high shelf on top turned into the bar. Food was set up in the kitchen. Everybody brought stacks of 45 records to supply endless dance music. Our neighbors, of course, had been given advance notice of the impending noise.

Carnival is celebrated as much in Germany as it is in Rio de Janeiro. The celebrations spread over several days with costume parties all over Germany. Every year we dressed in a different costume, and planning started long before Carnival. Once settled on a costume we wore it to all parties.

There always was a party somewhere. When the party was at our apartment, we not only had to fret over our costume but also had to decorate the room to the nines. Planning was as much fun as the party!

Birthdays and Holidays

When I was little, children's birthdays were not celebrated much. At first, it meant we would have cake and coffee, half coffee – half milk for children, on a weekday. Maybe a relative would stop by. I think after I turned twelve, nearby cousins and aunts would visit to wish me a happy birthday. It was not until Confirmation at age fifteen that I was considered semi-adult and counted when my birthday came around. Anyone who came stayed for coffee and cake. The traditional presents usually were books or a piece of china or something similar for the dowry.

From my twelfth birthday on, dowry presents were given. The most common were towels and *Sammeltassen*, a china set with plate, cup and saucer. This set was used for afternoon coffee and occasions when visitors came calling. Every set was different and made for a colorful table. Unlike linens, the dowry china was not stored away until marriage. The *Sammeltasse* sets were put to use right away when the occasion arose.

Mutti's birthday brought more relatives and they usually stayed through supper.

Uncle Helmut and Aunt Elschen's birthdays were close together. They let us know which day to come and celebrate. It was the same for Ingrid and Dorit when they reached their teens. Their birthdays were two days apart and they chose to have guests on the day between the actual birthdays.

Aunt Anni and Uncle Emil in Tempelhof and Aunt Hilda in Weisensee, celebrated their birthdays on weekends. It took several hours to get to their home and couldn't be fit into the weekday routines.

At Christmas and Easter, we stayed home unless we had a special invitation from Aunt Hilda or Aunt Anni.

1958
Margot, Werner und Heidi
At Aunt Hilda's birthday in East Berlin.

Oma's Birthday

Oma's birthday on August 24, in the middle of the summer, was better than all other birthdays and holidays. It was the highlight of the year! It was the only birthday that was celebrated on the actual day. The get-togethers did not start until 1950, a year after Uncle Helmut returned from Russia. Then her birthday became the one day when truly the whole family gathered. Family had a standing invitation and Oma knew to be ready to receive visitors by two in the afternoon. Coffee and cakes better be on hand because that was expected! Everyone also stayed for supper.

I looked forward to Oma's birthday because my favorite aunt, Aunt Hille, always came.

Aunt Hille was everyone's favorite aunt. She was not really a relative. She was engaged to Mutti's brother, Werner. After he died, she continued to be close to the family. In 1943, she married Erich, and did not have children. She doted on us, her four nieces, and I could not wait for her to arrive.

Preparation for the large celebration would start a couple of days before. Oma lived next to us and Mutti was helping her getting everything organized. Assorted salads were prepared the day before.

On the morning of the big day, Oma made three cakes: her special cheesecake with raisins in it, a crumb cake and a plum cake. Mutti reserved space at the bakery on the next block to bake them. We had coal or wood-heated ovens. They were not big enough to hold baking trays. We also could not regulate the temperatures. They could not be used for baking.

I helped carry one of the cake trays to the bakery in the morning. We walked into the rear of the bakery where the ovens were. The baker stuck a paper nametag into the dough for identification. When they were done, usually around 1pm, I made several trips to bring the trays home. Then I would make another trip with a large empty bowl to buy whipped cream at the bakery. The bakery produced freshly whipped cream all afternoon. No one would think of eating any cake without whipped cream!

Bowls and trays with Oma's bounty for supper already were taking up space in the small kitchen.

The table was set during the morning with the good china – the gold-rimmed white plates. After three table leaves were inserted, the table almost took up the entire living room. For Oma's birthday we had to borrow more china, as well as extra chairs from Aunt Schneider.

On the strike of two, the doorbell rang for the first time. Usually Oma's sisters and brothers, having traveled together on the train from a borough about an hour away, were the first to arrive. Uncle Arthur, Aunt Lotte, Aunt Anni and Uncle Emil made lots of chatter and excited exchanges, "How are you?" and "You're looking well," along with formal birthday congratulations.

Everyone brought bouquets of flowers. It was often my job to find a suitable vase, arrange the flowers and then find a place in the living room where everyone could admire them. Presents were not usually given, only on special milestones like the 70th birthday. Once Ingrid arrived we took turns with the flowers.

Visitors kept arriving. I often looked out of the wide open windows to see if I could spot Aunt Hille somewhere down the road. She was never one of the early visitors. If it was a weekday she came after work. Finally the bell rang and when Oma opened the door it was Aunt Hille! I got a big hug "How are you Heidekin?"

While there was space we, the children, were allowed to have our cake and coffee at the main table and listen. When there was no room for us, we took our plates to the kitchen and ate there.

In the early years most of the conversations were about where one could get what; which stores had the most supplies; the effort of finding a job.

Around suppertime, the talk would switch to reminiscing. By then Margot and Dorit already disappeared to play outside. Ingrid and I stayed inside because we did not want to miss any of the stories.

It was also our chance to monopolize Aunt Hille. We huddled next to her chair, and she always put her arms around us and held tight. She felt warm and soft. If we were quiet, the adults totally forgot we were there. Stories kept coming along with food that was ever present on the long dining table.

Everybody chimed in, as they all had experiences to share. Aunt Elschen and Mrs. Freier from the years they were evacuated, how difficult it was to get food, even with food stamps.

Aunt Hille was in Berlin throughout the war and spent many days and nights in bomb shelters. She kept busy looking after people's children; telling them stories, leading a sing-along, leading them in the dark through the rubble to safety after the house above them was a total loss, but the cellar held up.

When it was time to change the table setting for suppertime, Ingrid and I were put to work. We worked very fast because we did not want to miss any of the conversation.

We carried bowls with different potato salads; green bean salad; beet salad; a huge bowl with heated *wurst*; trays of sliced dark bread; baskets of crusty rolls; platters with assorted specialties everyone liked: head cheese; thinly sliced dried beef, sliced boiled ham, several varieties of liverwurst, sliced corned beef; a bowl with pickles and a small bowl with potato salad just for Ingrid and myself. The traditional Berlin version of potato salad has herring as one of the ingredients; both Ingrid and I did not like it.

Many hours were spent sitting, eating and catching up with people we only saw once a year at grandmother's birthday.

After supper everyone was really relaxed. The men usually had a beer or two and the women had a shot of *Eierlikör*, very good tasting liquor made with egg yolks. One of the benefits of helping was that Ingrid and I licked the liquor glasses clean in the kitchen. It was real tasty.

The evening was the time when Uncle Helmut and Uncle Erich had long conversations about the war and their years as prisoners of war in Russia. I remember the room being very quiet, just the two talking. I was also absolutely silent, not wanting to be noticed and sent out of the room with "You shouldn't hear this."

Uncle Helmut and Uncle Erich talked about the marches, how they went on for days and days and anyone who fell down, was left behind. They ridiculed the food, laughed endlessly about the straight faces the prisoners made when they were given water and it was called soup. They talked about the prison guards also, how they were very good-natured. Their duty seemed to be some kind of punishment too.

(For Uncle Helmut's war experiences turn to "Soldiers," page 173).

The aunts took turns helping with the dishes in the kitchen. The birthday party always came to an end at ten. The latest train the relatives wanted to catch was at ten-twenty and the relatives from far away did not want to miss it.

The routine never changed. As we grew up, Ingrid and I stayed at the table while Margot and Dorit were straining to get out of the house as soon as they had a piece of cake.

When Oma could no longer make her cakes or salads, it became Mutti's job and we still gathered at Oma's dining table for her birthday celebration. She lived to be 92.

Soldiers

August Sieg, Sr.

As far as anybody knows, Pappa's father, Opa Sieg, never was a soldier. There are no records.

August Sieg

Pappa completed army basic training before he started his business. By the time World War II started, in September 1939, he had a successful vegetable and potato business. Being a food supplier kept him out of active duty until March 1941. Through his entire duty, he was driving supply trucks in France, Russia and Czechoslovakia.

He was in Berlin during the last days of the war when the city was captured by the Russians. Pappa was sleeping in one of the cellars at our house when the Russians apparently stumbled upon him. He was shot and killed.

Alfred Sieg

Uncle Alfred, Pappa's brother, was in the infantry and wounded a couple of times. He was shot in the thigh during one battle. During surgery in the field hospital, they cut some ligaments, so he had a stiff knee and walked with a limp for the rest of his life.

At the end of the war he returned home with tuberculosis, with one lung completely diseased. Many people died at this stage. I believe it was 1947 when he agreed to an experimental surgery. The bad lung was removed and a rubber lung, like a balloon, took its place. This was making room in the chest cavity for the healthy lung to work freely. His good lung was not affected yet by TB. The surgery and long recovery were successful. Uncle Alfred lived to be 80.

Fritz and Erich Sieg

Pappa's step-brothers, Fritz and Erich, joined the Hitler Youth as was mandatory of boys by the age of 12. During the war they were mobilized in the infantry, being 17 and 15. Luckily they returned home without injuries.

Paul Gustav Richter

Mutti's father, Opa Richter, was already a tailor by trade when he enlisted in the army in 1911. He was an infantry soldier during World War I. After the war he pursued his profession as a tailor. He was a master, meaning he was certified to teach others.

As Hitler's party was rising, Opa joined the Nazi Party. He went to meetings regularly and rose in the party ranks as a civilian. At the beginning of World War II, he was borough leader; he was responsible to see that Party doctrine was followed in the several neighborhood blocks under his charge. He believed in Hitler and went along with everything the Nazi Party stood for. Although he wore a uniform during the war, he stayed in the barracks in Berlin. He disappeared at the end of the war. If he had returned to Berlin he would have been jailed, at the very least, for his active participation and co-operation, for things like reporting the presence of visiting Jews in his apartment building, or telling on a shop owner who was serving a Jew when it was V*erboten (*forbidden).

Many years later, actually after the Wall came down, Mutti learned that her father with her older sister, whom she never met, in the Spreewald region near Berlin, East Germany. He found refuge and anonymity in East Germany.

After the end of the war Nazi Party members first went to other European countries and then to South America where they started a new life without persecution. A few years after World War II was over, many Nazi War criminals were found and extradited from their safe haven countries over a span of many years. I do not recall of one being discovered in East Germany or Russia. Those countries did not co-operate in the world wide search for past Nazi Party officials.

Werner Richter

Mutti's brother Werner enlisted straight from school. He barely managed to graduate from school and found that the army suited him. He advanced easily and planned to make the army his career. Werner wrote regularly and there are a few letters relating his experiences.

He was engaged to Hilde Bahr, Aunt Hille, whom he dated since 1935. They did not have immediate wedding plans. In September of 1939, when Helmut married Elschen, he sent a letter of congratulations and also stated how envious he was.

In the fall of 1939, his unit was doing field exercises with live ammunition. Frugality is the German way and the army was no different. It was a soldier's duty to collect any ammunition, grenades, etc that did not go off and bring them back to headquarters. Werner picked up a hand grenade and stuffed into his coat pocket. He jumped over a ditch and the grenade went off, killing him instantly. Oma was devastated, because Werner was her favorite. His fiancée, Aunt Hille, was a great support for Oma, and she remained a member of our family.

Erich Piatzina

Aunt Hille, as we always called her, married Erich in 1943 while he was on leave for a couple of days. Erich was also in the infantry and was captured soon after they married. He was sent to a camp in Siberia and almost immediately became ill with tuberculosis. He was unable to work and received minimal food each day. He was one of the first prisoners to be released and sent home after the war ended in 1945.

Because of TB he was on complete disability and could not work. Aunt Hille was a very good accountant and worked full time while Erich cooked, took care of the house and Aunt Hille's invalid mother, Frau Bahr, with whom they shared an apartment.

Erich worked part-time in a used bookstore. I remember talking with him about books, what I was reading at the time and he suggesting books that I might like.

Helmut Richter

(Some of the following I heard often over the years as Uncle Helmut and Uncle Erich talked with each other about their years in prison camps. In the mid 1990s, I spent an afternoon with him alone, listening and taking notes, as he spoke freely about his war experiences. Many of the details he relayed I heard for the first time then.)

Helmut
1938

Uncle Helmut, Mutti's youngest brother, was drafted into the infantry in 1938. He was not much taller than Mutti, probably no more than 5'2". He saw his first active duty in August 1939. World War II started in September 1939. Before his unit was sent on a campaign in Russia, he married Elschen that same month.

His first duty was being a member of a spy troop. He actually was working at the rear of the troops, keeping an eye on enemy movement as much as possible. Cattle cars transported the troops to Russia. He was in Russia throughout except for a couple of home leaves.

In 1943, during a battle along the Dnjepr River 24 miles before Stalingrad, he was hit with shrapnel all over his backside, except the head because he wore his helmet. He was taken to the field hospital where he was treated without medication because none was available. Medical supplies reached the hospital seldom. Later he was transferred to a bigger field hospital for treatment and recovery in Gütersloh near the German border. Only surface shrapnel was removed. Throughout his life he went to a hospital for treatment every time shrapnel moved near the surface of the skin. At the time of this writing, he is 92 and shrapnel are still surfacing.

In January of 1944, he rejoined his troop in Poland near the German border. In February, they went back to the Russian front.

Later that year, they moved to Hungary. In Budapest they had to wait to join up with another troop. They camped on the banks of the Jassi River, where Romanians were on the other side of the river. Both sides kept an eye on the other. The troops got caught up with rest, maintained their equipment, and did laundry. Life was easy for about six weeks.

Suddenly one morning the Romanians attacked. Hand-to-hand combat lasted several hours, heavy at times with total quiet in between. Helmut shot several enemies. "You just have to do it," he recalled many years later. "It was kill or be killed when you are confronted by an enemy soldier." He continued, "Once I opened a dead soldier's shirt and found a family photo with seven children. It was so sad. Even in this battle situation you ask 'Why?' and just cry.

"We were captured by the Romanians who turned us over to the Russians." It was August 1944.

In the camp the prisoners were treated very well, doing routine labor for the Russians. After two weeks in the camp, they had to march to Odessa (Ukraine) by the Black Sea, an important war harbor for the Germans. There were several huge battles with the Russians, and the Germans lost. "When we arrived the harbor was jammed with dead bodies from the attacks. The stench was awful," Helmut recalled. "Bodies covered the water surface like logs as far as the eye could see. It was our job to clean up the harbor. We had to wade into the water, formed a chain and moved the bodies, one at a time, to dry land and made a pile with bodies. Later that day we dug huge graves. All bodies were buried at the end of each day. It took four weeks to clear the harbor."

Helmut contracted malaria during this time and was down to 76 pounds. "Of course I had to work every day. As long as you could stand, you had to work."

When the harbor was cleared, and all bodies buried, the prisoners were loaded onto cattle cars outfitted with bunk beds. The bunk beds had a layer of straw, but there were no windows and the heavy sliding door was locked from the outside. "We didn't know where we were going, but had a pretty good idea that it was Siberia. As far as we knew all prisoners were sent to Siberia."

The trip took four weeks. A hole in the floor of the cattle car was used as the john. The sick just did everything into the straw on the bunks. Once a day the train stopped, the door opened and the dead bodies were kicked outside. Then we got a bucket full of fresh water. Sometimes the straw was replaced with fresh. The door was shut and locked again and the train moved on.

Helmut was in a labor camp near Sverdlovsk, now Yekaterinburg, East of the Ural Mountains, known as Eastern Siberia. All 800 prisoners at the camp were laborers at the nearby Plywood factory. "It was very hard labor but good work. First we pulled the logs out of the river that accumulated daily, as they floated down from forests upstream. Then we moved them to the processing plant. We worked from early morning until evening, six days a week. As long as we worked we also had good and more than adequate food."

The men were grouped according to work, and that's also how food was handed out. Occasionally there were special work details. Helmut qualified for the job of unloading holds of ships with assorted supplies in the harbor. The prisoners had to walk two hours to get here in the morning, unload whatever ship was there, and then walk two hours back. "We got extra food," he recalled with a hint of a smile.

One incident Helmut remembered vividly. "We were unloading a huge hold of a ship loaded with barrels of alcohol. We thought we could get some alcohol while unloading. This one barrel turned out to be methanol alcohol instead of ethanol. Many men got very sick, out of 60, 30 were ill, luckily I didn't drink any. We carried the sick on the long two-hour walk back to the camp. The camp doctor pumped their stomachs, and ten of them died.

"We were paid small amounts of money for daily labor. No work, no money." The money was used to barter for things. "Once the war was over, the camp had a small store for necessities. But before that happened we had to go through a very cold winter with minus 38 Celsius (-36 Fahrenheit) for days on end. The barracks were not heated, and I was shivering all the time. I don't know how I made it through those hard months. I was living from minute to minute.

"It also seemed when it was the coldest, food was in very short supply. Early in 1945, supplies to the camp were sparse. We had what was supposed to be broth, ha! One bone for a whole barrel of water! One bowl of broth and a chunk of dark bread was our daily ration for a while that winter. We made that meal last. We chewed the broth, one small spoonful at a time, until there was nothing left on the tongue. Then a small bite of bread was chewed and chewed, swished around in the mouth until it was thinner than spit."

The guards at the camp were very sympathetic, and ate the same food as the prisoners. Although guards and prisoners did not speak each other's language, they got along. As long as one worked and followed the rules the prisoners were treated very well.

In March 1945, every worker in good standings was handed one postcard to write home. The postcard reached Elschen, Helmut's wife, on November 16. It was the first sign of life from him since 1943 when he wrote her from the hospital.

Once the war ended in May 1945, the Red Cross made regular visits and conditions and food improved. In the fall, the Russians started to let the wounded and sick ones go home. "Meanwhile the rest of us kept working at the wood factory."

"In late 1948, it was my turn to be part of a large group going home! I sent a letter to Elschen that I was in the next transport from the camp. She could listen to the radio announcements and find out when we would arrive." The Red Cross announced the arrival of trains with returning prisoners of war on the radio several times a day.

"After several days on the train in the cattle cars, the doors were opened and we were told to line up outside. The weak and ill were let go back on the train. We were grouped by numbers: group 1, group 2, group 3 and group 4. Then an officer stepped forward. He spoke perfect

German and introduced himself. He was a German Jew who immigrated to Russia early when Hitler started to single out the Jewish population. He told us that he was in charge of building a large bridge. The bridge was going to be part of planned road construction. A better road system was needed for the expansion of the Ural oil fields. He also told us, "If you work hard and the bridge can be completed in less than a year, you will all be free and can go home."

Helmut and his fellow prisoners worked in a huge stone quarry. The quarry supplied all stones for the bridge. "We lived in mud huts and worked from dawn to dusk, seven days a week. Pay was very good, and I saved most of it. The food was good too. But we were not allowed to write. Nobody was supposed to know where we were."

Elschen went to meet the train in Berlin as his letter announced. Of course, Helmut was not on it. Thinking the worst, she passed out on the platform.

"Once a week we were examined by a doctor. We lined up naked, the doctor walked behind us and checked our buttock area. I was told that this area shows what condition your body is in. If you are sick or emaciated to the core, that's where it shows. I always passed. I found that being short and stocky was an advantage over being tall and thin. The tall men seemed to weaken the fastest. Many lost a lot of weight with the quarry work and were emaciated. Those men had to step aside after the inspections. They were sent to other huts, separated from us by a high fence. I heard later that their food was cut back severely.

"A little over nine months later we had an assembly in front of the huts. The officer told us, "The project is done. You are free." I couldn't believe my ears. We had no idea how the bridge was progressing, we never saw it. My knees were shaking and threatened to buckle. "Do I dare get excited?" I kept asking myself. Then I kept telling myself 'Keep your knees locked.' I didn't want to look weak now and risk possibly being left behind.

"I was so impressed, and still am to this day, how the officer kept his word. He could have easily assigned us to another work detail. It didn't matter that we were Germans. He showed no bitterness towards us whatsoever. He promised. We did as asked and he kept his word. I will never forget that."

"We were told to stay outside while our huts were cleaned from top to bottom. No bugs or sand flies were left. We cleaned ourselves and got a complete set of new clothes and waited for the train to take us home. It came in a couple of days and two weeks later it slowly rolled into Berlin."

When the Red Cross announced the impending arrival of released war prisoners on the radio, they read the names of all men. Elschen always listened to those broadcasts and one afternoon in October 1949 she heard Helmut's name, and that the train was expected at 11:30 am the next day at Bahnhof Zoo, Berlin's main train station. She went to the station telling herself that he may not be on the train after all.

The train arrived on time and Helmut was home at last!

Christmas

The Christmas season was my favorite! It wasn't about presents or large gatherings. It was a quiet time, anticipated with restraint and the focus of being extra good. For weeks it was in the air and on everyone's mind. People sometimes would break into a smile for no reason at all or give me a wink acknowledging that something was up.

It was also about treats that were only available at Christmas time: *Dominosteine*, a square chocolate-covered cookie like a layer cake, only in miniature; *Lebkuchen*, a gingerbread cookie, sometimes covered with a very light sugar frosting; *Baumkuchen*, a many-layered cake that melted on your tongue; fruit gelee, a very firm Jell-O-like concoction in fruit and star shapes and *Stollen*. Many recipes for these date back centuries, especially *Stollen*.

Baking was not part of our tradition. Most kitchens did not have an oven with a thermostat, and the temperature was difficult to regulate. *Stollen*, taking many steps to complete, was only done in bakeries. The most famous *Stollen* comes from Dresden. *Stollen* is a yeast cake with lots of candied fruit that have been soaked in rum or brandy. It is baked in November and needs to be untouched so that it can mature until Christmas. By then the yeast dough has mellowed into a delicate cake.

One sweet that Mutti tried to make every year was *Marzipankartoffeln*, a butter and ground almond dough rolled into small balls and dusted with cocoa resembling potatoes. She made them every Christmas except the one when Margot and I ate all the sugar Mutti had hoarded. (See "Always Hungry", page 86).

The season included Advent – four Sundays of Advent leading to Christmas and ended with Three Kings Day, the 6th of January, after which our tree was taken down and the ornaments carefully wrapped and stored.

On that first Sunday of Advent, we gathered at the table at the traditional coffee time at four o'clock. The evergreen Advent wreath decorated with small pine cones, a red ribbon and four red candles, one for each Sunday, was the centerpiece on the table in the living room. Oma joined us as it was getting dark outside and at the table Mutti lit the first candle. The candle's glow cast mysterious shadows about the room. We had coffee and sampled a few *Dominosteine* and *Lebkuchen*. When I was little, my 'coffee' was more milk than coffee.

From a book of Christmas poems, stories and songs, we read some poems and decided which one we would recite in front of the tree on Christmas Eve. It's a tradition that all children recite a poem before they can receive a present.

December 1st, marked the day we could open the first of twenty-four windows on our Advent calendar. The calendar was always carefully chosen by Mutti, a different one for Margot and me. We leaned them against the kitchen window so that light would highlight the pretty Christmas season picture behind the opened window. The kitchen, being the warmest room, had the only windows not frosted solid.

Next in the chain of traditions was Saint Nikolas Day, December 6. The night before, the 5th of December, we put our spotlessly-shined shoes by the front door. Saint Nikolas visited all children during the night. He carried a big book full of notes of naughty and nice deeds of all. Depending on our deeds, he would leave a piece of coal for being naughty or some fruit or candy if we had been good in our shoes.

We could not wait to get up in the morning to check our shoes! We realized that Saint Nikolas knew everything because we always had a piece of coal – for naughty, an apple – for being good in our shoes. An evergreen twig stuck in one of the shoes also. The twig obviously fell off the plain tree that he carried along with a sack of goodies; a sign that he was really here.

Christmas markets also started after the first of December. We always went for a walk through the market near Town Hall in the evening. The mouthwatering smell of hot sausages and the sweet aroma of Glühwein, warm mulled wine with spices, greeted us long before we were actually at the market. Everything looked more special with lights. In the early years, we never bought anything but admired the wares in every booth: homemade wooden crèches, glass tree ornaments, beeswax tree candles, and many versions of gingerbread houses. Every booth was a discovery. A few years later a hot knockwurst on a crusty roll with mustard was our usual treat before heading home. Sausage never tasted better than on those cold December evenings!

Mutti took her time choosing the perfect Christmas tree. We asked her every day, "Did you look today?" When she finally came across the right Balsam Fir, she brought the tree home and stored it outside the living room window facing the street. There it was tied to the center stud of the window frame hanging upside down to stay fresh. As Christmas came closer all apartments had a tree hanging from the window. It was very reassuring seeing all those trees outside people's windows, waiting to be brought inside and decorated on Christmas Eve. We knew, once we had the tree Christmas, was getting closer.

As the Sundays towards Christmas added up, so did the lit candles on the wreath on Sunday afternoons. When all four candles were lit, the living room was much brighter and Christmas Eve was almost here. Margot and I rehearsed and memorized our chosen poem in private for weeks. We didn't want to stumble. It had to be perfect.

Christmas Eve

Christmas Eve is when all the magic is happening in Germany. Children don't see the tree before the evening ceremony. According to German tradition, the tree isn't there until an angel, *Das Christkind,* along with Santa Claus, *Der Weihnachtsmann,* bring it to your house in the early evening (fully decorated, of course).

What I remember most from those early years is Christmas 1945 at Oma's.

It was Christmas Eve and at about 2 pm, we were told to go into the kitchen and to stay there or else. Although it was mid-afternoon, it was already getting darker and darker outside. Margot and I were sitting in the kitchen on the two hard, white, wooden chairs matching the table and cupboard. The kitchen wall clock, centered over the table, kept time for us but was getting harder to see in the dim light. Electricity was rationed and used only if you had to; sitting in the kitchen did not qualify. The ornate hands on the clock seemed to move slower than usual. There was nothing for us to do but talk. We were egging each other on about what presents we might get. I can't remember what we fantasized about though.

Oma came to the kitchen to check on the coal stove a few times. She said very little and after adding a coal brick to the fire, she quickly left the room again.

Sometimes during that endless afternoon, we heard some rumpling in the hall; something got knocked against the kitchen door. We saw shadows moving slowly past the opaque kitchen door windows. And then there was silence again, interrupted once in a while with commotion coming from the living room.

I remember that the little hand on the clock was hovering near the bottom and the big one was almost straight at the top. Oma had given me a hint after I asked what time *Der Weihnachtsmann* was coming. She told me, "He usually comes when both hands form a straight up and down line." I knew time was coming near. Both Margot and I got very jumpy and nervous about our bad deeds of the past year. We could not remember being bad, but guessed that *Der Weihnachtsmann* surely had everything recorded.

Finally Mutti and Oma came, each took one of us by the hand and led us to the living room. Except for the burning candles on the tree, the room was dark. The tree was mesmerizing; I thought it was the most beautiful thing I had ever seen! The yellowish glow of the candles was very soft, warm and reassuring. It was absolutely silent in the room.

We were led in front of the tree. I can still feel the butterflies in my stomach and the lump in my throat as I was being nudged to go first, and recite the endlessly rehearsed Christmas poem. Afterward Mutti and Oma seemed very serious as they shook my hand and wished me "*Frohe Weihnachten!*"

I can't remember what our presents were. I guess they consisted of an apple, a few nuts, and a pair of awfully scratchy woolen knee socks, our standard presents then.

Christmas Eve always seemed to be the longest day. Throughout the day we were not allowed into the living room. Mutti was out of sight; we had to fend for ourselves. Oma would usually arrive just before six and shortly thereafter Mutti called us into the living room. The first sighting of the tree in the far corner of the living room with our silver, gold, red and blue glass ornaments and tinsel all over was especially exciting year after year. All lights were off; the candles on the tree were lit and cast their warm glow about the room.

One at a time Margot and I recited our Christmas poem facing the tree. Our voices were the only sound in the room. When we were little, the poem could be short. The older we were the longer the poem needed to be.

Finally Mutti lifted the cloth off the dining table where our presents lay. My presents were in one spot. We received one present each from Oma and Mutti as well as our own plate with assorted traditional Christmas sweets. I remember that one present always was a book and the other maybe a sweater or blouse. Margot and I gave small homemade presents to Mutti and Oma, maybe a paper star for the tree or a coaster made of felt for the table, things like that.

We admired each other's presents and then settled in for the traditional Christmas Eve supper of *Kartoffel Salat* and *Bockwurst* - potato salad and sausage. On Christmas Eve food was always plentiful.

Mutti turned on the radio. Programs included Christmas carols, poems, stories and distinct church bell ringing from well-known churches. We sang along with all the songs and hymns.

We did not go to church on Christmas Eve but after supper we went for a walk. Right after the war people were asked to put a candle for each family member who died or was missing in the window. Our windows were a double set of single windows; it was safe to put candles between the windows. We put four candles in our street-facing living room window; one each for Pappa, Uncle Werner, Herr Freier and Uncle Helmut, who was still in a Siberian prison camp. The tradition of placing candles in a window on Christmas Eve continues today.

The streets of Berlin were transformed by the candle glow; there were candles behind every windowpane. By now it was eight or so. Few people were about and hardly any cars, which was so different from the usual. It seemed surreal.

We did not get a lot of snow in Berlin but there were many snowy Christmases. I remember looking at the lit windows as we passed building after building. Some were lit with one candle; some had a row of them; our footsteps crunching into the snow making the only sound. I always looked forward to this walk, especially when it snowed.

Santa Claus

Christmases were always the same. Aside from the first Christmas I remember, there is another that is vivid in my mind - the one when Santa Claus came to our apartment. I think I was seven or eight.

We were already in the living room when we heard a series of hard knocks on our door. Oma answered the door and in came Santa Claus.

I could not believe my eyes. Even Margot didn't utter a word. Then Santa asked us to recite our poems. Being the oldest I had to go first. I don't know why, but my legs just didn't want to move the way they usually did. Stiff legged I walked to the tree and the words actually came out all right. I recited my poem flawlessly.

After Margot had her turn, Santa opened the large sack he was carrying. Santa gave me a large doll that I had been wishing for. I was so surprised I could barely say *"Danke schön."* Besides the dollhouse that Aunt Schneider had given us years ago, this was the first real toy - my first doll!

The next morning, *Der Erste Feiertag* (First day of Christmas and we also had a second and a third), I played with my doll right away. A baby must have a bath, of course. I set up a large pan with water and put the doll into the water. It did not take long for my doll to start falling apart. The doll was made out of paper maché and totally dissolved. Mutti hadn't noticed, she was in the kitchen and I busied myself in the living room. The doll could not be rescued. I was crying and crying. I was inconsolable. There was nothing to be done. I have been very careful with any presents ever since.

Christmas Day

Der Erste Feiertag, Christmas Day, was usually reserved for staying home with Christmas dinner served in the middle of the day. That was the day I could start and finish the book I received, interrupted only by meals. I was twelve when *Gone with the Wind* was my present and it took me three days to finish.

Christmas breakfast included the long awaited first slice of *Stollen.* Mutti sliced it thin. We could have it plain, with jam or butter; I liked it best smeared with sweet butter

Our traditional dinner was Mutti's roast leg of lamb, served with potato dumplings, sautéed kale and red cabbage. We anticipated that meal for weeks.

Mutti started cooking the vegetables a week before. First, she cooked the kale. I was always amazed at how much she bought, two shopping bags full, and when it was done cooking, the kale barely filled half a stewpot. Of course, in December it was cold enough for Mutti to store the pot on the sill outside the kitchen window.

Next came the red cabbage. Again, she had her standards. She did not like the vinegary, tart German version. The red cabbage pot then joined the kale on the windowsill. Mutti reheated both pots every other day. "Every time the vegetables get reheated they taste even better than the first time, probably the enzymes working." The smell wafting through the apartment was mouth-watering and I could hardly wait until Christmas Day. Christmas Eve came first though, when we ate the standard potato salad and *wurst* after the presents were delivered.

Christmas Day dawned early for Mutti. She had to start the coal in the roasting oven. When the oven was hot enough, she put the cast iron pan with the lamb in and regulated the heat by opening and closing the door. Again she stayed in the kitchen to make sure nothing got burned. Off and on she basted the roast and waiting for dinner became almost unbearable for us all! It seemed that it took hours and hours until it was ready.

Finally when the lamb and all the side dishes were ready, we could sit down at the living room table. For special dinners like Christmas, the table was set with a white linen tablecloth, napkins and Oma's gold-rimmed china. Oma came just before dinner was ready to join us. The tree candles were lit again while we were in the room. Those lamb roasts were the best; I could never get tired of it. After the meal we were already looking forward to leftovers.

Der Zweite Feiertag, Second day of Christmas, was the day for visiting relatives. That's when we went to Uncle Helmut's and spent a little time with Ingrid and Dorit. Sometimes we stayed for coffee and sweets, sometimes not that long.

In later years it was the day we visited Aunt Hilda in Weissensee, East Berlin. We left in the morning, loaded with extra food and came home after supper. I liked our trips to Weissensee. Werner did not spend any holidays with Uncle Alfred and Aunt Ruth and was at Aunt Hilda's already when we arrived. Aunt Hilda's boyfriend and a couple of other old friends were usually visiting too. We sat around the living room, went for a walk around the lake and went back to the apartment for another meal. The conversation was always very lively, filled with jokes and a lot of laughter.

New Year's Eve was almost as anticipated as Christmas! We had a late supper so that we could stay awake until midnight. Radio programs replayed events that happened during the year, as well as new music hits that appeared with dance music in between.

We reviewed the past year as it had treated us and also the hopes that we placed in the year that lay ahead, sipping *Glühwein* that Mutti made for the special occasion. Even when we were young, we were allowed to have a small glass.

When we looked back on the year past, I remember that the focus was on the positive; an unexpected treat we were given or an extra visit to Aunt Anni in Tempelhof - one of our favorites - or something funny we heard.

Our hopes for the New Year were similar; let the blockade be over, maybe all of the roof could be repaired and not just patched, maybe the summer will be warm so that we can be outside more.

So, when midnight came we opened the windows to the street to see and hear the fireworks. Everyone had firecrackers, little rockets and more. We wished each other *"Prosit Neujahr,"* Happy New Year, and joined the chorus outside shouting, *"Prosit Neujahr"* over and over to everyone.

I remember the murmur of anticipation in the pit of my stomach as I hoped that the New Year would bring something good, something special. I still feel it every New Year's Eve.

Christmas 1959
Visiting Aunt Hilda in Weissensee – East Berlin
Back: Werner and Margot
Front: on left Aunt Hilda, Heidi far right.

Missing Pappa

From the very beginning I always had a sense that my father was watching over me. Our neighbors and Pappa's business contacts had known him since the mid 1930s when he moved to Berlin. Everyone always spoke highly of him.

When we were out and about with Mutt, it was customary to chat briefly with the people you knew. Conversations were always formal, no matter how long people knew one another. "How are you, Frau Sieg and how are you, Heidi? Are you behaving and not giving your mother any worries?" My answer was usually a nod and then shaking my head. I was always very conscious not to upset my mother.

Then people would continue, "Oh, Frau Sieg, how sad that your husband did not come back. I will always remember the day when he brought me a quarter pound of butter...in the middle of the war...I hadn't tasted any for years!" Or, "Frau Sieg, I remember the last time I saw your husband when he had leave and I asked him what he hoped for...'I want to see my girls grow up' he said."

At those times I felt surrounded by love and continued walking with butterflies in my tummy. I asked Mutti, who was walking very quietly after meetings like this, about those comments. "Your Pappa just wanted to run his business and give you a good life. That's why he planned to move us into the countryside in Fehrbellin (approximately 60 miles northwest of Berlin). He thought it offered the best of both worlds, country life with the city nearby." Then with a deep sigh she added, *"Aber das Schickal hat es anders bestimmt* – but fate decided differently."

Pappa's father, Opa Sieg, suddenly died in Bochum in 1952. Out of the blue, I had the opportunity to hear more about Pappa from a circle of people unknown to me until then.

Mutti saw Opa Sieg as an ogre. The few times he visited in Berlin he would hang around with Alfred, flash lots of money in front of people at the neighborhood pub, brag about the well-behaved grandchildren and never gave us even 50 cents.

When he died, Uncle Alfred insisted we all go to the funeral. Mutti thought it ludicrous; she had little contact with him ever and Margot and I hardly knew him. But she gave in.

Before dawn we all piled into his VW Beetle: Uncle Alfred driving and Aunt Ruth in the front, Mutti and Aunt Elfriede in the back. Margot and I took turns in the little space behind the back where we had to curl up to fit. It was a long six-hour drive. I remember mostly being in the back, looking out the window. It was the first long trip out of Berlin that I can remember.

We arrived in Bochum just before the afternoon funeral. The church was packed; we had to sit in the front. But before we were allowed to sit, Margot and I had to stand in front of the open coffin and pay our respect for a while. We had no clue what we were supposed to do. I looked at the waxen face of grandfather and once in a while peered sideways at Margot to see what she was doing. She did the same. After a while someone pulled us back to sit down.

For me the best part came afterwards. Oma Sieg's small living room was full of friends and business people, sitting at long tables having dinner and lots of *Bier und Schnapps*. Margot and I ate something in the kitchen and then wandered about the living room.

It was the first time we met the step-grandmother and Pappa's half-siblings Fritz, Erich and Klara. We also got re-acquainted with Pappa's aunts and uncles who raised him.

At one point we were introduced as August's children and the murmur of approval was buzzing. Margot and I went to each and everyone, curtsied, shook their hands and introduced ourselves. Every single one recalled August as they knew him before he set off for Berlin. I was asked how old I was, how I liked school and when we would be driving back to Berlin. Over and over I was told how respected Pappa was as a hard worker and congenial fellow. Even if the same was repeated, I did not get tired of it, and wanted to hear more. I know I was smiling the whole time.

Of course, I was told very clearly that my father had died and although there was a grave to visit, Margot and I held out the hope that someone made a mistake.

In the early years it was not much of an issue. Many families were without a husband and father. In the late 1940s, more and more soldiers returned from prisoner of war camps. We heard of many instances where a man believed to be dead rang a doorbell and was greeted with disbelief and astonishment.

Uncle Helmut came back from Siberia in late 1949. Ingrid and Dorit had their dad back. The radio was full of stories of reunited families. Margot and I started to think that perhaps the body in the cellar was not my father's and he really was alive. We believed this to be a very good possibility. When we asked Mutti about it, she recited the overwhelming evidence, his ID card, uniform, size of the body, and that there was no doubt in her mind.

In the early 1950s Margot spent many an afternoon at a school friend's house. Her father, a baker, was home. Margot wanted a father. She wanted Mutti to get married so that we would have a father. She believed life would be better with a father in the house. Well, as far as I knew Mutti did not have any men friends, so how could she get married?

Margot came up with the idea of putting an ad in the 'Spouse Wanted Section' of *Heim und Welt* magazine. The magazine featured general help, travel and personal experience articles from home and abroad. The personal ad section in the back was filled with ads by single or widowed women, looking for husbands. After the war, there were far more women than men and this was an accepted venue to reach out.

I was not as dedicated to the cause. Would I like to have another person living with us? I went along with Margot's wishful thinking. We spent quite a bit of time debating what to put in the ad, often changing the wording way past lights out. Should we highlight Mutti's best qualities, how should we describe ourselves, should we mention children at all? We went round and round.

One evening, the light was out already, we were debating the ad when the door opened and Mutti came into the room. She turned on the light but stayed at the doorway.

"I've been listening to you two long enough. This is ridiculous! Forget about it!" Turning towards Margot, she said, "Yes, maybe life would be better with a father for you, maybe not. A man can make life more difficult and not solve a thing. I never wanted to get married. But your father came along and I did, and now I have the two of you to raise. It is not easy, but I will manage somehow. I have no intention whatsoever to get married again or live with somebody just so you can have a father."

She paused, "How do you know this would be a good father? The experience with my father, as husband and father model, was not good at all. I was lucky with your father, who was a good man. I do not want to tempt fate twice. I'd much rather be alone and at peace. I'm not saying never, because who knows? Just don't go on plotting! Forget about it! Not another word!"

For me, that was it. I really wished often that my father was with us, but I did not want to replace him with someone else. Margot did some daydreaming out loud once in a while when she knew Mutti was not around, mostly in the summer when we went on outings by ourselves when Mutti had a migraine.

When we were on the long trek to go swimming on a hot summer day, she imagined what we might be doing if Pappa were there; would he go with us? Better than that, he would drive us in his car, of course! Maybe Mutti wouldn't be having migraines and would come with us, too.

We both let it go, but once in a while we imagined what our life would be like had Pappa returned to us. Mutti even brought up the subject when a situation was leading her right to it. When she could not afford something, she sometimes said, "If Pappa had returned, things would be different. You would have a better life."

Many years later, when I was seventeen, I was hit out of the blue with the possibility that Pappa was alive. I was on the train riding home from work when I saw a man sitting across the aisle who looked just like Pappa! I could not help staring. He looked so much like him, the color of his eyes, the receding hairline of medium blond hair, that family trait mole on his forehead! Wow! Even in the late 1950s men were still returning from the war who had been given up for dead! Could it be? My heart was beating so hard I thought the woman on the seat next to me could hear it!

When the man got up for the next stop, I got up also. I followed him up the long staircase making sure not to be too close. At the top of the stairs, just before heading into the cool evening air, I stopped. It couldn't be. This man looks just like Pappa, but now it is 1959 and he would definitely look different from the old photos. I looked up again in his direction, but he was gone.

For a moment I stood still, staring in disbelief. Well, nobody I knew had seen me; now I was embarrassed for this whim. On the other hand, for a few minutes I had this wonderful, hopeful feeling. I carried it with me for a long time.

When I shared it with Mutti, she smiled and was very sympathetic. She said, "Maybe your subconscious, wishful thinking made you see him. Maybe you saw a man looking like Pappa; then again maybe you just saw him."

I was riding the same train every evening and scrutinized the passengers carefully, but I never saw this man again.

Relatives in Bochum

My grandfather, Opa August Sieg, moved from Ost Preussen (Poland since World War II) to Germany's Ruhr Valley in the early 1900s. He raised his family in Bochum and it remained his hometown. I heard about the relatives there often but only remember meeting Opa a couple of times when he was visiting Berlin in the late 1940s.

At Opa's funeral in 1952, I met the Bochum family: Oma Sieg, his second wife, and their children: Uncle Fritz, Uncle Erich and Aunt Klärchen, the youngest. All were in their twenties, still single and living at home.

Bochum lies in the heart of Germany's coal industry. Coal mines dominate the landscape and endless tunnels criss-crossed under the towns. Coal dust was in the air at all times and blanketed houses and countryside. Many houses were a bit slanted from collapsed tunnels underground. The floors in Opa's house were also slanted. It was an accepted fact that people lived with. Only if a building was in danger of collapsing did the mine administrators step in to help secure a structure.

Opa's vegetable and potato empire was in the backyard of his one-story building. Most buildings in the neighborhood were one or two-stories. Oma Sieg was in charge of the grocery store that occupied most of the house.

After the funeral, the family promised to invite Margot and me during vacations. We were asked to stay in touch and write. Mutti did. The following spring Aunt Klärchen sent a letter, inviting me to stay with them during summer vacation. Mutti was very touched that the family actually followed through. I think she had conditioned herself not to count on anyone's promises.

I was very excited and couldn't wait for summer to arrive. Transportation at the time was very different. There were trains and buses, but being eleven Mutti didn't feel it safe for me to travel alone. An alternative had developed in the last couple of years. More and more Berliners bought cars and some enterprising people created a shuttle service to West Germany using their cars. Mutti called the central headquarters, where the private cars and drivers were registered, and requested a ride for me. The service operated mostly on weekends. One was picked up at the front door in Berlin and delivered to the destination's address. This was the ideal way for me to get to Bochum.

Mutti sent a postcard to my aunt with the day and time of my estimated arrival. Packing a suitcase for me did not take very long. Practically everything I owned was washed and ironed and fit into one of Oma's suitcases with room to spare.

Sure enough, I was picked up on a Saturday at 6 am. Mutti paid the driver and we were off. Two other adults, one next to me and one in the passenger seat in the front, were also going to towns near Bochum.

Bochum is about 320 miles west of Berlin. Although the *Autobahn* went from Berlin to the west, it took a bit longer than usual to arrive anywhere because almost half of the mileage took us through the Russian controlled East Germany. At the checkpoint upon entering East Germany the driver was given a ticket with the time on it. The Russian had set a 25 mph speed limit through their sector and you better not drive faster than that. The ticket had to be handed in at the border leaving East Germany and the time traveled was checked.

It was very quiet in the car. Nobody said very much outside of pleasantries. Except for a couple of bathroom stops we drove straight through. Mutti had packed sandwiches and an apple for my lunch. We ate in the car as the driver pushed on. Food broke the silence. "Well, what do you have?" was the opening as we showed off our treats. I had my favorite liverwurst sandwich with mustard on dark rye. It smelled real good and was admired. We arrived in front of the grocery store in Bochum by mid-afternoon.

The driver went inside and brought Oma Sieg and Klärchen to the curb. After a hug from each we went inside.

Klärchen, I called those aunts and uncles by their first name, worked in the store with Oma. I was introduced right away as "my granddaughter from Berlin," to the customers inside. I don't remember exactly where I slept. Klärchen showed me a bed in an odd-sized room under the roof. I quickly piled my belongings on a nearby shelf and hurried back to the store.

Fritz and Erich were still on the neighborhood rounds selling vegetables and potatoes from their small trucks. As they drove into the yard I ran outside. Fritz was the eldest and far friendlier than Erich. Fritz engaged in conversation with me right away, but Erich didn't say much.

Everyone was cleaned up at suppertime. Erich ate quickly and left immediately after. He had a girlfriend, Marianne, and planned to get married soon.

It was an eventful day for me. I went to bed right after supper and fell asleep promptly.

Oma and Klärchen were very nice and friendly; it felt like I had known them forever. From breakfast on I had little jobs I could do.

I helped keep the store clean. In those days, everything was sold in bulk and cleaning around the bins was constant. Soon I was allowed to serve customers. Everyone was very indulgent and didn't blink an eye when I waited on them. Many of these people had lived in the neighborhood forever and if they didn't know my father, they knew of him.

I learned to concentrate on two things at a time, measuring and weighing while carrying on a conversation. "*Guten Tag, Heidi*, have you done this before? I would like a half pound of liverwurst, *bitte*."

"No, this is the first time. This is a little over. Would that be all right?" I tried to sound confident and friendly, imitating Oma.

"Very well. What grade are you in? I also need a quarter pound of sugar and one pound of flour."

"Would you like white or brown sugar? I'm in fifth grade and my sister is in fourth," I answered as I busied myself finding the right bins.

Everything was measured into paper bags. Smaller amounts fitted into blue cone-shaped ones and larger ones into rectangular brown ones. When the customer's order was complete, I wrote every item on a small receipt sheet and handed the bags over the counter. Then I added it all up and gave the sheet to Oma or Klärchen to double check. At first I was very nervous about making a mistake. But I did very well and soon Klärchen waved me off when I wanted to give her my tally. "You're a born *Geschäftsfrau* - business woman!"

Either Oma or Klärchen did the cooking. I don't remember the kitchen or helping there.

Over the truck garage in the backyard was a large apartment where Nowotchs lived. Tante was Opa's sister. Pappa was raised on their farm in Ost Preussen. During the war, we stayed with them on their farm to escape the Berlin bombings. After they fled the Russian invasion in 1944, they settled in Opa's apartment in Bochum.

I visited the family on many afternoons. Tante, Emma, Emilie, Friedrich and Willie, all remembered me as a busy toddler staying at their farm. One of them was always recalling a story about the farm, the horses, Pappa or something I had done. I loved to listen and I know it made me feel really good.

Fritz and I spent most evenings together. He, like Uncle Alfred, took me along everywhere. Whether he went for a drive or to the corner pub, he took me along. At the pub, he spent time sitting at the bar drinking beer and meeting buddies. He supplied me with endless quarters to keep the jukebox going. I was absolutely delighted, spending hours in that smoke-filled bar.

Fritz and Erich did not only sell vegetables and potatoes in the neighborhoods. They also had a couple of large trucks for long distance hauling of goods. Fritz took me along on those long drives to far away farms to buy their harvest. We went to the Netherlands for potatoes and southern Germany for vegetables.

The drive to the Netherlands was the longest. We left after supper. After a few hours driving in the darkness, Fritz was so tired from a long day (he usually got up around four) that he needed a quick nap before moving on. He pulled over to the side of the highway. With my lap as a pillow, he said "Wake me in two hours," and he quickly went to sleep. For two hours I didn't dare move a muscle, afraid to cut his nap short. It was pitch black all around and I had no idea where we were, but I was not afraid. I still remember how long those two hours seemed.

We arrived at the farm at 2 am. I was shown to bed and was asleep before they turned off the light. In the morning the truck was loaded to the very top with big sacks of new potatoes and covered with a tarp. The drive back seemed shorter, maybe because it was daylight. Fritz was very pleased with this load of early potatoes. New potatoes were eagerly anticipated; they had a sweeter taste and were more delicate, skin and all. Fritz was happy to bring the fist load of 'new ones' to town. He knew they would be sold out within a couple of days.

My vacation went by very quickly. The following year it was Margot's turn and in 1955 we both could stay with Oma and Klärchen. Fritz was married to Erika and we didn't see them much. We spent more time with Klärchen and Oma.

Margot and I were constant and very efficient helpers at the family store. The store was a member of a co-op that organized events for their customers. We went on a couple of Saturday afternoon bus trips with many of the store's customers, mostly women. We were the only young ones in the group, sitting in the front of the bus being announcers and cheerleaders.

The destinations were always a big restaurant in the country with outdoor entertainment. The drives in both directions were filled with singing. The microphone was passed along to those who wanted to tell a joke or short story. Time went by quickly. At the restaurant everyone settled in quickly for afternoon coffee and pastries. Shortly after a band started to play and everyone danced until it was time to get on the bus for the return trip. It was an afternoon of lighthearted fun!

The following year was my turn again and this time I stayed with Fritz and Erica who lived not far from Oma and Klärchen. I met Erika once when she and Fritz visited Uncle Alfred a couple of years before. Erica was like Fritz, and we got along well from the moment we met.

Erika and Fritz were parents of my newest cousin. Little Fritz was just one year old. I did not have to baby-sit much, because it seemed that every young girl in the neighborhood wanted a turn spending time with him.

Weekdays were workdays and something was always needed. Fritz was going to the open farmers' market every day and usually home by early afternoon after it closed. After lunch he got ready for the following day.

We never stayed home on Sundays. The extended family, Fritz and Erika's, usually met up somewhere: a picnic; the big town swimming pool; an air show at the Dortmund Airport; an outdoor restaurant.

Oma Sieg always stayed home. She was happy to have peace and quiet. Erich and his wife Marianne stayed by themselves, so I did not see them. He and his wife had their own business. There probably was some family stuff going on, but nobody talked about it.

In 1957, Margot and I both spent time in Bochum, again with Fritz and Erika. It was my first year at business school and I only had a two-week vacation. The stay was short but so much fun again. Erika was like our big sister with a wonderful sense of humor.

Remembering summers with our family in Bochum always makes me smile!

Religion

I was raised as a Protestant, but we rarely went to church. When Mutti was growing up, all Germans had to belong to a church. It was the law. One chose the denomination; Pappa and Mutti were Protestants, declared it and automatically paid a church fee every year with the income taxes. Mutti felt that in the years before and during World War II, all churches did not try hard enough to give people protection whether they were Christians or Jews. One of her first decisions after the war was to officially leave the church.

She detested the falseness of going to church every Sunday and then, in daily life, watching others ignore the Golden Rule, "Do unto others..." Leading by example, she made sure that I grew up with very clear directions of what was morally right or wrong. When there was a question about a decision, I can still hear her voice, "How would you feel if someone did this to you?"

She always considered herself last. For instance, when she had a lottery windfall in 1950, she shared it with everyone. Shoes for Minna, a blouse for Oma, a kitchen cupboard for Uncle Helmut and Aunt Elschen, until all was spent. At the time I did not understand why she gave so much away, even to people she was not very fond of. Later I recalled and understood her saying, "At the end of a day I want to go to sleep with a clear conscience."

Mutti wanted us to be exposed to religion from other sources than herself to be able to find our own preferences. When I was thirteen Mutti enrolled me in Catechism class at the Protestant church around the corner, where I was baptized. I studied the Bible every Wednesday evening with the minister and a few other students. I was not intrigued by the readings at all and if I was supposed to feel something, I didn't.

The two-year study culminated with confirmation. It is an affirmation of baptism and the traditional 'Rite of Passage' from being a child to being a young adulthood. Every church had its ceremonies. In East Berlin, where they adopted the 'no religion' policy of Russia, they held this ceremony, without the religious part, in a meeting hall.

Confirmation Day was a huge milestone, a once-in-a-lifetime happening. Planning and logistics took many months; the mail was the only communication then.

My dress in the traditional black color was made by Mutti's seamstress friend, her former landlady. We went by tram to many fittings, always preceded by a postcard setting the appointment.

Mutti mailed a notice to all the relatives. The mid morning confirmation ceremony was followed by a big lunch at home where the relatives joined in the celebration. Mutti saved for months. Weeks beforehand, Mutti bought extra food, whatever she could carry, to have enough for everyone.

The day before Confirmation I was sent to the beauty salon for my first perm. The hairdresser had permed Oma's and Mutti's hair for years and gave me the exact hairdo. What a disaster! I was really uncomfortable with those old-fashioned waves on my head. I wanted to cry but did not dare. Everyone was so happy for me. I liked the dress, but oh, that hairdo!

Mutti was busy preparing lunch of creamed chicken with fresh asparagus for the twenty expected guests the day before. Any chicken dish was very special, because at the time chicken was an expensive delicacy. I don't know how she did it in our small kitchen. Except for the hours getting my hair done, I was running errands for days to get things that were still needed.

My Confirmation Day, March 31, 1957, also happened to be the Sunday after high school graduation. The following Monday I started business school and my shop apprenticeship.

The day started early with the church ceremony, then onto the photographer for the official portrait. Uhg!

After that I rushed home to be on hand when the guests arrived for lunch. The relatives who had been to the church ceremony were there. Mutti's 'Chicken a la King' was outstanding! The chicken was tender, the asparagus and peas not over done and the cream sauce was smooth and silky.

After lunch I visited neighbors who sent congratulations, including Uncle Alfred and Aunt Ruth.

Werner was there, as well as Helmut, whom I would only see on weekends with my new job schedule.

The relatives from further away arrived around 3 pm for afternoon coffee. Traditional presents at the time were contributions for the dowry - towels, dishes, glassware, and flatware. Uncle Alfred and Aunt Ruth sent a charm bracelet. The dishes are long gone, but the bracelet I still wear today.

The day stretched from coffee time into the early evening and supper. After supper the dining table was moved along a wall to make room for dancing.

I had visited our neighbors to remind them that we would be celebrating and noise in the evening so that nobody would be upset. If a neighbor was upset, they usually knocked on the wall, or ceiling with a broom stick and once they had our attention, they yelled "QUIET!"

As the evening went on I was thinking ahead to Monday. I had to be at company headquarters at 8 am.

My Confirmation Day Portrait

Family Tribunal

In the early summer of 1957, a few weeks after I started going to business school, Mutti started to work at Osram. It was one of the largest employers in Berlin. The company was developing technology and manufacturing light bulbs.

Mutti worked at an assembly line. The camaraderie of her co-workers and knowing that she was useful was really good for her. She left the house at 6:30 am and came back about 4:30 pm. On the way home she bought groceries for supper. Other than working, her routine had not changed. She did not go out, have friends or dates.

Oma, living next to us, was now retired from her job. Margot and I made our beds and were supposed to keep the bedroom neat. Oma came in every morning to do light housekeeping for Mutti, and she also bought staple groceries occasionally. She cleaned some odd dishes, dusted and generally straightened everything.

One summer day in 1959, when I was seventeen, I was getting ready to go to the shop when Oma came in. I think I was doing my hair in front of the mirror in the living room while Oma was busying herself, working around me.

As usual, she kept a running commentary about every item she picked up. The comments were always about Mutti, and always critical. If there was still coffee in her cup, she picked it up with, "What a waste!"; if there was knitting in progress on a table, "She should have put this away!" I never said anything; I was taught not to talk back to adults. I ignored her comments.

On this particular morning a book and several magazines were on the small coffee table in the living room. Oma threw the lot onto a chair and started dusting, "What a waste of good money! This woman does not have any sense at all! All these extravagances! No wonder she doesn't amount to anything!"

I don't know what snapped. I turned to Oma and said, "Don't talk about my mother like that! You do nothing but grumble and criticize. What has anybody ever done to help her? She is always alone. All she does every day is to provide for Margot and me. Going to a movie and reading is all she does for herself! When you are not critical of Mutti, then you complain about us. Don't you ever have anything good to say?"

Oma stood frozen in her tracks. She stared at me with wide, open eyes. Then she turned and left the room.

I must say it felt good. I did not feel bad for having talked back to my grandmother. For once I did not have a knot in my stomach as I left for work.

My day was uneventful and I arrived home at the usual time. I rang the doorbell and Mutti greeted me with a serious look, "Uncle Helmut is waiting for you in Oma's living room."

Oma was sitting in her favorite reading chair by the window and Uncle Helmut was standing next to her.

I don't remember the exact sequence but it went something like this. Uncle Helmut asked, "Oma tells me that you contradicted her today. What do have to say for yourself?"

"Yes, I asked her not to criticize Mutti so much. Every morning is the same. She grumbles about everything and anything Mutti does or doesn't do. Oma does it all the time and I told her to stop it."

Uncle Helmut shot back, "This is intolerable, outrageous!" He continued, "You can't talk to your grandmother like that. Who do think you are? You are nothing. You know nothing!"

He looked at Mutti, "Edith, you are a total failure as a parent! What do you have to say?"

Silence.

Then Mutti said, "I stand by Heidi. She said nothing but the truth."

"From now on you are both expelled from the family. We don't want to have anything to do with you. We don't know you anymore." Looking at me he continued, "I'll tell Ingrid and Dorit to stay away from you from this moment on. You are a bad influence on them."

After a pause he looked at Mutti "What do you say to that?"

"Helmut, this is the first time someone stood up for me. I stand by Heidi." We both left Oma's living room.

During supper we rehashed the day. What I said to Oma; what Uncle Helmut said. I asked Mutti, "Does he mean it?"

"Oh, yes, you can count on that. It has always been like that in the family. Dump on Edith." She went on, "We'll be fine without the lot. You were so right. What have they ever done for me? Including Oma, nothing! Actually just the opposite is a fact!"

I didn't miss the family gatherings we were not allowed to attend. I did miss Ingrid's company at first. We had been buddies as long as I could remember; playing during school breaks, going swimming every week and later going to movies and parties together.

Once we had joined the working world, we had often met in front of her house after work a couple evenings a week. With neighborhood boys our age and a couple years older, we would chat the evening away, mostly about our daily experiences. It was quite a group. The girls all worked in shops. The boys aspired to varied careers, an architect, a medical doctor, a dentist and a surveyor. The tales of 'a day in the life of...' just never ended. I was cut off from all that in an instant. I knew I couldn't go there for fear of being spotted by Uncle Helmut. I have no idea how my sudden disappearance was explained to my friends.

Whenever I met Uncle Helmut or Aunt Elschen on the street, they looked past me. Ingrid and Dorit went on the opposite side of the street when they saw me to make sure they we didn't meet, obeying their father.

Mutti made some friends at work and joined them on outings. At the time I was already going out with Margot and her friends. I went with them more often now.

Leaving the Nest

I was eighteen and going on my first overnight, long-distance train ride. Not only was this my first long train ride, but I was also leaving home.

Traveling was not something I did often while growing up. I've been away from home alone before, but those were Health Department prescribed Spa retreats. Mutti always took me to the bus station were the group of children gathered to embark on the ride to our extended get-well vacations.

Our group would stay for six weeks at a place designed for children and consisted of spa treatments, lots of hiking, lots of meals and rest. We were chaperoned from the minute we left the bus station in Berlin until we arrived back. I had no decisions to make, I just had to follow the rules.

In the spring of 1960, I graduated from business school. I earned a regular salary and two weeks paid vacation, but the day-to-day business did not capture my interest. I had friends, lots of boys around, but I was not dating anyone. I went out every week-end. Although it was fun, it was always the same.

I don't remember exactly when it was. Sometime during the summer it was like having a vision. I could see a clear pattern of life that was laid out for me that was not inspiring. Actually it was depressing.

It was standard to live at home until marriage. To get an apartment of your own just wasn't done and in Berlin also next to impossible because of a housing shortage. I would always have to do as expected. Changing that pattern would be very difficult and I was not a fighter to go against convention.

The idea of working as an *au pair* governess started to swirl in my head. I still wanted to work with children. It was quite normal to spend a year away as an *au pair* especially if it was abroad, widening our cultural horizon. To leave Berlin with a job at hand would be acceptable. It would be an opportunity to be on my own and work and travel at the same time. When I approached Mutti with my idea she supported me wholeheartedly

I scanned the advertisements in good publications regularly when I noticed an ad from a family in Basel, Switzerland, looking for a governess for their three small children. It fit my requirements; it was in a foreign country and a family with small children, so I applied. I felt I had some experience to offer. After all, I had been a part-time governess for my young cousin since I was twelve. I was surprised, though, when the job offer came by return mail. I had a contract for a year, earning double my salary and would have my own room with a bath.

When I let the word out I was going to Switzerland for a year, everyone was surprised. "You are so close to Mutti and always so quiet. I never would have thought of you going off alone," I heard most. Minna said, "Oh boy, I have to sit down. I always thought Margot would be the one to take off," and later added "You'll see. You'll meet a young man and never come back." I strongly denied all. I'm just going away for a year!

Of course, I had to visit just about everyone I knew to say good-bye. They all had heard, after all this was a small neighborhood, and wished me well. "We know you'll succeed, and if you don't like it you can always come back."

The following weeks were quite busy. I needed a passport and had to give notice at my job. My free time was spent organizing my clothes and carefully sorting what I could fit into one suitcase to take with me. I saved every penny for the one-way train ticket.

Finally the first of November arrived, the day I would take the night train to Basel. I said my good-byes to Margot, "Write as soon as you can and tell me all about it," she said.

Then I knocked on Oma's door - even though she was not speaking to me. She just shook my hand and gave me a letter. In the letter Oma was telling me I should know how much my leaving is hurting Mutti. She also said to look out for myself and to be especially wary of men!

Before leaving the apartment, I packed a couple of sandwiches, an apple and a canteen of water to last me through the trip. Mutti and I took the tram to Bahnhof Zoo, the main train station.

Before she married, Mutti traveled often and mostly by train. She was bubbling over with advice. "Get a seat by the window if possible, so you can sleep better"; "Ask someone to help you put the suitcase in the overhead bin, because it is too heavy for you alone," and, "Sit on your purse when you get sleepy. It is safer."

The train was waiting at the platform when we arrived. It was already dark and although there were lots of people rushing around, the noises were sort of subdued. We looked for my train car and Mutti insisted on coming onto the train to look for a good compartment. There were a few empty ones but she suggested looking for one with people in it already, "It is safer for a woman alone if you already have an idea who will keep you company." She chose one occupied by several women and one man; no one had taken the window seat.

The man immediately offered to put my suitcase up. I left my coat on the window seat and went back on the platform with Mutti. Within seconds the conductor announced, "All aboard." Suddenly there was just time for one more hug and I scrambled up the steps to the compartment.

As I lowered the window, a gentle shrug of the train car let me know that I was leaving. I leaned out the window to wave. Mutti called, "*Pass auf Dich auf* – watch out for yourself. Write! Write!" As the trained moved faster, Mutti got smaller and smaller and then she was gone.

The women in the compartment urged, "Please close the window quickly, it is getting cold in here!" I hadn't noticed. Finally I claimed my cushy seat. Looking out the window I saw nothing but lights rush by. My companions settled in, we lowered the lights and one after the other fell asleep.

I couldn't sleep. I kept watching the window, hoping to see something but the East German countryside was dark, dark, dark. By mandate of the East German government, the train had to go fifteen miles per hour through the Eastern Zone that surrounded Berlin like a moat. It seemed to take a long time. Once we were in West Germany, the clickety-clack of the wheels increased sharply.

Slowly gray was emerging from black. It was getting light. With that, we were approaching Basel after the eight-hour trip. After a stop at the Border for *Passkontrolle*, passport checkpoint, the train slowly pulled into the station. I could not wait to meet my new boss and get started.

I really didn't know who to expect to meet me. This journey was taken on trust. Trust that the job would be all right. The train finally stopped and then I stood on the platform with my suitcase that held all I owned.

Chapter Four - On my Own

A new Day – A new Country

An elderly, distinguished-looking lady approached me on the train platform. "Are you Fräulein Sieg?" I nodded with relief. She shook my hand, "I am Frau Dr. Langer. There has been a change. Frau Lobel's governess decided to stay on and therefore she has no need for a governess."

I thought I was not understanding her right. But no, her German was perfect. I didn't have a job! I also didn't have a place to stay; no money for a ticket back to Berlin, no money period. In a split second, I was trying to figure out any options and came up with zero.

"What do you intend to do?" she asked.

"I don't know! I didn't expect this." I couldn't think.

"I'm prepared to make you an offer, if you are interested?" We stood face to face. "Can you cook?"

Without hesitation I said, "A little." I could count my cooking skills on one hand: making proper tea and coffee, boiling potatoes, making yummy sandwiches and making excellent whipped cream.

"Good!" she went on, "Our household of four adults needs a cook. And if you like to learn some of our cooking, I'll teach you." She offered a good salary, my own room and bath, and two half-days off.

I added a small explanation about my little cooking skills. "I really haven't cooked much. I'm not sure I can do the job properly."

"Oh, that's all right. I'm a good cook and can teach you everything. As a matter of fact, I think I really like the idea...if you want to."

I didn't want to go back to Berlin, because it would have been humiliating to return right away. Quickly I accepted.

Once I agreed to the new job proposal, I grabbed my suitcase and followed Frau Dr., that's what I called her, to her car. I was relieved that after the initial shock of possibly having to return home so quickly, luck was with me. I was very calm and trusted this woman. I had no idea of what to expect. I told myself to keep an open mind and tackle whatever came my way.

As soon as we left the center of town, the landscape quickly turned rural. It looked like the suburbs of Berlin with trees and single-family homes along winding roads. Soon open fields and woods were in view just beyond the homes. We arrived at their two-story villa within fifteen minutes.

A short walk from the garage brought us to the front door and the glassed-in foyer that was filled with plants along the walls. A lush, bright red bougainvillea was spreading its branches. It was so welcoming, that I felt at ease immediately.

We went directly to my room, which was off the large, tile-covered hall. It was spacious, plenty of room for a bed, a desk, a table and chairs and still more room to move about easily. Off the bedroom was my own bathroom. What a luxury!

I quickly unpacked and joined Frau Dr. in the kitchen. She was starting lunch with explanatory comments along the way. "You'll meet the family soon. They come home for lunch almost every day."

Being in a foreign country wasn't so strange after all. Frau Dr. spoke very good German with occasional lapses into *Swyzerdeutsch*, the Swiss-German dialect that's like a foreign language. At first, I couldn't understand a word. She continued, "I'll make lunch and dinner today, and you watch and take notes. Tomorrow you'll start cooking."

At 12:30 sharp, a car with the rest of the family pulled into the driveway. Herr Doctor, the daughter and her friend came into the kitchen for introductions. He was probably in his sixties, very slim and serious-looking but breaking into a smile easily. He was a vice president at one of the pharmaceutical firms in Basel. Their daughter Anna, in her mid thirties, was working in a research lab at the same company. Her friend Rose, studying for a doctorate at Basel University, was staying with the family rear round. She was renting a bedroom that once was their married daughter's room, for a small fee.

As is European custom, everyone was addressed formally by their last name. Herr and Frau Dr. with their family name, the younger members I called Miss Anna and Miss Rose. All were friendly and easygoing.

The family went to the dining room and I brought the lunch Frau Dr. had prepared to the table. I ate at a small table in the kitchen and was glad to have a little time by myself. My head was swirling, trying to process all that had come at me this day. I didn't sleep the night before on the train and everything was new and strange, but I felt very calm.

After about a half hour I heard the bell signaling that they were finished and I cleared the table before serving the coffee they all enjoyed after lunch. When the dishes were in the dishwasher and the kitchen cleaned, I was ready for a dose of fresh air.

I did not mention the fifth member of the family: Boy, an aging purebred boxer dog. Except for a small parakeet, I was not familiar with house pets. Frau Dr. gave me a few tips about food and water needs for Boy and also suggested that I could take him along if I went out. Boy's stubby tail was wagging wildly and he looked at me expectantly when I was moving towards the door. I could not leave him behind.

We headed out the door, across the quiet narrow street. I found a path leading through a field to the nearby forest. Except for birds and squirrels I didn't meet anyone. It was very quiet. Boy enjoyed the pace. By law, dogs had to be leashed at all times, but he was on a very long leash and led the way. Boy and I became fast friends and would take this two-hour walk in any weather almost daily.

Once back, Boy went for a long nap. His bed was in the hall. After a few days I found him sleeping in front of my door. His bed was moved next to my bedroom door and he was mine from then on.

I headed back to the kitchen by four and had time to do a little snooping. The room was oblong with stove, sink, dish washer and long counter space on top on one side. The opposite wall was floor to ceiling cabinets with shelves of varied heights. They held everything one could possibly need. I saw pots and gadgets that I had never seen, and no clue about how to use them.

Supper would be simpler than lunch. Lunch, the midday meal, was the main hot meal of the day as I was used to in Berlin. Supper usually was sandwiches, with a few exceptions. Frau Dr. explained their usual supper routine and at precisely 6:30 everyone was at their place in the dining room and by 7 they were done. Cleaning up was quick.

I went to my room and knowing that I was expected to be in the kitchen by 6 am, I fell into bed and was asleep immediately.

Kitchen Boot Camp

My day in the kitchen started at 6 am. Frau Dr. arrived a couple of minutes later to show me what was expected and where everything was.

The breakfast routine was easy: Coffee, warm milk in a separate pitcher so that everyone could make their own half coffee - half milk mixture, Muesli cereal, sometimes eggs, jams and butter at the table. The coffee pot was put on a warming light to keep warm. A toaster was on the sideboard in the dining room where everyone could make their own.

I ate my breakfast in the kitchen with my coffee all black. After the first morning I was familiar with breakfast and prepared everything myself from then on.

After breakfast, cooking school started in earnest. Frau Dr. had a menu mapped out for a whole week. The milkman brought fresh milk every morning. If meat was needed, she called the butcher in the morning and they delivered within a half hour. A wagon with fruits and vegetables stopped at the house every other day where she picked out what she wanted. A truck from a Swiss grocery store chain, loaded with everything from eggs to rice, stopped on the street twice a week. This was different from what I was used to. Less time spent shopping, more time for cooking.

During the first couple of weeks, Frau Dr cooked all meals commenting as she went along, "This is a white sauce and by adding spices it can be used in many dishes, same with a basic brown sauce"..."Always, always add liquid to dry ingredients, not the other way around, there will be no lumpy sauces this way." I was watching and taking notes.

Another one of the important rules for success, she insisted, "Never leave the kitchen when cooking, as things can happen fast – like scorched sauces or burnt onions. If you have to, take the pan off the heat." She did this with all parts of any recipe.

I learned the importance of planning and timing. Always starting with the item that takes the longest assures that everything will be ready at the same time. I paid particular attention to that.

When lunch was ready, I bought everything to the table and retreated to the kitchen, still taking notes while I ate.

After kitchen clean-up, I had a couple of hours to myself. If it was not raining, I took Boy for a walk and enjoyed the fresh country air.

In the afternoon we started all over. This time I prepared a sauce Frau Dr. made in the morning while she watched, or we talked about menu planning or the family's food preferences and dislikes.

Frau Dr's cooking was based on French basics. But because the southern region of Switzerland bordered on Italy, many dishes we made were Italian.

A new food world opened up to me. Pasta, rice, and polenta - I knew of, but never cooked. I found that spaghetti could be delicious. What I tasted now was very different from my memories of pasty mush with a red sauce served at elementary school lunches. I loved the spaghetti sauce I learned to cook and experiment with. Actually my love affair with Italian food was in full bloom!

Fennel, eggplant, zucchini, Belgian endive - were vegetables I had not even heard of. Belgian endives in salads or *au gratin* are still some of my favorite foods.

I was familiar with basic herbs and spices but rosemary, basil, tarragon and curries I had not used.

Chestnuts for dessert? I thought chestnuts were only good for kicking along the sidewalk after they fell off the trees. Now I found that they can be cooked several ways. They are delicious when braised with red cabbage. Chestnuts can appear many ways for dessert. My favorite is *Mt. Blanc*: chestnuts are peeled and boiled, then mixed with sugar, brandy and whipped cream, then mashed like potatoes. Finally the mixture is put through a ricer – one of those foreign gadgets in the kitchen – creating a fluffy mountain on top of a bed of meringues. It all just melted in my mouth. Out of this world! One could drizzle melted chocolate over the top, but to me that was overkill.

Soufflés for dinner, soufflés for desert, soups, braised dishes, vegetable pies – today's quiche – omelets - all made easier in a fully equipped, modern kitchen. By that I mean an oven with a thermostat and a cook top with five burners, very different from the kitchen at home.

In Berlin, Mutti still used a wood heated oven for roasting. Temperature was regulated by varying the opening of the oven door. Of course, that does not work for the fine baking that I was trying to master now: meringues, almond cake, apple strudel, baked Alaska and many varieties of cookies.

After two weeks of daily intense lessons, Frau Dr. decided I was ready to let loose. "I think you have a handle on the basics and it'll be good to be on your own. I am nearby and if you have any questions or need help, just come and get me." She also said, "Now you know how we eat. We would really like to taste some of your dishes from Berlin, some of your favorites!"

I sent an 'SOS' letter to Mutti, asking for some recipes for regional dishes like *Königsberger Klopse* and stuffed cabbage; lamb and green bean stew, one of my favorites, that I would like to make.

After about ten days, a very thick letter from Mutti arrived. She answered my plea and wrote the recipes I asked for in detail. The letter opened with:

'I have serious doubts that any good will come of this. Did you not tell them that you never showed any interest or aptitude for cooking?! I am worried!' I just laughed! My interest was very high and my aptitude seemed to be on track.

Once I was left to my own devices I was a little nervous. But soon concentration on the steps I had to remember took over and I did not have time to worry. I aced chopping and prep work right away. Having watched Mutti in the kitchen for so many years made this part easy.

To have a meal completely ready on time was most important. At first I mapped out my morning up to serving time at lunch by the minute. If I needed boiling water for veggies, I wrote down the time I should put the pot of water on the stove; when it should be boiling; how often to check food for doneness and when they should be ready. I continued this timeline for a long time before I trusted my memory.

My aim was to appear very accomplished and to ask for as little help as possible. I discovered a thick cookbook in one of the cabinets and I leaned on it heavily for information. I hid the cookbook, opened to whatever recipe I need at the time, in a cabinet drawer close to the stove. I followed the recipes and if I heard anyone approaching the kitchen I slammed the drawer shut with a quick push with my hips. If Frau Dr. knew my routine, she never let on.

I was very happy in my kitchen domain and loved cooking. I also found that I had very reliable taste buds. When a sauce or soup seemed off, I relied on tasting and adjusting until it was right.

Frau Dr. was never critical, and she believed there were many ways to reach the same results. When something burned or didn't turn out for other reasons, she just said, '"Well, I guess you'll have to try again." When I asked for advice, she was always patiently ready. The family's reaction encouraged me to be unafraid and forge ahead with my kitchen endeavors. Now I know that it was the perfect learning environment for me.

My days in the kitchen started at 6 am and I was usually finished by 7:30 pm. When one meal was completed, I started to plan the next. I was like a dry sponge thrown into water. Everything was stored somewhere in my brain to be recalled as needed. Luckily the kitchen was my only domain. The family also had a cleaning woman, laundry person, one woman who came just to do ironing, and a gardener.

The first big test came seven weeks later. The family's relatives from Paris arrived for the Christmas holidays. With Frau Dr.'s input, I planned several dinners with up to seven courses for twelve. Christmas Eve, Christmas Day and New Year's Day were the most formal and longest dinners. Having a refrigerator helped with the preparations. For some meals I started three days before the actual dinner. Meanwhile I also had to prep and serve breakfast and lunches.

Frau Dr. and the entire family were all smiles. Every meal was a success. It was my graduation from kitchen boot camp!

Quiet Times

During the first few weeks I was completely immersed in the routines of my new job. The days were filled with new experiences. My head was spinning with learning and absorbing. I went for a long walk with my new buddy Boy every day. Other than that I didn't leave the house for weeks. I wanted for nothing.

I didn't miss home or the parties I'd been used to. Sure I missed Mutti and our talks but I was not homesick. I enjoyed my peaceful existence. Nobody was telling me what or what not to do. No one was criticizing me. No one was arguing around me. I was content.

In my room I listened to the radio, again my window to the world. At first I went to bed early, not even taking the time for a luxurious bath and was asleep soon after. After a few days I stayed up longer and started writing. Every week I wrote long letters to Mutti, filling her in about the house, the family and my work. She was very good in turn keeping me up-to-date on all the neighborhood news. Margot, my favorite aunts, all our neighbors and my former colleagues were getting post cards. I didn't have to go to the post office. I simply left money for postage along with my mail in the mailbox. Definitely new to me. That would have never worked in Berlin!

On my half day off, I took advantage of the yard surrounding the house. The front was landscaped and taken care of by a gardener. The backyard had a huge vegetable garden, berry bushes and fruit trees. If the weather was at all nice, I took a book outside to read. Sometimes I took Boy for longer than our usual walks to explore the surrounding countryside.

The weeks sped by. After I successfully executed the menus during the holidays, the family invited me to join them at lunch when they didn't have company. I started to be a regular at the table. I served the meal and then took my place. The different age groups made for interesting conversation about politics, sports and their work.

Herr Dr. was involved in developing a non-sudsing dishwashing liquid (not on the market at that time). Our dishes were his testing ground. He came into the kitchen saying, "Let the dishes sit without rinsing for an hour before turning on the dishwasher." Sometimes he asked me to wait longer. After they went through the cleaning cycle, he came to check the result. At first sudsing was a problem, but within a couple of months that disappeared and the dishes always were clean.

Miss Anna was working in a lab, doing research on a vaccine for malaria and often shared the setbacks or small victories. Her friend Rose was bogged down with studying and frequently moaned about papers that always seemed to be due. Becoming more a part of the family made me even more comfortable in my new life.

Miss Anna liked to go on Sunday drives, preferably on roads she had not been on before. During the week she used the tram or car pooled with her father. She drove her little car only on Sundays or vacations. On my free Sunday afternoon she asked me to come along. Of course, I loved that! It reminded me of adventurous Uncle Alfred.

Miss Anna would drive until we were away from Basel, which only took a few minutes. Then she stopped the car and pulled out the road map. She picked one of the roads and started driving and then it was my job to keep track of where we were. I had to check out all crossroads as we approached them to see where they were leading. According to my report, she would either turn or continue on the road we were on. We drove around for about two hours before she would head back home. This two-hour radius went over winding roads and rolling hills of the *Voralpen*, lower Alps, and through many small and neat villages. Sometimes it looked like we were driving through storybook photos. When there was the ruin of a castle on a hill, we'd stop to hike up the hill to see what was beyond. I became familiar with all the roads in this two-hour radius and it contributed greatly to a sense of belonging.

We'd talk about traveling and life in general. She had been to Africa several times and her fluency in French and English was very useful there. She encouraged me to continue English classes to retain what I'd learned over the years, "You'll find it useful, especially if you continue living in other countries."

Only once did we get lost. Miss Anna turned onto an unmarked road and then she took many turns that were not on the map. We drove for miles and miles never seeing any road markers or street signs. We ended up in an old town surrounded by a moat and high walls. We were way past the two-hour radius and would not make it back home in time for supper. Miss Anita stopped at the one restaurant in town and sheepishly called home to let them know that we were lost and would be home later. The family would have to fend for themselves at supper time.

Frau Dr. enjoyed classical music and opera. When a special concert was broadcast on the radio, she always asked me to join her in the living room and listen.

Once in a while I was invited along when the family went to a special outdoor concert or the opera. At the time a young mezzo-soprano was the talk of the town. The family had tickets for *Carmen* where we heard the still largely unknown Grace Bumbry. It was such a treat!

During this year with the family I was introduced to many firsts. For some Sunday dinners, they made reservations at well-known outdoor restaurants. I was not used to eating in restaurants. It was something new. In Berlin we sometimes stopped for coffee and a pastry when we were window shopping in the city or on a Sunday outing in the Grunewald Forest.

I was invited along on an outing to the tradition of *Spargelessen,* an asparagus eating feast. The Swiss were no different when it came to enjoying this spring ritual. It was 1961 and many fruits and vegetables were only available during their normal growing season. Asparagus season was especially anticipated. At traditional *Spargelessen,* asparagus with the choice of several topping or sauces was served in large quantities and little else. Sometimes very thin slices of raw ham were on the side or a green salad was offered. We drove to their favorite restaurant in the country that grew their own asparagus, the white European kind. "From the field to the table in minutes. It doesn't get any better," Herr Dr. kept saying.

Escargots were definitely new and a strange dish, but I loved it immediately. On occasion the family took a drive into neighboring France, "To find the best Escargot."

A small farmhouse on a back road often turned out to be a cozy restaurant, serving classic French country cooking that included escargot. A dozen snails per person, lots of crusty French bread to soak up the garlicky butter and a green salad was the standard order. If someone was still hungry, another dozen was on the way. White wine rounded out the meal perfectly. It became easy to make snails myself and it still is my all-time favorite treat!

After many months spending time by myself and going into town only to buy necessities, Frau Dr. suggested that I might like to join a group of young women in town. One of the churches in Basel was hosting a weekly meeting for women, mostly foreigners. The group met Wednesday evenings.

'Why not see what the people are like,' I thought, and headed to town the following Wednesday.

New Friends and Ex-Pats

Sundays and Wednesdays were my half-days off. Once a month I had a full Sunday free. Tuesday and Thursday evenings I was taking a course at the Community College. On Miss Anna's suggestion, I signed up for an English Conversation course. I heard of a meeting for young women in the basement of an old church in Basel every Wednesday and I decided to find out what it was all about.

In the basement of the ancient church, I found the assigned room. I opened a heavy wooden door in the hallway and walked into a brightly lit room full of animated chatter. A group of women were sitting in a large circle and all seemed to talk at once.

Miss Müller organized this club as a venue for foreigners to meet, share experiences and explore the country together. She was a Swiss native, in her fifties, petite, full of energy and with a very sharp mind. It was very common in the 1950s and 60s to spend a year in a foreign country. She knew it could be difficult to meet other people, especially in a closed society like Switzerland. "The only place to meet people is in bars and that is not a place for respectable young women," she repeated often.

As introductions were made I learned that the majority of women were from Germany and almost all had positions in households. A few Austrians were there, and one woman each from France, England and Denmark.

It was a friendly group, an informal club, and I decided right away to join them every week. Miss Müller led the discussions. Sometimes it was about current events, and sometimes she'd ask us to share something from our hometown. She had held this meeting for many years and received lots of mail from former members. It was customary to stay abroad for one year. If you were more adventurous, you would find a new job for an additional year. Most often it would be in another town or country. There had been quite a turnover in the club.

When she got letters from former club members who had traveled to other countries, she read them to us. Most of the letters came from the United States. The women described their job experiences; not all of them were positive. The oft-repeated complaint was that they accepted a job where the family paid for their travel expenses and the women were 'stuck' for a year in job situations they did not like and they did not have a way out. After listening, we discussed how this situation could possibly be handled and then listened to the next letter.

Most evenings, though, were spent planning outings for the following Sunday. Often we agreed to meet at a tram or train station to take us into the countryside for an afternoon hike. We all had the same schedule. Once a month we had a full Sunday off. So, on those Sundays we could go further into Switzerland for exploring. We took the earliest train we could find to spend the day in Zurich or other larger cities that we had not been to. It was always fun to explore an unfamiliar town together.

The church owned a small cottage near Zurich and when it was available we would leave Saturday evening, spend the night at the cottage and return to Basel late in the evening. We cooked, hiked, played games and generally were mostly silly.

Out of the large group seven of us gravitated towards each other. Sigrid, Helga, Doris, Gerda, Janine and Margit became my new friends. In addition to Wednesdays, we met every Sunday whether or not there was an organized outing. We met either at someone's house or explored more of Basel and the surroundings.

We also often met Wednesdays as soon as we were free and could make it into town. Most of the times we went shopping. I felt very rich. I was paid well and didn't really have any expenses. We spent time in the upscale shopping area. When I saw shoes or a sweater or blouse, I treated myself. I didn't have to look at the price tag, because I knew I could afford it. It was such a change from my life in Berlin. It felt really good. It was a very carefree time for me. After an early dinner we headed to our club meeting.

Our club gatherings rarely lasted more than a couple of hours. By 8 pm or so there still was a lot of time left and we didn't feel like heading back to our homes. We did what Miss Müller tried to prevent. We headed to Club 49, a well known nearby bar.

Ex-Patriots in Basel

Club 49, in the center of Basel, was known as a place where foreigners gathered. That's were our group was headed after the club meeting at the church. As soon as we stepped into the crowded room, the seats at the bar were vacated for us. The small room was filled with men and German voices. Francois, the bartender, made us feel very welcome.

Francois poured a tall cool beer for each of us and in a very short time knew our life stories. Within a few minutes he made introductions to the men crowding around. We all met someone from our hometown, and the majority came from Berlin.

Club 49 turned into our home away from home. The church club and bar patrons merged into a large group, sometimes we were twenty strong. All dates started at the bar. They were not really dates. Everyone was just friends. All food and drink was Dutch treat. If anyone was dating, she stayed away and joined the group again when she wasn't dating anyone.

We met at the bar and then decided where to go next. We went to a movie, to a restaurant, to a show or we stayed at the bar and just talked. Our talks often centered on food that would lead to a shared home cooked dinner.

As soon as we could all agree on a date, we planned a dinner; who would bring what, and who would be cooking. On a Sunday we met at one of our friend's rental apartment in Basel and cooked meals we remembered from home. We cooked dishes like potato pancakes with sour cream and applesauce, cabbage rolls or pot roast with potato dumplings along side, foods that were not on any restaurant menu here. With all burners in use, the kitchen stove's gas meter required a quarter every five minutes to keep the gas on. Since our cooking took several hours, one person was responsible for the supply of quarters. The men in our group only knew the most basics about cooking and really appreciated those home-cooked feasts.

Many Sunday afternoons were spent getting into the countryside. Depending on where we were headed we went by tram or car-pooled. During the summer months we went hiking or to a swimming pool; ice skating or skiing in the winter. In the summer we occasionally met in town, riding bicycles and touring.

Once in a while we'd plan to spend a Sunday driving around in the rural area surrounding Basel or to nearby France. We drove along back roads until we saw a pub in a nice setting and made that our stop for the day. Since we all appreciated good food, we spread our lunches over several hours. Before we ordered we scrutinized the menu in detail. We made sure that we ordered every item and then shared.

On one of these outings I was confronted with dislike of Germans. The first time it happened I was on the way to the rest room. As I passed a table someone said, "Damned German." I turned around as the man looked at me and spit on the floor. I was shocked. This never happened before. I couldn't believe it! It never occurred to me that people would hate me because I'm German. My knees were shaking

"Better get used to it," my friends back at the table said and relayed similar stories. "The only place it hasn't happened is at Club 49. Probably because all customers are foreigners. Here we are in the countryside, the place is full of Swiss. The war was over fifteen years ago, but people are acting as if the war is still on."

Of course, when a group of eight or ten strong walks in anywhere they get noticed. As soon as we spoke, everyone knew we were German. We worked at keeping our voices down but it really did not make any difference. Once a young man walked up to our table and let go of a barrage against, "Hitler's kind. You Nazis should stay home."

That was just too much for me. I couldn't keep quiet. "What do you know about us? I was a baby during the war. What have I done to you?" Of course, he was not interested. The confrontation continued. I relayed some of my mother's and father's history. He was not interested. Finally with a condescending smile he said, "Amazing how all of a sudden all Germans were good Germans. Ha!" and walked away.

I was really upset. What did it all have to do with me? After calming down, I had to admit that any conversation with someone who vented against Germans was useless. My friends were right. This attitude against Germans is not going to change for a long time. As long as I choose to live in a foreign country I better get used to it. Even young people my age, who grew up after the war, were talking as if they had been there. They were echoing what they heard around them. This strong anti-German feeling will be passed from generation to generation.

It took me a while to realize and accept that all this was not against me personally but the German culture I represented, making me a target for anyone who chose to vent. From then on I ignored any anti-German comments coming my way. When slurs were made, I talked to myself, 'What does he know? Who knows what his parents did during the war?' Outwardly I pretended not to hear.

Where Were You When "The Wall" Went Up?

Traveling was always on my mind. I reveled in this newfound freedom of not having to think about restrictions. No *Ostzone*, East Germany, that surrounded Berlin to travel through. No travel paper checkpoints. I could just go.

I accumulated some off time and turned it into several long week-ends. It only took a couple of hours by train to get to the Alps. It took just a little longer to arrive in Switzerland's southern most county bordering Italy, the Ticino and palm trees. Often these trips were planned with friends but I would go ahead by myself if the others couldn't make it. I became very comfortable traveling by myself.

I divided my two-week paid vacation time. One week I spent at a mountain lake resort in the Alps. I will never forget the shock of jumping into the ice-cold water of the Brienzer See and thinking my heart was going to stop. Nobody told me that the lake is always freezing from glacier run-off. Hiking to some of the mountain tops and viewing the town that shrunk to the size of a pinhead put life into perspective. I realized how insignificant human beings are.

Another week I spent on the Costa Brava in Spain. Tourism hadn't arrived yet but the coastal towns were busy building hotels as if they knew that a boom was coming. It was very inexpensive and I chided myself for not planning a longer stay. Barcelona and the coast offered variety and a lot to discover. Going to a bull fight was, of course, a must. The arena was packed with Spaniards applauding, shouting "Ole" or booing if a matador was not performing. I could not get into the excitement. I would have much rather been on the beach.

During the summer of 1961, I was invited to stay with my friend Sigrid in Klosters, near St. Moritz. The area is famous for the ski resorts and also for hiking and mountaineering in summer. Sigrid worked for a family with three children, who spent the month of August there. I was curious to explore the area that I had heard and read so much about. I helped with Sigrid's chores, giving her more free time to come along with me.

We took a gondola from the center of town to the top of a ridge and then hiked from there. Another time we went to St. Moritz, had lunch in a highly- rated restaurant. The food was good, but not that good and the servings were tiny. We had hearty appetites and miniscule portions were not what we expected for the prices they charged. A side trip to the Diavolezza range, near the Italian border, was eye opening. This Alpine region has snow year round. It was the first time I was in snow up to my knees in August! We lounged in an outside café and watched daring skiers schussing down steep mountain slopes. That was impressive.

Sigrid's employer offered me a deal. In exchange for a free train ticket, I would take their eight-year-old son Norman, with me at the end of my stay. The grandparents would meet the train in Zurich during the fifteen-minute stop and take Norman so he could spend a few days with them.

On Sunday, August the 13th, we took the train and both enjoyed the mountain scenery and the dining car. It was a special treat to be served there, outfitted and run like a fancy restaurant. A very mature Norman and I played games of who could out class the other when ordering lunch. It was a lot of fun.

The train arrived in Zurich a little after 2 pm. We spotted the grandparents right away from the compartment window. They were the only wildly-waving couple on the platform. They hugged Norman and then turned to me with a somber look, "Have you heard the news?"

"No. What news?"

"East Germany started to build a wall early this morning between East and West Germany and it goes right through Berlin. Nobody can get in or out. West Berlin is totally isolated."

I was stunned. I didn't know what to think. I was thinking of Mutti and worried how she was going to take this. The blockade came to mind when Russia tried to isolate Berlin in hopes of taking over the city.

I almost panicked. I wanted to go to Berlin right away to assure myself that all would be all right. But right now I had to get to Basel first. It was time to get back on the train.

The grandparents sent me on my way, "We hope that the Allies will stay strong, not give in to the Eastern regime and support the Berliners. Best of luck to you and your family."

The two-hour train ride seemed like an eternity. Every time I checked my watch only five minutes had gone by. Now I heard other passengers talking about the audacity of the act of building a dividing wall. People were very sympathetic even when they knew I was German. The general opinion was this wall would stay. "What can any Government do about it? Make War? I don't believe so."

I was not hopeful. I planned to call Aunt Schneider in the apartment under us, hoping she could get Mutti to come to the phone. I would tell Frau Dr. that I had to go home for a few days.

I indulged in a taxi to get to my room in Basel as fast as possible. I quickly found Frau Dr. and, of course, she agreed to additional days off to go home, "Stay as long as you need."

From the telephone in the hall, I called Aunt Schneider. She promptly answered. She went right to the heart of the matter, "I don't know what to think. My family is visiting right now, and we're all in shock. We are glued to the radio waiting for updates. Let's hope the American, French and Brits stick together and don't give us up to the Russians!"

Finally Mutti was on the phone. She said she was a nervous wreck. "The East has tried everything to make it difficult for people to leave their wonderful country. Obviously it didn't work. Now they're gonna build a big fence. I don't know how this will end. If the East takes over Berlin, I don't think I can stand it"

"I'm coming home on the first train tomorrow" I blurted out.

"No! I don't want you to leave Switzerland." I couldn't think. 'I can't go home? What does she mean?'

"We don't know what will happen. Will they let us travel through the East zone or will West Berlin be more isolated?" She continued, "It is very comforting for me to know that you are safe. If things go bad, maybe you can help us later to get out. We will know more in a few months." That pretty much was our conversation.

I had dinner with the family. We discussed all the possible things that could happen in Berlin. I relayed in detail the non-cooperation of the Russians with the other three Allies: American, British and French after the war years. So far the three Allies had not taken a strong stand against Russia. A formal protest against some action by Russia, that was contrary to the Allied's agreement forged after the war, was all they did. Mutti was right, we have to wait. Only time would tell.

Back in my room I realized that I was totally drained. I was beyond worrying. Never in my life had I been as exhausted as when I fell asleep that night.

(History background is included in 'The Blockade and Beyond' Page 88).

Uncertain Days

The installation of the Wall between East and West Germany on August 13, 1961, became known as The Berlin Crisis. The situation slowly evolved during tense weeks and months that followed.

Newspapers and radio were my most immediate sources for information. I listened to the radio constantly. At first I didn't leave the house, afraid to miss any breaking news. Although Mutti was sending letters with updates, the mail was taking longer than usual to reach me. Mutti did not have a telephone. Aunt Schneider's phone was to be used only in emergencies.

During the most recent years, East German citizens had been fleeing to the West in record numbers. The Allies had been waiting to see what East Germany would do to contain its people. The Wall was all along the border separating East and West Germany and going through Berlin. All border crossing were closed to keep East Germans from going to the West. They did not cut off West Berlin's travel and supply routes that were going through East Germany to the West. The Allies saw the Wall as a sign that it may be all the Soviet Government would do. They sent a formal protest because the new barrier was against their agreement.

The agreement made by the Allies dated back to the end of World War II. America, France, Britain and the

Soviet Union defeated Germany and were going to occupy the country. They divided Germany into four equal parts, each getting a section that would be under their jurisdiction. Berlin, the capital of Germany, was in the middle of the region to be under the Soviets. The three other governments were not willing to concede the capital totally to the Soviets. At a meeting in Potsdam, they agreed to divide Berlin, as they divided the country, into four sectors. Citizens were to be free to move within all of Berlin.

In 1948, the Soviets went against their agreement by cutting off all roads going to Berlin in an attempt to win Berlin as a whole. The blockade was not successful. The Americans, French and British started a massive airlift, bringing supplies into Berlin that kept Berliners from starving. After more than a year, the Soviets conceded, and all supply routes were opened again.

There were no visible borders or barricades within the city. The Allies simply drew lines through Berlin to establish their sectors. We only knew that we were going into a different area as we passed posted signs advising 'You are now entering the American Sector,' for example. Each country stationed troops in their area. Was the Wall another attempt to isolate the city?

President John F. Kennedy immediately wanted to assure West Berliners of the support of the U.S. He sent retired General Lucius Clay to Berlin, who had been Military Governor of the U.S. occupied zone during the blockade and held in high regard by Berliners. Vice President Lyndon Johnson also flew to Berlin. Johnson and Clay maintained high visibility in the days following. President Kennedy also announced the reinforcement of U.S. troops.

The following Sunday, August 20, the enforcement troops marched through East Germany to West Berlin. The troops, arranged in a column of 491 vehicles and trailers, lined up in groups of five carrying 1,500 men. They assembled at the Helmsted-Marienborn Autobahn checkpoint on the West German border. East German guards counted all personnel as they entered East Germany. The column was 100 miles long and covered the 110 miles to Berlin in full battle gear. East German police watched them all along the Autobahn.

When they arrived at the outskirts of Berlin, they were met by Clay and Johnson. Then the troops paraded through West Berlin to a cheering crowd. Berliners felt reassured.

Several months after the barbed wire was rolled out to start the Wall, the U.S. government informed the Soviet government that it accepted the Wall as 'a fact of international life' and would not challenge it by force, even though it violated the Allied's post-war Potsdam agreement.

By Christmas time, crossing into East Berlin was allowed for selected visitors with a permit. But not West Berliners; they had to wait another two years until a limited amount of permits were issued to them at Christmas. For the next few years Berliners could only get permits at Christmas to visit their relatives. It took until 1971 for West Berliners to be able to apply for a visitor's permit at any time.

A few months after the appearance of the Wall, it became clear that West Berlin was not in danger of becoming occupied by the Soviets. I could go home anytime. With danger averted, I planned to go home for Christmas.

My year in Switzerland would be ending then also. I realized that I was not ready to move back to Berlin. I could not imagine going to work in a retail shop again. Most of my friends from the club were feeling the same way. We started to put feelers out to see what positions may be open for the following year.

Sigrid's family knew of nearby neighbors who may be looking for a governess. I let her know immediately that I was interested. It sounded almost too good to be true, because this was the kind of job I was looking for all along.

One evening I went to meet this couple at their home. Mr. and Mrs. Guidi had two boys, ages four and two, and a newborn daughter. The husband was working for a pharmaceutical company, just like Herr Dr. The wife was a registered nurse but was now a homemaker. We liked each other immediately.

The two-year-old was having heavy asthma attacks and that was the reason they were considering hiring an *au pair*. These attacks could last through the night and with a newborn in the house, they needed help. The family was living in an apartment on the top floor of a three-story building in a suburb of Basel. They were in the process of building a single-family home nearby to be completed the following fall. My quarters would be a small apartment in the partial basement of the building until they moved into their house. I was hired to start right after the New Year. Life was good.

I boarded the train to Berlin for my Christmas vacation with nervousness. Would it feel different?

All seemed normal until I saw the Wall. Mutti was not as depressed as she was in August, but she was actually optimistic. She trusted the support of the Allies and life was almost back to normal.

Mutti and I walked to the Brandenburg Gate where the new border was most visible. Being confronted by this divider, it took a few minutes to accept what I saw. At this time a cement barrier was in place as well as barbed wire on both sides of the Wall. Beyond it, to the east, a 100-yard deep strip of 'no-man's land' was visible with guardhouses in regular increments along the line. It was meant to keep anyone from escaping to the West. It was effective. Since August, many people tried to flee. Some made it using clever ways, including digging a tunnel from east to west under the 'no-man's land' strip. Others were shot either trying to run across the barren stretch of land or attempting to swim across the Spree River that was part of the new border.

Mutti and I stood in silence, staring across the Wall. I became very familiar with Soviet Government tactics while growing up in Berlin and knew that the Wall was going to be part of Germany forever. Who knows when we would see Aunt Hilda, stuck in East Berlin, again?

The Wall
with the 'Death strip' separating East and West Berlin.

Getting my Wings

Living with three young children was a new pace, which was quite different from my job as cook the year before. Daniel (4), Adrian (2) and the infant Martina were now part of my daily routine. It was only a few years since I took care of my cousin Helmut daily after he was born. I was back in the 'taking care of children mode' quickly. The boys were well behaved and the baby had her own schedule. Adrian was the one with the asthma attacks that concerned the family. He was allergic to dust and mold.

Adrian's attacks varied in frequency and duration. The apartment was cleared of anything that could hold dust or mold: horse hair mattresses, carpets, houseplants, etc. The children's room, shared by the three, also had no curtains. Curtains could harbor dust.

When he had an attack, Mrs. Guidi and I took turns sitting by his bed with a vaporizer pump. It was a hand-operated device and required staying power. We erected a makeshift tent with sheets over Adrian's bed to keep the moisture in this area. It always helped immensely. Soon Mr. Guidi bought an electric humidifier for the children's room. We spent most of the day in this room only venturing into the other rooms at mealtimes. I took the children on long walks after naptime in the afternoons. Adrian never had an asthma attack while outside. We actually could see a decrease in attacks and that made the parents hopeful that he could get completely well.

As Adrian's asthma attacks decreased, Martina developed an eating disorder. She rejected food. A few minutes after she started drinking from her bottle, she simply threw up. The milk reappeared with great force arching high over us. At mealtime we spread plastic on the floor where she was being fed. It was a puzzlement, because she seemed completely normal with a good disposition otherwise. The doctor determined that she was processing food extremely slowly. As her stomach got filled it sent the excess back out.

Over time we learned to give Martina her food in very small amounts at a time. Milk and all other food was given by spoon. A small spoon of food and then waiting for several minutes to see how her body reacted. This actually worked. Only if we made the spoon too full or did not wait long enough did she throw up. Feeding time lasted an hour, sometimes more.

Mrs. Guidi and I worked as a team. We took turns feeding Martina while the other spent time with the boys. We also traded off housework. The reference from Frau Dr. included my cooking experience. Shortly after beginning to work for the family Mrs. Guidi said, "I really don't like to cook. I'll do the cleaning, laundry and ironing of the children's things if you would do the cooking for us." It sounded like a good deal to me and it was.

The months went by quickly. I enjoyed my little apartment on the ground floor. Mrs. Guidi never used her bicycle and it became mine for the duration. I went everywhere on the bike, even rode it into town to the club and meeting friends at the bar. I hailed a taxi to go home when it was dark. The taxi driver put the bike in the trunk, at no extra charge. I used the tram only when it rained. My work schedule was the same as the year before. Wednesday and Sunday afternoons were my time off. Every other Sunday was completely free. On those days my friends and I made it a point to explore a town or place we had not been to before.

At the club meetings the talk often centered on going to America for a year. By now we explored Switzerland and neighboring countries thoroughly. If we were not ready to go back to our hometowns, where would we want to go next?

Letters kept coming from young women who had gone to the U.S. The idea of going to America was intriguing. We could go as a group at the same time, which seemed less daunting. Who would be interested? The process would not be as easy as it was traveling and working within Europe. Out of the twenty or so, I, along with fifteen others, became committed to go. It sounded like a good idea.

We started to make inquiries at the American Embassy in Zurich. We would need to apply for a work visa and would need an employer in the U.S. in order to get the visa. I was not yet twenty-one and would need the permission of a parent. I felt Mutti would give her permission but I was a bit uneasy about how she would take this. Going overseas would be a bigger trip than I had ever taken. I decided not to mention it to her yet. Who knows, I might not even go.

The Guidis were very involved with the construction of their new home. The site was only a short drive from the apartment. It was an even shorter walk because we could take a short cut up a steep bank. The couple had blueprints at home. After reviewing them, they went to check the site daily after the crew left. I walked to the site often with the children to check on the progress. The boys loved visiting their future rooms. I had watched remodeling projects at Uncle Alfred's house but this was the first time I watched a house being built from the ground up. It was interesting to see foundation, water pipes, electrical wiring, heating systems, and plumbing being installed according to plans and it would all work when the time came. The home was ready without a glitch in August.

This was quite a change from the apartment. The main floor was at street level with kitchen, living/dining room combo, a master bedroom suite and a bedroom for each child. Below was the other level with my room, several guestrooms, a dry-goods storeroom, a root cellar and a large playroom. It was basically a basement. The house was built into a hillside, with one wall below ground but the opposite fully exposed. All rooms had large windows with an expansive view of the rolling countryside, just like upstairs.

Mrs. Guidi knew that I could sew. We took on making the entire window coverings for the house. She brought home rolls and rolls of material to be made into curtains. We set up the sewing machine in the playroom. When not cooking, I was busy making curtains. By the way, the old white and red striped kitchen curtains from the apartment turned into a summer dress for me a la Scarlett O'Hara in *Gone with the Wind*.

The kitchen was twice the size of the one in the apartment. One afternoon Mr. Guidi arrived home with a sack of coffee beans. "My brother sent them from Brazil. They are green, meaning they still need to be roasted before we can make coffee." This was something new to me. Nobody I knew roasted their own coffee.

Guidis had a coffee-roasting machine that I hadn't noticed before. The contraption looked like a cross between a pressure cooker and butter churn. The machine was operated manually. I poured beans into the pot, closed the lid and started turning the handle while on medium heat on the stove. The handle 'churned' the beans under the lid and made a scraping noise while I was at it. It was moving the beans around so that they were evenly exposed to the heat. By constantly moving them they also would not burn. After roughly twenty minutes the beans started to take on color. Slowly they turned brown. Soon the color changed faster. I stopped every couple of minutes to check the color by opening a peephole in the top off the lid. When the beans reached rich reddish, chocolate brown, I stopped and quickly emptied the beans onto large baking sheets. They cooled off fast and were ready to turn into a delicious coffee the morning.

After my first batch of roasting beans, I found out more I didn't know. The oily steam released by the beans stubbornly settled everywhere; in my clothes, my hair and throughout the entire house. After a while it didn't seem such an appetizing smell. I learned to prep for this experience. I put on my oldest clothes, wrapped my hair in a towel. Kitchen doors were closed tightly with towels along the threshold to keep the smell from escaping. Nobody was allowed to open the doors until I gave the all clear. Then, no matter the outside weather, I opened the kitchen windows wide and turned the stove fan on high.

Another first was roasting lamb over an open fire. The new house had a large raised fireplace in the living room. Shortly after moving in, Mr. Guidi was prepping some lamb to roast for a special supper. He told me, "Tonight I'm the chef, cooking lamb my favorite way." He inserted garlic slivers all over the meat and then rubbed it with salt and crushed rosemary.

The fire made with apple tree logs from an old tree in the yard soon created hot coals. Mr. Guidi put an elevated grate over the coals and put the lamb on. We were all sitting around the fireplace watching. After a little while a wonderful aroma started to emerge from the fat dripping into the coals. When the meat was done, it was crusty outside and pink and juicy inside. So far I had tasted only well-done lamb. This was delicious, and still my favorite way to enjoy lamb.

I went on several trips with the family. They rented a house in the Ticino, in southern Switzerland at the Italian border. We spent three weeks in a small town at the edge of Lago Maggiore. We went swimming every day in the lake with a backdrop of snow capped mountains. This Italian region of Switzerland was particularly scenic. Palms dotted the shores of Lago Maggiore and Lago Lugano. Very lush landscaping, small towns with quaint, narrow alleys and villas built into the hillsides where everywhere. I had my regular times off and traveled to other towns and lakes and into Italy every free minute I had.

We also spent three weeks in Klosters, a ski resort in the Swiss Alps. The children went to ski school daily and so did I. I had dreamed of skiing since I was very young, but I did not think I would actually get the opportunity to do it. Daniel and Adrian quickly advanced. They went straight down the bunny slope when I was still doing the snow plow, the beginner's technique. Soon, though, I caught up and we all graduated to other slopes.

One day Mrs. Guidi's brother took Daniel and me on a day trip. We took several lifts and gondolas to the highest peak in the area. We skied in this upper terrain above the tree line all morning. I skied and skied without falling down. It was exhilarating and I loved it. After a hearty lunch in a chalet restaurant that was packed with skiers we had to start heading towards the valley. The long winding descent on many wide and sometimes very narrow trails took over an hour. When we finally took off our skis, I considered myself a skier.

Mutti visited during her summer vacation. This was her first vacation away from Berlin since she started to work a few years ago. She stayed in the apartment for ten days and kept me company while I worked. I took her along everywhere including to the women's group and Club '49. My friends loved having someone else to tease and she was a good sport.

I had saved some of my days off and we spent three days sightseeing and hiking in Lucerne, by the Vierwaldstättersee, a lake in central Switzerland. We didn't laze around. The town, boat rides and hiking trails were waiting for us.

During one of the dinners I gathered my courage and brought our conversation around to what I might be doing next year. I relayed what I had heard about going to America during the club meetings, how many girls have gone to work in the states. I blurted out, "I think I would like to go to America and I need your permission. Of course, it could take a while before I get a visa."

Mutti looked at me silently for a few minutes and then with a sigh she said, "You'll be twenty-one soon and will not need my permission. If you need it, I will gladly give it." She continued, "You have made a very nice life for yourself here. I can see that it is doing you good. I understand that you would want to continue on.

"You may not come back if you go to America. Don't worry about leaving your homeland. It has taken your father, kept him from raising you. You have done everything you were supposed to and in turn your Fatherland has done nothing for you. You do not owe it a thing. If I were you, I would do exactly the same. I'm too old to start over. You go. I'm sure you will do well."

It took a big load of my mind. I was relieved not to have any more secrets. The relationship with the Fatherland is very important to Germans. I was a little surprised at her words. She rarely revealed her innermost feelings. Her comments showed me how bitter she was about the events in her life.

Having Mutti's support would make all decisions that may come my way so much easier.

1962
With Mutti in Lucerne

A Big Decision

What's next for us? This was the major topic of conversations at the weekly club meetings. Every young woman in our group was at her job for a year, a common practice when working in another country. After the year was up we had to find another job or head back to our hometown.

The talk always came to 'How about America?' Since the end of World War II, America – the U.S. - was the dream goal for many. Many young women married GIs and went to America, the land where everything seemed easy and plentiful. We, of course, knew of several former club members who went to America to work and for whom it did not work out. Actually it was the same with the marriages. The women had no idea of what life in America was like or even where they would be living. We did not consider marrying a GI to go to America as an option.

Fifteen of us decided, "Let's all go at the same time, and then we won't be alone there." We would need a work visa, a green card. None of us could afford to just travel in the United States. Getting a visa could take a long time. Some people had to wait up to five years to get one.

In late summer we called the American Consulate in Zurich to learn more about the process of obtaining a green card. We should come to the consulate and complete an application. It would be simpler than mailing back and forth. It was decided to go to the consulate in October when everyone was back in Basel from vacations.

A week before our visit to the consulate in Zurich, we were going to settle on the details of the trip. At our Wednesday club meeting my friends dropped out of the going-to-America plan. Several decided to go back home instead. Others felt that going to the United States was too ambitious and daunting. So many things could go wrong and they may get stranded in a strange land with a strange language. At the end of the meeting, every single one of my friends had changed her mind. I was stunned and very disappointed.

I told the group that, "the decision to go to America had not been easy for me. I'll still try to get a visa and go."

During the years living by myself, I learned to go on outings alone. I would have missed a lot had I stayed home every time a planned trip was canceled by friends at the last minute.

Since Mutti had given me the go ahead a couple of months ago, I had gotten used to the idea of living in the United States for a couple of years. I was reading travel books and articles about the U.S. to learn all I could. I also continued the English language class at the community college. I decided to go ahead by myself.

A couple of days before taking the train to the consulate in Zurich, my friend Margit called. This was unusual, because we did not call each other. Meetings and trips were always planned ahead. "Heidi, I've been thinking about America. If you like, I will go with you," she told me. This was a great surprise. Margit was not part of the group that originally wanted to go.

"I don't know why I decided to join you. I don't know any English, but many of the other girls don't either. I guess I should be ok and you know a little."

I was overjoyed and relieved that I would have a buddy. I didn't really want to go to America alone. Margit and I always got along well, and she was a friend I could count on. We planned to meet at the Basel train station a couple of days later to go to the consulate.

We filled out the visa application. The clerk gave us a list of things we needed to bring before it could be processed. We needed our birth certificate, a passport, a criminal record check from every place we ever lived, three character references, all vaccinations to be current, and proof of employment in the United States. When we had everything in hand, we should call for an appointment. At the time of the appointment we would also get the required physical check-up by a consulate approved doctor and a lung x-ray at a clinic.

Margit and I decided to start gathering all we needed and get back to the consulate after our Christmas vacation at home. At home we could get started with the criminal record check at the police station. Securing a job would be the biggest hurdle. We didn't have any connections in the U.S.

I knew that Mr. and Mrs. Guidi spent a year in New York after they were first married. I approached them with my plans for the future. First, they let me know that I could work for them until I got a visa. That was a relief; I didn't have to find another position after my year with them was over. Mrs. Guidi also said, "We have good friends who live in New York. Mr. And Mrs. Boden have three children and they always are looking for a nanny. Mr. Boden works for the pharmaceutical company's New York branch that my husband is with. He and my husband are in touch often. I will write a letter and find out if you could be working for them. Maybe they know of a place for Margit also."

I let Mrs. Guidi know that both Margit and I intended to pay for our travel expenses. From the letters by girls working abroad, we had learned this was creating the most problems. Employers often paid all expenses in exchange for a one-year commitment. Flying or going by boat was very expensive. Having the employer pay expenses was often the only way young women could go to the states. Many times the job did not work out but the girls were then stuck for a year and very unhappy.

During my Christmas vacation in Berlin, I didn't mention anything about New York to anyone. However, I kept Mutti up-to-date on the status of my America plans.

The borough police station that was across the street from our house had merged with one near city hall. The officer on duty used to be stationed at the Waldstrasse precinct and knew Pappa. I had known him since childhood. "What do you need this document for?" he was curious. I told him. He said, "You know that getting a visa for the United States can take a long time. My daughter has been waiting for three years now. Best of luck to you, Heidi." He continued, "Come back next week and I'll have the paper ready for you."

As I headed back home I was glad that the document would be ready before I was going back to Basel. I was hoping that it would not take three years for us to get a visa. Three years! What could I be doing while I was waiting? I decided not to think about that, just focus on getting all the required documents together for the next appointment at the consulate.

Back in Basel, Mrs. Guidi had a letter from the Bodens in New York offering me a position as governess. They also included a letter from acquaintances, the

Bridges family, stating they needed a housekeeper and would hire Margit. This was great news.

Margit and I made an appointment at the consulate for the end of January. This would give us enough time to get the background checks from the Basel police stations. On January 30, a Wednesday, we took the train to Zurich.

The consulate found all needed papers in order. We were told that it would not take very long to get a visa and to look into our travel options to New York for this year. We felt very encouraged. We went to the required health check-up and chest x-ray. Now, we had to wait.

We arrived back in Basel in time to go to a travel agency for information on ship passages to New York. Flying was too expensive. It was way over our budget, about 2,000 German Marks. We learned that a ticket for a boat passage in a shared cabin would cost us around 800. It still was more than we had saved at the time and knew that we better not spend any money unless absolutely necessary. At least we knew. We reported everything we learned to Ms. Müller and the group at the club meeting later that evening. Everyone was really excited for us but none decided to join us at the last minute.

A good distraction was my upcoming twenty-first birthday, Saturday, February 9. Twenty-one is a major milestone, according to German law, twenty-one is the age of maturity. A party was in order. I reworked my favorite, but dated dark green wool dress into a more fashionable one. What was a shirt dress turned into a cocktail dress. The front became the back; buttons were replaced with a zipper on the low cut back; long sleeves turned into puffy elbow length ones. It was ready the day before the party and I felt very stylish.

Guidi's volunteered their house for the celebration. They would go to Zurich for an overnight, and the children would stay with the grandparents.

Twenty of my friends and fellow ex-pats joined me. We ate and drank and danced and then we ate, drank and danced some more. The last one left at four am. Margit stayed over and helped clean up. The grandparents were bringing the children back at noon. The house was prim and proper again by the time they arrived.

On Monday, February 11, the consulate called. I passed the check-up and x-ray and my visa was ready.

Margit had a clean bill of health also. This was much faster than anticipated.

At the consulate the following day we asked how come we got a visa so fast? "Every country has a quota for different nationalities. There are very few Germans applying for visas in Switzerland. We never reach the quota."

It was February 12, the visa had to be activated within four months, or we would have to apply again. Now we were in the hot seat of getting to New York in time.

Ready to Cross the Big Pond

I still couldn't believe how fast everything happened. It only took a couple of months versus all the stories of 'it takes years to get a visa to the United States.' Still in disbelief, Margit and I often kept looking at each other and burst out laughing. America was the country everyone wanted to go to.

I called Mutti to let her know. I figured Aunt Schneider wouldn't mind getting her to come to the phone although it was not an emergency. "I envy you. I always wanted to go to New York. Maybe I'll get to visit you." Then she went upstairs to get Mutti.

Margit and I realized quickly that we better make a plan for all to become real. Our first stop was the travel agency. We booked a passage in a shared cabin on the 'M.S. Berlin' for a May 14, 1963, departure from Bremerhaven with arrival in New York May 24th. There were ships that covered the distance in five days. We chose the M.S. Berlin because it would give us a ten-day vacation. Once in New York we would be working for a year without a holiday.

My ticket to New York was 850 German Marks. I was not very good at saving money. There had been no need so far. I had half of the needed amount and made a deposit. I would be able to come up with the balance before ending my job with Guidis at the end of April.

Through Guidis we contacted both families who had promised jobs just outside New York City. Indeed, they would meet us when the ship arrived in New York in May.

On the surface life went on as before. But now, when I was not at the club or with my ex-pat friends, I was busy planning. I sorted through my belongings, made sure all my clothes were in good condition. I counted down the days.

My last days with the Guidi family came quickly. We had enjoyed each other. The children, the parents and I had spent an eventful sixteen months together. And now it was time for good-byes at the Basel train station. The boys waved until the platform disappeared from view.

I arrived in Berlin on a Saturday. My boat ticket was paid up before I left Basel. After buying the train ticket I had very little money left. More expenses were coming my way. What to do? Mutti didn't have any extra to loan.

Mutti suggested getting a job for two weeks. It would give me the needed extra cash. Good suggestion, but how can I find work on this short notice?

On Monday I went to the shopping area in the center of Berlin. A help- wanted sign at Kaiser's Kaffee, a coffee chain store, got my attention. The owner of this busy store, selling coffee in bulk as well as chocolates, needed an additional sales clerk. After I recited experience working in my grandmother's grocery store one summer I was hired on the spot. What a relief! It would solve all my financial worries. I already felt guilty, though, because I didn't tell the owner that I would be there for only two weeks. But I kept it to myself because I was sure I wouldn't have been hired.

I reported to work the following morning and went right back to bantering with customers while weighing coffee or truffles. It was really a very fun job for these two weeks.

In the evenings I was getting my suitcases ready. When I went to Switzerland the first time, I had one suitcase. Now I was filling two and had to decide what to leave behind. Once all I was taking was assembled I divided everything between the two cases. One was packed with the clothes needed during the voyage. Everything else went into the other. The one to get stored in the ship's hull until arrival in New York had to be at the dock three days before departure according to the guidelines from the travel agency.

I also made my good-by rounds to friends and neighbors. By now they were all used to saying good-by to me. This would be a much longer journey. Everyone was admiring my sense of adventure and was wishing me well, some with a tiny bit of envy. Uncle Alfred promised, "If you stay there long enough, I'll come and visit."

Minna was sure I would not come back, "My, once you are there why would you want to come back? Berlin isn't that beautiful! We are still struggling to recover."

She continued, "You'll meet a young man and get married. Remember that I told you so!"

I shook my head, "Noooooooooooo. Margit and I want to work in New York for a year or so, saving our money and then go to San Francisco."

"Well, remember what I said. They must all be blind not to snatch you!" With that Minna, Mutti and I had a good laugh.

Hanging over me was what to tell my boss on my last day? He had mentioned several times that he was pleased with the job I was doing. Payday was every Friday. It was customary to receive cash. When my turn came on that last day I apologized over and over how I had to quit. I said, "I was on waiting list for this trip to America and didn't think it would happen this fast."

He was, of course stunned. He took a deep breath and then he said, "Wow! That's a surprise! You sure had your best poker face on these two weeks. I guess I have to hire a new clerk."

At the end of the day he and the other three clerks wished me well. "Hope this works out for you." I was relieved, smiling all the way home.

Mothers Day, May 12, was my last day at home. Mutti and I were alone. Margot had graduated from high school and refused to go to the university as was originally planned. She was an *au pair* in the south of France at the time.

Mutti and I had a lazy day with coffee time in the afternoon. I went to the bakery for our treats. The owner knew what I would be asking for; a Napoleon for Mutti and my favorite *Windbeutel*, cream puff, for myself. I had been buying those at this bakery often. The baker's wife wouldn't let me pay for it, "Have a safe journey and *toi,toi,toi* - good luck - in America." Oma came to say good-by reminding me, "to be very careful out in the world."

For the rest of the day I was busy with last minute packing and repacking of my suitcase and large travel bag. I must have moved things between those two vessels a hundred times. I was determined not to open the suitcase until I was in our cabin. What I needed in the meantime had to fit into the travel bag.

Early in the morning of the thirteenth, Mutti went to work after a final sleepy hug. I headed to the bus station. Minna waved from her living room window as I

252 | Heidemarie Sieg

climbed into a taxi. The bus to Bremen left at seven. I was so focused on getting to the bus on time that I didn't have time to think about where I was going.

Margit and I had a room reservation in Bremen where we would meet later that day. All went according to plan. My bus arrived on time in Bremen. Our hotel was within short walking distance of the bus station. I was thankful. Lugging my suitcase and large travel bag was really cumbersome. Margit arrived right after I checked in. We congratulated ourselves on how smoothly everything had proceeded ever since we applied for the visas. We treated ourselves to a nice dinner and a movie.

I was restless during the night. I woke up often. I remember thinking 'What if I don't come back?'

The next morning we both woke up early. At seven in the morning, the hotel's dining room was already filled. We learned they were our fellow passengers, anxious to get going. Because we didn't know when the first meal on the ship would be served, we filled ourselves with scrambled eggs, bacon, rolls and lots of coffee. Back in our room, we locked up our suitcases. We were ready.

I was looking forward to traveling on an ocean liner. There were so many unknowns. Nobody I knew had traveled on a ship. Oma's sister Marty did in the early 1930s, when she immigrated to Argentina. She died in the mid '50s. Couldn't ask her for advice. I did not let any emotions enter my thoughts. I told myself that I will be all right if I pay attention, follow any rules and then just be myself.

I concentrated on the schedule we had made. Leave right after breakfast for the train station. Be at the pier as soon as possible. Better to wait there than at the hotel. Anything could happen. We didn't want to leave anything to chance. No need to add stress by leaving late.

The train went from Bremen directly to the pier at Bremerhaven. The pier where the SS *Berlin* was docked was humming with activity when we arrived. People as far as the eye could see. Some standing still, most of them hurrying around. Slowly we made our way to the ship.

The line going up the gangway to the entry deck was moving extremely slowly. We checked the suitcases to be delivered to our cabin near the base of the gangway. Suddenly I heard, "Heidi! Heidi! Over here!" I looked towards the voice. It was Uncle Lutz. He brought Aunt

Schneider to the pier. She was just visiting his family in Hamburg.

"We couldn't let this opportunity go by! How often are we close by when someone we know goes to America." I was so surprised. I knew that Aunt Schneider was visiting in Hamburg. But it never occurred to me that she would make the trip to the pier. They had flowers and a card for me. We chatted until remaining passengers were encouraged to board the ship.

Finally Margit and I walked up to the entry deck. The loudspeaker kept reminding visitors to leave the ship. It was close to noon, the departure time. We found space along the railing and scoured the crowd for Aunt Schneider and Uncle Lutz. We found them fairly far up-front waving with all arms.

Suddenly the ship's horns were blowing loudly several times. The gangway was taken up. The lines to the dock released and the ship slowly inched away from the pier.

We threw streamers, waved and screamed, "*Auf Wiedersehen! Auf Wiedersehen!*" again and again as loudly as we could.

I was on the way to America.

Postscript – Berlin 1989
Published by my local paper, *The Times Argus,* Vermont.

When the Wall Came Down

"We have to change our thinking. Suddenly nothing is impossible anymore," an older man next to me reflected, as I was watching a sea of East Germans spill through the Wall into West Berlin, my hometown.

November 9, 1989 brought a new milestone in history. The Berlin Wall crumbled.

This was the first good news since the end of the war. I immediately bought a plane ticket from New York to Berlin, to celebrate with my family.

West Berlin was in an early Christmas-rush chaos. My reserved, elderly mother, light-footed like a teenager and bursting with excitement, tried to relay all events at once.

She told me how the Russian cellist Mistlav Rostropovitch, moved deeply by the East Germans' action, chartered a private plane from his Paris residence and went directly to Checkpoint Charlie. Below the new Wall graffiti "Charlie retired," he played a half-hour of Bach in memory of those who died trying to escape.

"Can you believe it yet?" she continued. "They are free! It's monumental; it can make a sick person well."

I couldn't wait to go to the Wall. Mother and I went to one of the new crossings at Potsdamer Strasse near the Brandenburg Gate.

Heavy pedestrian traffic headed towards the Wall. We were swallowed by the crowd. I got butterflies, like waiting for my first date. Finally, a big gap in the Wall was in sight.

Jammed like sardines, we watched thousands of East Germans test the new policy. Going across the border with just a stamp in your passport? Unheard of! East German police, *Vopos,* actually smiled and merely waved people by.

As they crossed over, we cheered and applauded in the cold until hoarse. They waved back and slowly filed by, five or six across, like a slow motion movie. Exuberant shouts of, "*Willkommen!*...Isn't it great!...Where are you from?" filled the air.

Many would stop for a moment, take a deep breath, look around, and with a teary smile hug whoever was close. Suddenly I dissolved into tears of relief and joy. I was so proud of their courage. They are really free! Despite the evidence in front of me it was difficult to absorb the fundamental changes.

Men and women around us were wiping away tears, shaking their heads and murmuring, "I can't believe it...I can't believe it." People kept coming. After a while they all looked the same, turning into an undulating, endless ribbon of muted blue and gray.

Moving around the city was a challenge. Lines everywhere! Once in a bus or store, it was nearly impossible to get out. Getting to work was a major production for Berliners. "My ride usually takes fifteen minutes," an irritated cashier told me. "Today our bus couldn't get on the belt-way. Gridlock! It took an hour, and I had to stand all the way! But I'm sure it'll let up after the holidays," she added with a shrug.

The German Democratic Republic's (GDR) miniature cars, Trabants, have no emission control. Because their special gas mixture is not available in the West, they kept running out of gas and clogging the roads.

Berlin's administration slowly turned the city into a somewhat orderly madhouse. To ease traffic and pollution, the mayor of West Berlin, Walter Momper, appealed to East Germans to park their cars at the border and use the public transportation free of charge.

Greyhound buses from West Germany helped the taxed transportation department. Bus drivers, in unfamiliar territory, often got help from natives calling out bus stops.

Because the East's ancient phone system was out of order, *Vopos* and West Berlin traffic police installed army field telephones to coordinate additional crossings. Within a few days bulldozers and cranes tore thirteen new holes into the Wall. Now there are twenty-five crossings in an out of West Berlin. Traffic was heaviest at crossings close to West Berlin's center.

East Germans were showered with gifts at border crossings. Coca Cola, Mars Bars, soap, detergent samples, and more, were handed out. Kaiser's, a grocery store chain, gave away 170,000 bags containing a pound of coffee and a chocolate bar. Young women bundled up against the cold, welcomed men, women and children with carnations sent by Holland. Because West Berlin is blanked out on all road maps printed in the GDR, visitors received a city map.

The Morgenpost, Berlin's major daily, printed a special travel guide to ease the adjustment to a strange city. It featured: a subway and bus map, complete with time schedules; traffic laws and road signs; bank locations, shopping districts and information centers. All free or reduced fees for museums, concerts, theaters, and movies were listed. Practical tips – i.e., enter buses in front, exit to the rear, and "It pays to shop around" (East Germany has a uniform pricing system) – were also included.

By now, the normally stoic East Germans were moving about either happily smiling or totally dazed. They repaid the goodwill with politeness, cheerfulness and generally by coming out of their shell.

The Red Cross, Salvation Army, and the French, British and American armies pitched tents at all crossings and throughout the city. They assisted with information, hot food, and makeshift shelters in gyms. People had been sleeping in their cars, huddled in malls, hotel lobbies and subway stations.

Radio station SFB functioned as a clearinghouse for private homes offering a free room, sometimes just a living room sofa. After the first week, over 24,000 private accommodations became available.

The flow of humanity was unending. After ten days of the new policy, 12.3 of the total 16.7 million East Germans had travel visas. Border police counted over 800,000 people going into West Berlin in one day and finally gave up counting. But, as the authorities had hoped, only a fraction requested permanent stay in the West.

Buses and charter planes brought in thousands of tourists wanting to witness history. I must have given directions in English to at least half of them. Four lads from Ireland in Berlin for the day, wanted to know: "How far to the Wall? Where's the best crossing to watch people come over? Do we have to wait long to get into East

Berlin? How do we get to the 'Spy Bridge?' What's the quickest route back to the airport?" They would be able to fit everything into the day, except the bridge.

Until November 9th, only selected diplomats were allowed to cross *Glienicker Brücke,* nicknamed Spy Bridge. It crosses the Havel River to Potsdam in a wooded, remote, rural section of Berlin. It's true, East and West exchanged spies here at odd hours through the mist rising from the river for years. Today it's one of the new crossings.

Laws regulating store and banking hours were suspended. Restaurants and shops remained open after hours and on Sundays. Extra help was hired. Some Berliners volunteered. One woman walked into a coffee house on the *Kurfürsten Damm,* "Do you need any help?" The owner grabbed her immediately. "Please! If you would make coffee. We can't keep up."

Bank clerks worked seven days a week to pay 100 German marks ($55) welcome money, issued by the West German government. During the first three days, 135 million Marks were paid out in West Berlin.

East Germans are used to standing in line early at home if they want to get any of the sparse merchandise. Crowds milled patiently at the shops in West Berlin long before they opened. They were amazed at the supply in the West. Even when goods were sold out the previous day, shelves were stocked again the following morning.

People, three and four deep, marveled at window displays. Everything from hardware to food was thoroughly eyed and discussed. "Why so many kinds of salami?" one woman wondered. "You only need one!"

Families dominated the crowd. Baby carriages were loaded with packages like shopping carts. Everyone carried white plastic shopping bags bulging with sought after fruits and meats. It seemed that every family bought a boom box.

Toiletries, cosmetics, watches, toys, walk-mans, chocolates, and disposable diapers were hot sellers. And bananas. Bananas are unheard of in the GDR. Groups of three, four, and more, eating bananas huddled on sidewalks everywhere.

West Berliners in the street helped as soon as they saw anyone consulting a map, and I was happy to do my part. When heading in the same direction, I took people along and used the opportunity to ask their impressions and thoughts.

"We have to catch up with twenty-eight years of progress," one man said in awe. "After free elections, re-building can begin in earnest."

Another muttered, "I'm going home. The people, the noise, the sights! I'm tired!"

My cousin's husband, Peter, who literally jumped over barbed wire into West Berlin in 1961, was skeptical. "The same people are still in power. I don't trust them."

Neither East nor West Berliners felt reunification important. East Germans want to build up the country's economy, their standard of living, and hope to be able to join the European community as equals.

To the East of The Wall

On a bright, calm Sunday my sister and I explored East Berlin where I hadn't been since 1960. East Berlin was a ghost town. No color, people or sound. Everyone was in the West.

East Berlin is a treasure chest of old architecture, bridges, museums, and churches, dating as far back as 1230 A.D. Knowing that I wasn't surrounded by suppression made a visit East enjoyable for the first time in my life. We 'touristed' until dark. Many times we walked in the center of the street for a better look at the facades of buildings. It was wonderful.

We finished the day in *Ermeler Haus*, a restaurant in a restored building overlooking the Spree River. As one of only two occupied tables, we took our time eating and drinking away the mandatory exchange money in 1760s splendor. (One cannot go into East Germany without exchanging valuable 25 West German Mark for almost worthless East Marks and it had to be spent there).

Tearing Down The Wall

Back in West Berlin, I wanted a piece of the Wall and found I was not alone! More crowds. Everybody tried to pry a piece off this structure with anything from nail files to jackhammers. It sounded like a stone quarry. Berliners nick-named them Wall peckers.

Police, patrolling in pairs, often turned strangers into a brotherhood of conspirators. East Germany lodged a complaint against Wall peckers. One West Berlin officer approached a young man with a wink, "I'm giving you a warning that you are destroying public property and could be arrested." Our tools quickly slipped into pockets and knapsacks. When the policemen, walked away we stood around giggling, waiting for them to disappear around the bend. One man followed to the corner, gave an "all clear," and the chipping continued. The lookout was rewarded with a white and blue graffiti chip.

I attacked the Wall with great satisfaction, equipped with a mason's chisel and hammer. I pounded and pounded until I got my chunk of the Wall to take home and remember.

Berlin, November 1989
Chipping away at The Wall.

Credits

All photographs are the property of the author, except:

Page 44: Street in Berlin, 1945

Page 236: The Wall

The above photographs are in public domain.

*

Historic data has been cross referenced at *Wikipedia.*

About the author

Heidemarie Sieg, Heidi, lives in northern New Mexico with her husband Trent Smith.

She loves to paint, hike in the mountains, tend her flower garden and is also working on her next book *Nine Lives and More*.

CPSIA information can be obtained at www.ICGtesting.com
Printed in the USA
BVOW08s1127271113

337505BV00002B/161/P

9 780984 302451